LAND FOR THE P

LAND FOR THE PEOPLE?

The British Government and the Scottish Highlands, *c.* 1880–1925

EWEN A. CAMERON

First published in the Scottish Historical Review Monograph Series
in 1996 by Tuckwell Press Ltd
This edition published in 2009 by John Donald,
an imprint of Birlinn Ltd
West Newington House
10 Newington Road
Edinburgh
EH9 1QS

www.birlinn.co.uk

ISBN 978 1 906566 13 5

British Library Cataloguing-in-Publication Data
A catalogue record for this book is available
from the British Library

Typeset in 10/12 Baskerville

Printed and bound in Great Britain by Bell & Bain Ltd, Glasgow

for

MY FATHER AND MOTHER

Contents

Tables

Acknowledgements

I am grateful to the Cross Trust, the Carnegie Trust for the Scottish Universities, the Scottish Education Department, and the Universities of Glasgow, St Andrews and Edinburgh, for funding the research for this book.

I have benefited from the assistance of the staffs of the Bodleian Library, Oxford, the British Library, Churchill College, Cambridge (Political Archives Centre), Edinburgh University Library, Glasgow University Library, St Andrews University Library, the Highland Regional Archive, the Mitchell Library, Glasgow, the National Library of Scotland, the Public Record Office, the Scottish Record Office, and the Staffordshire County Record Office.

I am grateful to the following for facilitating access to their private archives: the Duke of Argyll, Sir Donald Cameron of Lochiel, the Clan Donald Centre, Mr Neil Hunter of Hunterston, Mrs Sheena Linzee-Gordon of Cluny, Mr John MacLeod of MacLeod, Mrs F. Raven-Smith of Ardtornish, the Marquess of Salisbury, and the Viscount Thurso. Mr John MacLeod of MacLeod was unique among the owners of private archives in imposing a charge for the use of his muniments, namely £50 for the first day and £15 for each succeeding day (plus VAT).

I owe particular thanks to Jennifer Carter and Don Withrington for pushing a rather aimless student in the direction of Scottish History. I have benefited enormously from the inspirational supervision of Professor Allan I. Macinnes and the assistance of Professor A. A. M. Duncan. Professor R. H. Campbell suspended his disdain for the pursuit of Highland history and was a constant source of encouragement. Professor T. M. Devine examined the Ph.D. thesis from which this book stems with characteristic methodological rigour, and has been of considerable assistance in the development of my interests since then. The University of Edinburgh gave me a job! My colleagues in the Department of Scottish History, Michael Lynch, John Simpson, John Bannerman and Helen Dingwall, have provided the ideal atmosphere for a young scholar to begin his career. Alison and Sandy Grant have worked far above and beyond the call of duty in editing the text. Fiona Watson, John Young, Ronnie Lee, Andrew Mackillop and Bill Knox contributed in their different ways to the enjoyment of research. Sally Ford, with love and forbearance, has put up with much over the past two years; without her, this book would not have been completed.

I owe an immeasurable debt to my parents for their support during what must have seemed an extended career as a student. Indeed, it was through their roots in the very different crofting communities of Stronaba and Idrigill that I first came to be interested in the issues discussed here.

None of the above shares any responsibility for the views, or the errors, contained in this book.

E. A. C.

Abbreviations

AJBP	A. J. Balfour Papers
BL	British Library, London
BLO	Bodleian Library, Oxford
BoAS	Board of Agriculture for Scotland
CBP	Campbell-Bannerman Papers
CDB	Congested Districts Board
EUL	Edinburgh University Library
HRA	Highland Regional Archive, Inverness
KEP	Kilmuir Estate Papers, HRA
KLTR	King's and Lord Treasurer's Remembrancer Department
NLS	National Library of Scotland, Edinburgh
NS	*Northern Scotland*
PD	Hansard, *Parliamentary Debates, House of Commons*
PP	*Parliamentary Papers*
PRO	Public Record Office, London
PWLC	Public Works Loan Commissioners
SCRO	Staffordshire County Record Office, Stafford
SEG	Skene, Edwards and Garson
SEGP	Skene, Edwards and Garson Papers, Edinburgh
SEP	Skeabost Estate Papers, HRA
SGM	*Scottish Geographical Magazine*
SHR	*Scottish Historical Review*
SJA	*Scottish Journal of Agriculture*
SLA	Scottish Liberal Association
SLC	Scottish Land Court
SLFP	Scottish Landowners' Federation Papers
SLPF	Scottish Land and Property Federation
SRO	Scottish Record Office, Edinburgh
TGSI	*Transactions of the Gaelic Society of Inverness*
WEGP	W. E. Gladstone Papers

Introduction

Historiographical Perspectives

In the history of the Highland land question, the period from 1886 to 1919 is characterised by four major pieces of legislation by the British government: the Crofters' Holdings (Scotland) Act, 1886; the Congested Districts (Scotland) Act, 1897; the Small Landholders (Scotland) Act, 1911; and the Land Settlement (Scotland) Act, 1919. In addition there were two important Royal Commissions: 1883–4 saw the 'Royal Commission of Inquiry into the Condition of Crofters and Cottars in the Highlands and Islands of Scotland', better known, after its Chairman, as the 'Napier Commission'; and 1892–5 saw the 'Royal Commission (Highlands and Islands) 1892' which, for rhetorical reasons, was better known as the 'Deer Forest Commission'. The four Acts and the reports of the two Commissions lie at the heart of this book.

Although the book concentrates on the period from the 1880s to the 1920s, it is important at the outset to explain the wider historiographical context, especially in view of the controversy over sources and the wide range of approaches which can be found in the work of previous historians. A major body of work has examined the history of the Highlands between 1750 and 1880; this is a vigorous and well-developed literature, although major areas of enquiry are still to be opened up. Surprisingly, given the amount of writing that has been generated, we are still unclear on many aspects of the Highland Clearances – though recent literature has drawn attention to the fact that the dynamics of Clearance were not uniform over the entire period from the mid-eighteenth century to the mid-nineteenth.[1] The financial structures behind the policy of Clearance and the whole institution of Highland landed estates are a second area in which pioneering research is under way. The work of Malcolm Gray, the first economic historian to turn his concentrated attention on the Highlands, has been particularly important. In his 1953 study of the Highland economy,[2] and in a series of introductions to a new edition of the *Statistical Account*, Gray repeatedly emphasises the theme of the diversity of economic and social

[1] A. I. Macinnes, 'Scottish Gaeldom: the first phase of Clearance', in T. M. Devine and R. Mitchison (eds.), *People and Society in Scotland*, vol. I *1760–1830* (Edinburgh, 1988); T M. Devine, *The Great Highland Famine* (Edinburgh, 1988).

[2] M. Gray, *The Highland Economy, 1750–1850* (London, 1953)

conditions in different areas of the Highlands. In particular, he draws attention to a basic difference between the northern and western parts of the Highlands and the southern and eastern parts. This is a point to which many other historians have returned. It is of particular relevance to this study, as the diversity of conditions in the Highlands was not reflected in government policy during the period under consideration: instead, the 1886 Act set a pattern whereby a single regime covered the majority of the parishes in the crofting counties. Indeed, from 1911 to 1955 the successor to the 1886 regime applied to the whole of Scotland.

Perhaps the most important recent development in the general literature on modern Highland history has been the plethora of studies focusing on the central topic of migration. This is important for a number of reasons; not only is it part of the wider theme of Scotland's paradoxical demography in the nineteenth century, but it also exposes critical facets of crofting society, and furthers the theme of the identification of a crofting area hinted at in Gray's work. The context for the ensuing discussion of this topic has been established in two seminal articles by T. M. Devine. Here, and in later work, Devine demonstrates the importance of temporary migration to the crofting community.[3] Building on Gray's distinction between the south-east and the north-west Highlands, and on a body of unpublished studies of specific areas, he argues that the former region – closer to Lowland towns, earlier and more comprehensively exposed to commercial pastoralism, and less affected by landlord-induced congestion during the kelp boom of the nineteenth century – was more affected by permanent migration of population to the towns and cities of the Lowlands. The north-west Highlands, by contrast, produced fewer permanent migrants. Instead, the population, forced to look for supplementary income after the creation of the crofting communities and the decline of the kelp industry, resorted to temporary migration. The consequence of this attempt to finance a valued way of life through the proceeds of labour outside the crofting region was that there continued to be a 'vulnerable society', which collapsed in the 1840s and, after a period of recovery, suffered badly again in the 1880s. Thus the economy and society of the crofting region were directly linked to the state of the industrial economy in Lowland Scotland and beyond. It is a profoundly depressing commentary on the effects of forty years of government intervention in the Highlands that the same equation of industrial depression and Highland poverty was as true in the 1930s as in the 1880s. The present book will attempt to explain why, through political inability and

[3] T. M. Devine, 'Temporary migration and the Scottish Highlands in the nineteenth century', *Economic History Review,* 2nd ser., xxxii (1979); T. M. Devine, 'Highland migration to Lowland Scotland, 1760–1860', *SHR*, lxii (1983); also, e.g., Devine, *Great Highland Famine*, pp. 146–70, 192–221.

unwillingness, the nettle of congestion was never truly grasped by the various policy-makers in the period under discussion here. It is this failure which links the 1880s and the 1930s.

Moving from the more general literature, there is much to be gained from a brief examination of works with a more specific bearing on the subject matter of this book. Much of these have concentrated on the 1886 Act. There has also been some discussion of the politics of the 1911 Act, partly because they became one of the issues in the developing conflict between the Liberal government and the House of Lords in the period from 1906 to 1911. The 1919 Act has been discussed in more detail recently, but the 1897 Act, and the Congested Districts Board which it created, have been largely ignored, despite a mass of documentary evidence concerning them.

The 1886 Act has usually been discussed in the context of preceding rather than succeeding events. Thus Eric Richards's *History of the Highland Clearances* includes a chapter on it, which argues that the Crofters Act represented the end of the Clearances and that 'it represented unambiguous gains for the crofters at the expense of the landlords; the Crofters Act was a great victory for the common people'.[4] The same author also draws attention to some of the Act's stagnating influences: in his study of the Cromartie estate, he claims that the Act interposed statutory relations between landlord and tenant, whereas previously a more informal relationship, which could benefit the crofter, had existed.[5]

The bulk of James Hunter's important but controversial book, *The Making of the Crofting Community,* is concerned with the years between 1850 and 1890, while the period from the 1890s to the 1920s receives cursory treatment.[6] *The Making of the Crofting Community* is important because it was the first survey of the modern history of the Highlands; further, it reacted against a historiographical tradition which, during the preceding decades, had been attacking the 1886 Act and classic crofting conditions as being outmoded and in dire need of reform.[7] The controversy surrounding Hunter's book stems from its specific aim, which was to write a history with the crofter at the centre. This technique conveys the impression of the crofter as a figure of unique virtue, universally oppressed by a monolithic group of landowners; thus there are elements of the work which resemble ahistorical propaganda rather

4 E. Richards, *A History of the Highland Clearances. Agrarian Transformation and the Evictions, 1746–1886* (London, 1982), chap. 15, 'Crofters, landlords and the public conscience, 1855–1886'; quote from p. 494.

5 E. Richards and M. Clough, *Cromartie. Highland Life. 1650–1914* (Aberdeen, 1989), p. 307

6 J. Hunter, *The Making of the Crofting Community* (Edinburgh, 1976).

7 D. J MacCuish, 'The origin and development of crofting law', *TGSI*, xliii (1960–3); D. J. MacCuish, 'The case for converting crofting tenure to ownership', *TGSI*, xlvi (1969–70); F. Gillanders, 'The economic life of Gaelic Scotland today', in D. C. Thomson and I. Grimble (eds.), *The Future of the Highlands* (London, 1968)

more than vigorous historical exposition. Hunter makes some large claims for the historical importance of the 1886 Act, seeing it, indeed, as the culminating event in the making of the crofting community. He argues that it gave statutory authority to long-standing popular notions about Highland land tenure, and, more controversially, that the combined effect of the crofters' agitation in the 1880s and the 1886 Act marked a watershed after which the political influence of the landowner declined as that of the crofting population rose.[8]

Other important commentaries include the work of I. M. M. MacPhail and I. F. Grigor. MacPhail's *Crofters' War* is the culmination of a life's work on the crofters' agitation, and was preceded by a series of important articles in the *Transactions of the Gaelic Society of Inverness*.[9] His is a notably sober assessment, although he also concludes his study in 1886. He agrees with Hunter that the Act was deficient, from the crofters' point of view, in that it did not include provision for giving them more land. However, he goes further than most in referring to the downside of the legacy of the Act; the perpetuation of small crofts is discussed, as is the lack of 'incentive ... for the introduction of modern methods of cultivation'.[10] MacPhail's book is, specifically, a study of the 1880s, so the charge which can be laid at the doors of others, of failing to consider the following decades, is less relevant. Nevertheless, this is not to deny that the history of the 1880s, and the 1886 Act, can be most usefully considered in the context of the subsequent period.

Both intellectually and methodologically, Grigor's work follows that of Hunter. His *Mightier than a Lord* is an examination of the Crofters' movement up to 1886, relying heavily on press comment and official publications. His subsequent doctoral thesis is an extension of this study. Both works are deficient in their systematic analysis of landlordism, despite the assertion that it is 'the key to nineteenth-century Highland Affairs'.[11] In his thesis, Grigor attempts to discuss the 1886 Act in the context of a triangular debate between the crofters, the government and the proprietors – a debate which concludes with the 1886 Act representing a signal victory for the crofters. However, this conclusion is pre-ordained, as the author has not used any evidence which would produce an understanding of the landlord position; nor has he used the

[8] Hunter, *Crofting Community*, p. 167.

[9] I. M. M. MacPhail, *The Crofters' War* (Stornoway, 1989); I. M. M. MacPhail, 'The prelude to the Crofters' War, 1870–1880', *TGSI*, xlix (1974–6); I. M. M. MacPhail, 'The Napier Commission', *TGSI*, xlviii (1972–4); I. M. M. MacPhail, 'The Skye military expedition of 1884–85', *TGSI*, xlviii (1972–4); I. M. M. MacPhail, 'The Highland elections of 1884–86', *TGSI*, l (1976–8); I. M. M. MacPhail, 'Gunboats to the Hebrides', *TGSI*, liii (1982–4).

[10] MacPhail, *Crofters' War*, p. 172.

[11] I. F. Grigor, *Mightier than a Lord* (Stornoway, 1979); I. F. Grigor, 'Crofters and the Land Question, 1870–1920' (Glasgow University Ph.D. thesis, 1989); quote from ibid., ii, pp. 18–19.

vast bulk of government records which shed considerable light on the period from 1886 to the mid-1920s.

The argument that the Act was part of the larger story of the declining position of the landed classes has been taken up in David Cannadine's *Decline and Fall of the British Aristocracy*; although it is based almost entirely on secondary sources, Cannadine has received some praise from reviewers for his consideration of the 'Celtic Fringe'.[12] And because the Crofters Act was passed in the 1886 Parliament, which was dominated by Irish Home Rule, it has impinged on the consciousness of some historians of British political history.[13] But, otherwise, British historians have shown only fleeting concern for the Highlands – which has been mirrored, ironically, by the minimal attention paid by Highland historians to the British political context of crofting legislation, and to sources outside Scotland.

The comparison with contemporaneous events in Ireland is an obvious one. Both countries had small tenants who employed a rhetorical version of their own history of oppression to good political effect. Both countries had a popular movement concerned with the land issue, which took direct action and was involved in mainstream politics. Both countries were the subject of innovative land legislation which interfered with proprietorial privileges. However, within this basic framework of similarity, there are important divergences of experience. The intensity of events surrounding the Irish land war is considerably greater than that of events in the Highlands. It is difficult to avoid the conclusion that this intensity was derived from the relationship between the land issue and the wider issue of Irish nationalism; in contrast, involvement in wider political issues was a destructive force in the Highland Land League. In the context of government policy, the contrast between the positive reaction to the concept of land purchase in Ireland, and the consistent and resourceful rejection of it by Highland crofters, is particularly striking.

Alongside this historical treatment of the 1886 Act, there has also been some polemical discussion. This emerged around the Act's centenary in 1986. For instance, in the collection of writings and images, *As An Fhearran*, it is stated:

> The significance of the 1886 Crofting Act for the Highlands and Islands is, therefore, difficult to exaggerate. It not only halted the Clearances, but represents a watershed which has shaped the subsequent history of the land and its people. The Crofting Act

[12] D. Cannadine, *The Decline and Fall of the British Aristocracy* (London, 1990), pp. 59–60; J. M. Bourne, Review of Cannadine, *Decline and Fall*, in *Twentieth-Century British History*, ii (1991), p. 386.

[13] See, e.g., W. C. Lubenow, *Parliamentary Politics and the Home Rule Crisis: The British House of Commons in 1886* (Oxford, 1988), pp. 196, 343–4.

legislation continues to shape the pattern of life in the Highlands to this day.[14]

This was the prevailing tone of the comment in that year. A different note has been struck, however, by Allan Macinnes in an article entitled 'The Crofters' Holdings Act: a hundred year sentence'.[15] He argues, in a highly polemical fashion, that the Act 'wrote the unbalanced use of land into the statute books' and 'perpetuated rather than corrected the pervasive abuse of land in the Highlands'. This is certainly an important corrective to the hagiographic tone which had predominated. But, by seeming to extend his criticism to the conduct of crofters in the twentieth century, Macinnes has won few friends. An unfortunate and unhelpful attack on the Scottish Crofters' Union, led at that time by James Hunter, obscured the historical content of the article, and as a result, few of the issues were debated meaningfully in the response by Hunter. The argument put forward by Macinnes, and also by MacPhail, that the Act perpetuated congestion, was not entirely new. J. B. Caird and H. A. Moisley had argued in the 1960s that the Act had stifled innovation in the crofting community: the fossilisation of land-holding and the ageing of the communities perpetuated this problem, as young, innovatory, crofters could not break through the accumulated conservatism of the older generation.[16]

The historiography of the 1886 Act has suffered from the polemical tone which has soured the debate. Support for the Act has been seen by some as a test of loyalty to modern crofting in a threatening era. The most notable failure has been the lack of any detailed examination of its operation. In particular, the important work of the Crofters' Commission, set up by the Act to deal with crofting rents, has not been systematically analysed.

The 1897 Act and the Congested Districts Board have been largely ignored by historians, with the honourable exception of A. S. Mather. Using basic printed sources, he has attempted to put the Board's work into perspective. He relates it, in various writings, to the land settlement activity following the statutes of 1911 and 1919. In an important 1988 article, the whole period is related to renewed government activity following the Highland Development Act of 1965.[17] Other comment by

[14] M. Maclean and C. Carrell (eds.), *As An Fhearran: From the Land* (Edinburgh, Glasgow and Stornoway, 1986), p. 6.

[15] A. I. Macinnes, 'The Crofters' Holdings Act: a hundred year sentence', *Radical Scotland*, xxv (Feb./Mar. 1987).

[16] J. B. Caird and H. A. Moisley, 'Leadership and innovation in the crofting communities of the Outer Hebrides', *Sociological Review*, ix (1961).

[17] A. S. Mather, 'The Congested Districts Board for Scotland', in W. Ritchie, J. C. Stone and A. S. Mather (eds.), *Essays for Professor R. E. H. Mellor* (Aberdeen, 1986); A. S. Mather, *State Aided Land Settlement in Scotland* (O'Dell Memorial Monograph, no. 6, Department of Geography, Aberdeen University, 1978); A. S. Mather, 'Government agencies and land development in the Scottish Highlands: a centenary survey', *NS*, viii (1988).

geographers on the 1897 Act has been limited to spurious comparisons with the Highlands and Islands Development Board [hereafter the HIDB]. The longer perspective taken by Mather allows him to place the importance of the Highland land issue in its psychological, as well as its political and ecological, context.[18]

The 1911 Act, in contrast, has occasioned a good deal of comment. This is due not so much to its contribution to Highland history as to its political context. The 1911 Act extended crofting tenure beyond the seven original crofting counties to the rest of Scotland, and also created a mechanism for the creation of new holdings on privately owned land. Both provisions were highly controversial: the Liberal government needed three attempts to pass the bill before it eventually became law in 1911. Because of the difficulties with the House of Lords in this period, it is dealt with in a number of textbooks on British history.[19] It has also been studied more closely, by John Brown in a 1968 article, and by Leah Leneman in the introduction to her recent study of post-war land settlement.[20] The comments by these authors, and by Hunter (who discusses the issue briefly),[21] tend to locate the Act simply as part of the straight conflict between a Liberal government and a Conservative-dominated House of Lords. This ignores important complexities in the debate, for there was a substantial, cross-party, body of opinion among Highland MPs and some Highland proprietors. Thus Lord Lovat, a Conservative peer, argued that a land settlement bill for the Highlands alone should be passed: the Lowlands could be catered for in the English arrangements, by which county councils had responsibility for land settlement. The government chose to ignore these entreaties, leading some to argue that the bill was being cynically used to foment conflict with the House of Lords at the expense of progress in the Highlands. It was not until changes were made in an attempt to mollify Lowland agricultural opinion, and after the passing of the Parliament Act of 1911, that the bill was passed.[22]

Similarly, the historiography of the operation of the 1911 Act has concentrated on the spoiling role of the proprietor; Hunter and Leneman have been particularly keen to stress this argument. They

[18] K. J Kaye, 'The use of the countryside by the urban state: Scotland's north-west seaboard and islands', *SGM*, cvi (1990), p. 91; A. S. Mather, 'The alleged deterioration of hill grazings in the Scottish Highlands', *Biological Conservation*, xiv (1978).

[19] R. C. K. Ensor, *England, 1870–1914* (Oxford, 1939), p. 393; P. Rowland, *The Last Liberal Governments: The Promised Land, 1905–1910* (London, 1968), p. 114; N Blewett, *The Peers, The Parties and The People: The General Elections of 1910* (London, 1970), pp. 380–3, 400–3

[20] J. Brown, 'Scottish and English land legislation, 1905–1911', *SHR*, xlvii (1968); L. Leneman, *Fit For Heroes? Land Settlement in Scotland after World War One* (Aberdeen, 1989), pp. 5–8.

[21] Hunter, *Crofting Community*, pp. 192–3

[22] *Glasgow Herald*, 29 May 1908, Memorial to the Prime Minister with reference to crofter legislation, SRO, SLFP, GD325/1/12, 'Conference between certain members of the House of Lords and the House of Commons, 4 Jun 1908'

tend, however, to underestimate the extent to which the Act's structure was a problem. The Board of Agriculture for Scotland [hereafter the BoAS], which was set up to implement the Act, was in no doubt that it was the legislation's imperfections that were the real problem. The point was made more forcefully by J. P. Day in his *Public Administration in the Highlands and Islands* – the only adequate overview of public policy towards the Highlands. However, Day's book is not without its problems; most obviously its antiquity. It was published in 1918, but had been completed before the outbreak of the First World War. As it is based on official printed sources available at the time, little penetration of the policy-making process was achieved. The lack of historical perspective, consequent upon the fact that it was written contemporaneously with many of the developments discussed here, means that its main value is as an interim report of the development of public policy in the Highlands up to 1913.[23]

The 1919 Act, perhaps the most efficient piece of legislation in the period, has been analysed at length by Leneman. This Act strengthened and simplified the 1911 procedure for creating new holdings on privately owned land, and, further, gave the BoAS power to purchase land for the purpose of land settlement: the largest number of new holdings were created in the period from 1919 to 1930. Leneman's book, however, is based almost solely on government records, which leads to a pedestrian recounting of the individual schemes of land settlement which were undertaken, and there is insufficient analysis of the policy as a whole. The 1919 Act is presented as part of the post-war reconstruction policy. In reality, the deficiencies of pre-war machinery were a much more important incentive for government action than the rhetoric of the 'Fit for Heroes' policy would suggest; indeed, the ex-service preference in post-war land settlement in the Highlands created as many problems as it solved.[24] The Highland land problem had little to do with the First World War. Instead, it had a great deal to do with the long-standing demand for land, and the associated policies to cope with this, which had been implemented since the 1880s and must be considered in that context.

The legacy of the 1919 Act, in creating a large number of new small crofts which were exposed to the grim economic conditions of the 1930s, has been underestimated. Analysis has concentrated instead on the extent to which the Act saw the official reversal of the Clearances. Accounts of the 1930s have not given sufficient emphasis to the structural problems which are inherent in the idea of an agricultural

[23] Hunter, *Crofting Community*, pp. 193–4; Leneman, *Fit For Heroes?*; pp. 11–12; J. P. Day, *Public Administration in the Highlands and Islands of Scotland* (London, 1918), p. 228.

[24] Leneman, *Fit for Heroes, passim*; SRO, Crofting Files, AF67/387, Memo by H. M. Conacher (Secretary to the BoAS), 'On economic conditions in the crofting counties'.

unit which was so small that it necessitated another source of income;[25] this is an ideal system only so long as the secondary source of income can be assured.

Thus, despite an interesting historical debate on the 1886 Act, the period from 1886 to 1919 has not been well served by historians of the Highlands. It has usually been treated as an unimportant addendum to the more important and interesting events of the 1880s; and general textbooks tend to deal with it briefly, merely recounting the dates of the Acts. This has created two historiographical deficiencies. First, the progress of legislation is seen as a straight line leading from 1886 to 1919. That was certainly not the intention of the Liberals in 1886. Gladstone and Harcourt saw the 1886 Act as a recognition of historically valid common rights, not as the beginning of a new code of legislation. The four Acts are not a straight line of policy development. There is, in fact, an ongoing debate between, on the one hand, the concepts of dual ownership, reflected in the 1886 and 1911 Acts and in Part II of the 1919 Act, and, on the other, peasant proprietorship, reflected in the 1897 Act and in the 1919 Act, Part I. The compulsory creation of new holdings on privately owned land was deeply unpopular with landlords; they were much happier to divest themselves of all responsibility for new holdings by selling land to government institutions who could then do what they liked with it.[26] Secondly, the bulk of the writing has concentrated on the 1886 Act to the exclusion of the succeeding legislation; consequently, the importance of the 1886 Act has been exaggerated. As noted above, several authors regard it as a watershed. Hunter's argument – that it marked the virtual end of proprietorial influence with the government – has been particularly influential. But, in fact, proprietorial influence on government, particularly of the Conservative variety, remained strong.[27] The developments of the period from 1886 to 1919 have been confused with the consequences of the 1886 Act because the former has been studied so superficially. This book, therefore, is an attempt to fill that gap.

A Note on Sources

The two issues of sources and perspectives in Highland history are inextricably linked; indeed, the issue of sources has become almost as controversial as some of the substantive historical issues. Highland history tends, in places, towards the emotive, and sources have become identified with particular groups in Highland society. It seems to have

25 Hunter, *Crofting Community*, p. 206; J. Hunter, *The Claim of Crofting: The Scottish Highlands and Islands, 1930–1990* (Edinburgh, 1991), chap. 1.

26 E. A. Cameron, 'Politics, ideology and the Highland land issue, 1886 to the 1920s', *SHR*, lxxii (1993).

27 E. A. Cameron, 'The political influence of Highland landowners: a reassessment', *NS*, xiv (1994).

become the practice to label sources and to assume that a particular kind of history will result from their use. This sectarian attitude to sources and perspectives has been a dominant trend in the historiography. But the use of a wide range of different sources for the purposes of this book has led to a realisation that the convenient labels attached to various groups of material are misleading in that they conceal the diversity of evidence contained within them.

Although use of a multiplicity of sources is a feature of the present approach, this is essentially a study of government policies, and the weight given to the sources reflects this. Government records, both published in the form of *Parliamentary Papers* and manuscript in the form of Departmental files and Cabinet Papers, are the basic source of information. There are several points worthy of emphasis here. First, there is an important coincidence between the establishment of the Scottish Office in 1885 and the passing of the Crofters Act the following summer. In its first few months of existence, the workload of the new Office was regarded as light and the position of Secretary for Scotland as none too onerous. However, once the Crofters Act was passed and the agitation showed no immediate signs of dying down, this perspective was altered. The crofters' agitation allowed the Scottish Office to bargain effectively with the Home Office for the transfer of sole responsibility for law and order.[28] The administration of police and military expeditions, intended to quell the agitation, gave rise to a large number of files. These contain a vast amount of information, as within them are contained regular reports by police constables from all over the troubled areas, which comment on the regularity and punctuality of rent payment, on the incidence and proceedings of public meetings and on other events concerned with the agitation. A second important process generating a significant amount of source material was the work of the institutions set up after 1886. The Crofters' Commission was a vital body for the Highland policies of both Liberal and Conservative governments in the period from 1886 to 1895. The files containing its correspondence illuminate the way this body was used in a highly political fashion in this period. The Congested Districts Board, established in 1897 in an attempt to facilitate crofter land purchase, has particularly voluminous source material relating to it; in the past, however, this had not been examined systematically by historians. Detailed material can also be found concerning the Board of Agriculture for Scotland which was established to succeed the Congested Districts Board in 1912.[29]

[28] H. J. Hanham, 'The creation of the Scottish Office, 1881–1887', *Juridical Review*, pp. 220–4.

[29] The Police reports and other material relating to attempts to quell the agitation can be found in the SRO, Home and Health Department Miscellaneous Files, HH1. The material relating to the Crofters' Commission can be found in Department of Agriculture and Fisheries, Crofting Files, AF67/1–31. Department of Agriculture and

There are also two areas of central government sources which proved especially useful. After 1919, the Board of Agriculture had access to money made available by the Public Works Loan Commissioners. Applications for this money were vetted by the Treasury through their eyes and ears in Scotland, the King's and the Lord Treasurer's Remembrancer; the resulting series of correspondence sheds important light on the attitude of the Treasury to the peculiarly Scottish policy of land settlement. Negotiations for money for land settlement can be followed by this means. Tensions between government departments (in this case the Scottish Office and the Treasury) are an important theme of any study of government policy, and this is no exception.[30] The second area of central government material is the records of the Cabinet and its Committees. After each Cabinet meeting, the Prime Minister sent a report of the proceedings to the monarch; such reports can be employed to follow the course of a bill through Cabinet. Both the 1886 and 1911 Acts had complicated gestation periods, and these reports proved an important source in understanding them. In addition, the lengthy memoranda prepared by the Scottish Office for circulation in the Cabinet can provide an insight into the reasons for a particular course of action or line of policy, and the records of Cabinet Committees provide vital detail on the process of the ongoing review of policy. This is particularly notable for the review of the expensive policy of land settlement in the early 1920s: important shifts of emphasis in the policy were carried out on the recommendation of a Cabinet Committee, but were never announced in public.

All these sources are essential for penetrating the public statements of governments. They are the only systematic route to an understanding of the policy-making process. But when using them, it is important to understand the audience for which they were intended. None, of course, was written with the public in mind: the strictures of the closure rules on this type of public record ensure that they were written with the assurance that they would not be made public for many years. This fact allows much unguarded comment by officials and politicians alike. Moreover, memoranda written for the internal workings of the Scottish Office structure must be read differently from those written to another government department. In the latter case, especially when the Treasury was concerned, the normal requirement of sceptical appreciation of the contents of a historical source is especially important. Awareness, where possible, of the perspective of the individuals involved in government correspondence can add extra insight. For example, during the tenure

Fisheries, CDB Files, AF42, run to over 9,000 in number, and many of them cover the day-to-day work of the Board. A selection containing material relating to policy-making or implementation has been used for the purposes of this study. Information concerning the activities of the Board of Agriculture for Scotland can be found in Department of Agriculture and Fisheries, Estate Management Files, AF83

30 See SRO, Exchequer, KLTR Files, E824

at the Scottish Office from 1906 to 1912 of John Sinclair (from 1909 Lord Pentland), his Permanent Under Secretary for Scotland was Sir Reginald MacLeod, heir to the Dunvegan estates in Skye – who obviously had a very different outlook on Highland issues from that of Sinclair, as became clear in 1910 when he resigned and stood as a Conservative candidate.

Although these are government sources, in the sense that they are generated by government, the official perspective is not the only one to be gleaned from them. The records of the Crofters' Commission and the Congested Districts Board are replete with letters from landlords, crofters, local authorities, political parties, and pressure groups (for example, landowners' and farmers' organisations). Occasionally, verbatim accounts of special events are included among normal government memoranda. This is the case with the record of the efforts of the Crofters' Commission and the Congested Districts Board to relocate the crofters of Sconser in 1900: this 'government' source gives the only verbatim account of the stated reasons of the crofters for their reluctance to leave their overcrowded and unhealthy township. A similar case arises with the Congested Districts Board's attempts to encourage the crofters of Kilmuir to purchase their holdings. Thus there is a danger in making value judgements about the type of evidence likely to be discovered in a particular source, and a similar danger in the attachment of convenient labels to such source material.

A supplementary method of penetrating the policy-making process is through the private correspondence of the individuals involved. This has been done here to analyse the politics behind the making of the 1886 and 1911 Acts. It affords an opportunity to examine the way in which coalitions, often containing surprising partnerships, were constructed in an attempt to get legislation through Parliament. Such correspondence can illuminate the private thoughts of ministers and the opinions of those outside the official policy-making process.

Next, in an attempt to examine the reactions to government policies, it has been found necessary to examine as wide a range of estate papers as possible. Much of value can be found here. The correspondence between proprietors and factors is full of unguarded comment about the impact of the new legislation and institutions on estate management. However, estate papers are relatively little used by historians of this period – except in those studies based on one collection of material.[31] Indeed, the use of estate papers has come to be thought characteristic of an approach recently dubbed 'landlord apologia'. One historian has argued that as a result of the study of estate documents, 'the people upon whom estate managements imposed their policies have been

[31] Neither Hunter, *Crofting Community*, nor Grigor, *Mightier than a Lord*, uses estate papers in a systematic fashion. Comments in the bibliographical essay of the latter display a markedly sectarian attitude to literature and sources.

almost completely neglected'. The inference is that somehow estate papers are a 'landlord source', used by authors 'whose sympathies lie with Highland landlords', to write a particular kind of history.[32]

But late nineteenth-century estate papers are, in reality, an extremely diverse collection of materials. As well as the internal correspondence of the estate management structure, they often include letters from official bodies such as the Crofters' Commission or the Congested Districts Board; and frequently, too, there are petitions from crofters or cottars on a wide variety of issues. These are not 'landlord' sources in content, nor do they necessarily lead to a sympathy with the complete works of landlordism. Indeed, if we are searching for evidence to damn the conduct of landlords and their representatives, we could find it in abundance, in their own words, in estate papers.[33] Thus, once again, it is extremely misleading to attach labels to a particular kind of evidence. This is a most important point, as Highland history has been plagued by sectarianism between historians who take different approaches to its study, and tend to reject various kinds of evidence, such as estate papers on the one hand, or oral evidence on the other, as incompatible with their world view.[34]

The final area of source material employed here, and by other historians of the period, is the voluminous evidence given by crofters, landlords and factors to the Royal Commissions of 1883 and 1892. This has been used effectively by others to 'put the crofter at the centre of his own history'.[35] The evidence heard by these Commissions was significant, in that it was the first time the crofters had spoken publicly, in a systematic fashion, in a manner which was often critical of their landlords' conduct. We should, of course, pay testimony to the significance of that step and to the courage involved in taking it. Yet that does not mean that the factual content of the evidence itself should be taken as objective truth. A great deal of rhetoric was involved, and the

32 B. Wilson, Column in *West Highland Free Press*, 26 Mar. 1993; a lively correspondence ensued over the following weeks on the subject of approaches to Highland history. See also Hunter, *Crofting Community*, pp. 4–5.

33 The attitude of Major Fraser of Kilmuir to his crofting tenants comes across all too clearly in his numerous letters to Alexander MacDonald, the Portree Solicitor and Banker who acted as his factor. See HRA, Kilmuir Estate Papers [KEP], AG INV 10. Much of the material here is that used by I. M. M. MacPhail over the years. It was known to him as 'the MacDonald and Fraser Papers', and was formerly located in the legal firm of that name in Portree. This firm ceased to exist in the early 1980s, and the archive material came under threat, until saved by Mr Allan Lawson of the HRA. The correspondence between Alexander MacDonald and Lachlan MacDonald of Skeabost is now in the HRA, Skeabost Estate Papers [SEP], AG INV 11. The correspondence of MacDonald and MacLeod of MacLeod has been returned to Dunvegan and can be found among the muniments there. The material recently catalogued by the National Register of Archives (Scotland) is the detritus of the collection, and contains none of the material used by MacPhail or by myself.

34 See the contrasting comments in Hunter, *Crofting Community*, pp. 1–5, and P. Gaskell, *Morvern Transformed* (Cambridge, 1973), p. 25.

35 Hunter, *Crofting Community*, p. 5.

statements have to be read with this in mind. This is particularly important in the case of the 1892 Royal Commission, when the crofter evidence was organised by Donald MacRae of the Highland Land League and the landlord evidence was co-ordinated by George Malcolm of the Highland Property Association. Much of the evidence was retrospective, involving testimony on the history of particular townships over the whole course of the nineteenth century. The testimony is excellent evidence of the collective state of mind of the crofting community in 1883 or 1892, but is not a reliable source for the events of the earlier nineteenth century.[36] The principal significance of the evidence to these Commissions lies not so much in their impact on policy, which was minimal, but in how they drew the attention of public opinion to the plight of the crofting community.

The final major body of source material utilised here is the considerable body of newspaper and contemporary periodical comment. As well as the national Scottish press, such as the *Glasgow Herald* or *The Scotsman*, which commented extensively on Highland issues in the period before the First World War, there was a vibrant local press in the Highlands. This was notable for the wide range of editorial opinion in the various papers. The *Inverness Courier* and the *Northern Chronicle*, also published in Inverness, tended to be highly critical of any crofter action which involved illegality, and to be greatly approving of any landlord initiative. At the other end of the spectrum stood papers like the *Scottish Highlander*, the *Oban Times* and the *Highland News*. The *Scottish Highlander* was published by the well-known Inverness journalist, historian and political activist, Alexander MacKenzie, and was notable, and valuable, for the amount of space it gave to the activities of the Highland Land Law Reform Association. After the *Scottish Highlander* went out of business in 1893, the most consistent advocate of the crofter cause became the *Oban Times*, although its radicalism was tempered by 1914. These are valuable sources for the varying reactions to the policy initiatives taken by governments. But, of course, an awareness of the political orientation of the newspaper in question is essential for its use as historical evidence.[37]

The approach to sources adopted for the purposes of this book centres on an attempt to employ as wide a range as possible. No historical source can be completely free from error, and all sources are partial views of a given situation. This necessitates an open-minded

[36] Some writers have tried to use it as such; see D. Craig, *On the Crofters' Trail* (London, 1990).

[37] Some of these local papers are not widely available. The NLS has the *Northern Chronicle* and the *Scottish Highlander*; Inverness Public Library has these and the *Inverness Courier*. All the papers are available in the Newspaper Library of the British Library at Hendon. A complete run of the *Oban Times* can be found in the offices of the paper in Oban, and access for readers can be arranged. The NLS has recently acquired a microfilm copy of the *Oban Times*.

approach to the various sources discussed here: the material in one can be used to complement or contradict an impression given in another. Thus, while the conclusions presented here no doubt will not – and indeed should not – generate universal agreement, it must be stressed that they have not been formulated on the basis of wilful disregard for any particular type of source material.

CHAPTER ONE

The Making of the Crofters' Holdings (Scotland) Act

The immediate politics of the 1886 Act extend back to the beginning of the 1880s and go through various stages which increase in intensity, from the involvement of local government, to analysis by Royal Commission, and, subsequently, to policy formation by the Cabinet after informal consultation with favoured proprietors. Examination of these politics neatly introduces the themes which are pursued in the rest of this book.

The series of incidents which have become known as the 'Crofters' War' preoccupied governments of both parties throughout the 1880s. The agitation arose from a complex interplay of economic and cultural forces in the post-famine Highlands. There was a series of disjointed outbreaks of agitation in Wester Ross and Lewis in the 1870s, but the most concerted phase of the agitation, lasting from 1882 to 1888, began in Skye.[1] This chapter considers the impact of the Crofters' War on government policy towards the Highlands, during the period from 1882 to the passing of the Crofters' Holdings (Scotland) Act in the summer of 1886. The government's responses both to the various demands of crofters and proprietors, and to political worries about the effect of special treatment for crofters on tenurial relations in the rest of Scotland, form the focus of the analysis.

The making of the Crofters Act can be divided into three periods. First, from 1882 to 1883, the crofter issue developed from an administrative to a political one, and its impact shifted from local to central government. The establishment of the Napier Commission in 1883, and the course of its work over the following year, helped to establish the question as regionally specific. Although the Commission's direct impact on the content of legislation was minimal, its importance in raising this question cannot be underestimated. The second phase, in 1884, was dominated by an attempt by the government to marginalise the Crofters' movement by encouraging proprietors to build a partnership with their tenants, through concessions on the issues of rent, compensation for improvements, and extra land. A growing realisation

[1] MacPhail, 'Prelude to the Crofters' War'; Hunter, *Crofting Community*; Devine, *Great Highland Famine*; D. E. Meek, 'The land question answered from the Bible', *SGM*, ciii (1987), pp. 84–9.

that this would be insufficient saw the onset of the final period, from 1885 to the eventual passing of the Act in mid-1886.

I

Trouble started in Skye in 1882, when the celebrated crofters of The Braes, near Portree, asserted their 'historical right' to graze their stock on Ben Lee. This was land which the proprietor, Lord MacDonald, now used for the grazing of his own sheep. The crofters' defiance of sheriff officers' attempts to uphold proprietorial legal rights culminated in the dispatch of a force of police to Skye. The ensuing confrontation between the police and the crofters was the first to have an impact on local and central government.[2] The Commissioners of Supply for the county of Inverness were the first to have to deal with the consequences of the events in Skye. Before the reform of Scottish local government in 1889, which saw the creation of a system of elected county councils, it was the commissioners who were responsible for policing the county. By late 1882, as the agitation spread from The Braes across Skye to the western district of Glendale, the county authorities became concerned that their police force was inadequate to maintain law and order in Skye – at this time the entire county of Inverness was policed by 135 men. An additional thirty-five could be found, but it would take time to train them for the difficult duty of policing the disturbed districts of Skye. In November the Police Committee resolved that it was 'quite unable to enforce the law and secure the maintenance of peace in the County without aid from the central government'. The Lord Advocate was unimpressed by this view. He informed Sheriff Ivory, the sheriff principal of Inverness, that he considered the county authorities to be responsible by statute for the policing of the county. Aid from central government would go no further than authorisation by the Home Secretary to recruit extra police from whatever source they considered appropriate. In the event, forty extra policemen from Glasgow were drafted in to help deal with the situation.[3]

In 1882 the crofters' agitation was an administrative problem. Certainly it was serious enough to cause problems in the relationship between local and central government, but it was not yet the political problem it would soon become. There was no structure by which the crofters could articulate their demands. This was partly remedied by the formation of a formal Crofters' movement. The London and Edinburgh Highland Land Law Reform Associations [hereafter the HLLRA] and

[2] H. J. Hanham, 'The problem of Highland discontent, 1880–1885', *Transactions of the Royal Historical Society*, 5th ser., xix (1969); MacPhail, *Crofters' War*, pp. 36–52; Hunter, *Crofting Community*, pp. 133–7.

[3] HRA, Inverness-shire Commissioners of Supply Papers, R/13, County of Inverness, Police Committee, resolution, 2 Dec. 1882; J. B. Balfour to William Ivory, 3 Nov. 1882

the Sutherland Association provided a forum for sympathetic political activists in urban Scotland and beyond to raise the grievances of the crofters and present them to a wider audience. The crofters themselves temporarily acquired a political voice through the sittings of the Napier Commission in 1883. However, it was not until 1885, following their enfranchisement under the third Reform Act, that they were able to have an independent political impact. Nevertheless, through the voice of the Crofters' movement and the actions of sympathisers in Parliament – such as Charles Fraser-Mackintosh, MP for Inverness Burghs, and Donald H. MacFarlane, at that time MP for Wicklow in Ireland – the government began to be made aware of the grievances of the crofters. In late 1882 and early 1883, as the agitation took a firm hold in Skye, moves were made to persuade the government to create a Royal Commission to examine crofting conditions. This was the first of a series of political moves in which the origins of the legislation of 1886 can be discerned. However, as will be seen from the discussion below, legislation was far from the mind of the government at this stage.

As early as August 1883 MacFarlane had appealed to the government for a Royal Commission. He pointed to the insecurity of the crofter, who could be legally evicted at only forty days' notice, and he contrasted it with the position of the Irish tenants, who had received a measure of protection from Parliament in 1881. The Lord Advocate, speaking for the government, argued that 'no adequate ground' for the setting up of a Royal Commission had been demonstrated. Before such a step could be contemplated, a clear legal problem, and some suggestion as to an alteration in the law to deal with it, would have to be identified. In an intimation of one of the themes of the debate on crofter legislation, he argued that the crofting population was not purely an agricultural population, but could independently improve its position without Commissions or legislation, through wage labour.[4]

Despite the public appearance of a categorical refusal of a Commission, the government considered the issue with some care in private. The Ministers involved in the issue were the Home Secretary, Sir William Harcourt; Lord Rosebery, who was a junior minister in the Home Office with special responsibility for Scottish affairs; the Lord Advocate, J. B. Balfour; and the Solicitor General. The Lord Advocate was strongly against a Commission, fearing it would only encourage agitation and the non-payment of rent. More importantly, there were political objections: a reluctance to consider special treatment for the crofters, and the difficulties in defining the geographic area to be covered by a Commission. It was argued that the crofter problem could best be dealt with in the general legislative framework employed for landlord–tenant relations. On the other hand, while a fear of giving

[4] *PD*, 3rd ser., vol. 273, cols. 766–83, 4 Aug. 1882.

special recognition to crofters existed, there was also an awareness that it would be dangerous to refuse a Commission and then, in the face of mounting agitation, to concede one at a later date, when demands would have escalated. By November, therefore, Harcourt had come round to the view that a Commission was unavoidable. This was based not on any profound sympathy with the crofters' case, but on the political grounds that a Commission would be a safer option at that time than in the future. He still had the worries of the summer over the geographic remit and the possibility that such a move would 'open the floodgates of the Highland land question'. The Prime Minister agreed, but wished the matter to go before the full Cabinet before a policy decision was reached.[5] In the past, Gladstone had accepted the idea of tenant right, based on a history of customary rights, most notably with regard to Ireland – he had used such arguments in the internal government debate leading up to the Irish Land Act of 1881. But at this date there was no sign that such thinking would be applied to Scotland. Indeed, Gladstone did not espouse it in a Scottish context until early 1885, during the debate leading up to the first Crofters' Bill.[6]

When Harcourt declared in Parliament in March 1883 that a Commission would be appointed, his objective was probably to try to take the heat out of the agitation. This view is strengthened by the fact that he announced that both the remit and the geographical scope of the Commission should be as general as possible.[7]

The Commission was to be chaired by Lord Napier, a Border peer, retired diplomat, and amateur social scientist. His colleagues were Sir Donald Cameron of Lochiel, at that time Tory MP for Inverness-shire; his fellow landowner Sir Kenneth MacKenzie of Gairloch, a noted Liberal; Charles Fraser-Mackintosh; and two Gaelic scholars, Alexander Nicolson, sheriff of Kirkcudbright, and Professor Donald MacKinnon, first holder of the Chair of Celtic at Edinburgh University. Representatives of the Crofters' movement argued that the Commission lacked a true crofter representative: Lochiel, MacKenzie of Gairloch and even Fraser-Mackintosh were all labelled as landowners. The HLLRA had recommended Alexander MacKenzie, the Inverness journalist, historian and genealogist, for the Commission, but Harcourt chose not to act on this suggestion. MacKinnon and Nicolson, as scholars, were not expected to provide a radical input. Harcourt had received a

[5] BL, WEGP, MS Add. 44476, fos. 245–7, Memo by the Lord Advocate, 7 Sep. 1882; MS Add. 44197, fos. 144–6, Harcourt to Gladstone, 25 Nov. 1882; MS Add. 44546, fo. 40, Gladstone to Harcourt, 25 Nov. 1882.

[6] C. Dewey, 'Celtic agrarian legislation and the Celtic revival: historicist implications of Gladstone's Irish and Scottish Land Acts, 1870–1886', *Past and Present*, lxiv (1974), pp. 56–63; R. F. Foster, *Modern Ireland, 1600–1972* (London, 1989 edn), pp. 395–7, 412–14; R. D. C. Black, 'Economic policy in Ireland and India in the time of J. S. Mill', *Economic History Review*, xxi (1968).

[7] *PD*, 3rd ser., vol. 277, col. 797, 19 Mar 1883

recommendation on MacKinnon's behalf from Lady Gordon Cathcart, the proprietor of Benbecula, South Uist and Barra; had this been widely known in 1882, MacKinnon would surely have been distrusted by the crofters. As for Nicolson, he took his seat on the Commission after declaring his Liberal allegiance to Harcourt and laying the problems of the Highlands at the door of 'Tory Lairds, factors, and their subordinates'. Many proprietors were unhappy at the political composition of the Commission, Lochiel being the sole Tory.[8]

Contemporary worries concerning the Napier Commission were political. Retrospectively, its most important characteristic can be identified as the antiquarian and historical interests of many of its members. Apart from Nicolson and MacKinnon, Fraser-Mackintosh was a noted antiquarian and Napier was a keen student of history and anthropology. This was important, because much of the crofters' rhetoric during the agitation had focused on their historical case for the restoration of lands which had been removed from their use by proprietors over the previous century and more. There had been a significant upsurge of interest in the history of the Highland land question in the early 1880s – especially with the publication of Alexander MacKenzie's *History of the Highland Clearances*.[9] This work was as important for its polemical denunciation of the actions of proprietors as for its scholarly analysis of the Clearances, something which was not without relevance to the origins of the agitation. The historical emphasis became more important once the crofter evidence to the Commission began to be heard. Crofter delegates were not discouraged from giving their own versions of the course of events in their townships over the preceding generations, in an attempt to justify their demands for more land and a more secure tenure. Further, the concept of the township, which had been destroyed by the time of the Clearances, was rehabilitated during the 1880s. The third volume of W. F. Skene's *Celtic Scotland*, published in 1880, had been devoted to this theme, while John Stuart Blackie was to give considerable attention to historical aspects of the land question in his evidence to the Napier Commission.[10]

One of the most important political questions, once the composition of the Commission had been decided, was the geographical area which it should cover. To restrict the area of its remit to the districts where the agitation was strongest would limit its political impact. But there were problems of definition if it were to include all areas where there were 'crofters' and 'cottars'; these were vague terms which had different

[8] BLO, MS Harcourt, dep. 114, fos. 101–2, Alexander Nicolson to Harcourt, 14 Mar. 1883; fos. 104–5, Lady Gordon Cathcart to Harcourt, 14 Mar. 1883; fos. 110–12, John MacDonald to Harcourt, 13 Mar. 1883.

[9] A. MacKenzie, *A History of the Highland Clearances* (Inverness, 1883).

[10] W. F. Skene, *Celtic Scotland: A History of Ancient Alban*, vol. III: *Land and People* (Edinburgh, 1880); *PP*, 1884: XXXVI, *Report of the Commissioners of Inquiry into the Condition of the Crofters and Cottars in the Highlands and Islands of Scotland*, pp. 3372–86.

meanings in different parts of the country. Napier himself was concerned about the status of Caithness: this was a low-lying county 'not inhabited by the Celtic race'; on the other hand, its population complained of the same grievances as those in the north of Skye, who were among the most vocal crofters. Then there were other fringe areas (such as Highland Perthshire, upland Banff and Aberdeenshire, and southern Argyllshire) where it was a matter for debate whether crofting conditions existed or not. In the end, it was left to the judgement of the Commissioners to decide their itinerary. One factor to be borne in mind was the need for a reasonably prompt report: an exhaustive inquiry, spread over a long period, would defeat the government's object. The Commission displayed an awareness of the political dimension to this debate by carrying out the 'heavier portion' of its work in the Hebrides first.[11]

The work of the Commission in its tour of the Highlands, taking evidence from crofters, proprietors and others, did not pass without controversy. There was claim and counter-claim concerning the role of the Crofters' movement. There is no doubt that there was action by activists like John Murdoch and Alexander MacKenzie, encouraging people to give evidence and assisting in its preparation. This kind of activity gave the Crofters' movement an opportunity to establish contacts and organisation in the grass roots of the crofting community – a source of strength which it had lacked until then.[12] In addition to the claims that the HLLRA was interfering unduly and distorting the evidence of the crofters, it was claimed that crofters who criticised estate managements in their evidence were the victims of reprisals. Such allegations struck a raw nerve in the proprietorial community, which responded by vigorously denying that there was any truth in them. At the forefront of this denial was a delegation led by the duke of Argyll, and including representatives of Skye, South Uist and Ross-shire estates, who stated their case to the Lord Advocate at the Home Office.[13]

A number of points can be made to clarify the position at the end of 1883, when the Napier Commission returned to Edinburgh to write its report. The agitation had developed from its disparate origins and now had a significant impact on local government in the Highlands. Thanks to the help of articulate and well-connected activists in Parliament and to continued agitation on the ground, the crofter question impinged on the

11 BLO, MS Harcourt, dep. 114, fo. 116, Napier to Harcourt, 17 Mar 1883, fo. 131, Lochiel to Harcourt, 13 Jun. 1883; J. P. Maxton, 'The problems of land tenure in the Highlands of Scotland', *Proceedings of the First International Conference of Agricultural Economists* (1929), p. 36.

12 HRA, KEP, AG INV 10/29, William Fraser to Alexander MacDonald, 22 Apr. 1883, 24 Apr. 1883, 4 Nov. 1883; SRO, Mackintosh Muniments, GD176/2633/31, The Mackintosh to Allan MacDonald, 15 Oct. 1883.

13 SEGP, deed box A6, Lady Gordon Cathcart, no. 6, bundle 14, 'Proceedings at the Home Office on a deputation to the Lord Advocate with reference to Scotch Crofters, 2 May 1884'.

attention of the Liberal government. The demand for a Commission had been voiced and eventually granted by the government in the hope that it would have an effect in quelling agitation. One of the major problems faced by the government in setting up the Commission had been how to limit its sphere of operations to an intellectually and politically defensible region, and yet to cover a wide enough area to ensure maximum impact in the disturbed districts of the Highlands. The compilation and publication of the Napier Commission's Report was the start of a vigorous debate on the most efficacious method of dealing with the crofter question which culminated in, but was not ended by, the passing of the Crofters' Holdings (Scotland) Act.

The Royal Commissioners had not achieved a unanimity in their view of the evidence after the completion of their investigations. Social and political divisions were evident. Despite their political differences, the two major landowners, Lochiel and MacKenzie of Gairloch, had reservations concerning the progress of the Commission. Lochiel had cast doubt on the value of much of the evidence he had heard from crofters, and felt sure that he would not be able to accept the fundamentals of the report once it was written, since Napier's ideas were paramount and he counted on the support of Nicolson, MacKinnon and Fraser-Mackintosh. Lochiel was aware of the dangers of sacrificing principle for the pursuit of superficial unanimity; as a Tory, his signature would be used by the Liberals to point out that the report had cross-party support. In the end, both he and Kenneth MacKenzie signed the report but appended dissents from the most critical section of the report dealing with land.[14] Napier had done his best to bring all the Commissioners together. He had been aware that this was likely to be difficult with regard to land, a subject on which the members of the Commission held 'divergent views'.[15]

The details of the Commission's Report with regard to land were striking. This section was largely penned by Napier, in the absence of agreement among his colleagues. He had been impressed with the complaints of crofters on the insecurity of their tenure, and also with the importance of increasing the size of the individual holding and of improving the quality of agriculture in the crofting areas. He aimed to accomplish these ends through a system of improving leases, township organisation and assisted emigration, backed up by limited security of tenure. Tenants with holdings of more than £6 annual value were to have a secure tenure and be given leases of thirty years' duration which would contain a programme of improvement for the holding. Tenants in holdings of less than £6 annual value were to remain outside the scheme, and would be catered for by a scheme of voluntary emigration. To include them, Napier felt, would perpetuate the ills he was trying to

[14] Hatfield House Papers, 3M/E, Lochiel to Salisbury, 2 Dec. 1883.
[15] BLO, MS Harcourt, dep. 115, Napier to Harcourt, 1 Nov. 1883.

eradicate. A recreated township system was to be the centrepiece of the scheme. The township was to be responsible for the 'possession and administration' of common pasture; all settlements of three or more holdings with common pasture, or a history of such within a forty-year period, were to be constituted as townships. Napier, unlike Lochiel, had been impressed with the crofter evidence to the Commission, as is clearly seen in his reasoning for the recreation of the township. He argued that it was valid because it had a 'basis of operation in the customs of the country' and a 'distinct existence in the sentiments and traditions of its component members'.[16] There were also provisions to govern vacant holdings and subdivision, designed to eradicate congestion over a period of time.[17]

Lochiel and Kenneth MacKenzie both dissented from the idea of the township, arguing that it would be inflexible and would damage proprietorial rights. Lochiel also made a pertinent point which he would echo many times over the next few years. He queried the geographic boundaries in which the scheme was to operate, pointing to the diversity of conditions in many Highland counties, and arguing that the parish was too small a unit of definition. An additional problem was the lack of conformity between estate and parish boundaries.[18]

A clear theme of social and even moral, as well as agricultural, improvement runs through this section of the report. It was stated that the aim was 'to stimulate the people to shake off the torpor which besets them' and to help form 'habits of industry and self respect'.[19] This, according to Napier, would be the long-term solution to the Highland problem. Furthermore, it would be a solution transcending governments and legislation.

The Irish Land Act of 1881 was constantly in the background in the ongoing debate on the Highland land issue. Napier's scheme, however, was a rejection of the application of this statute to the Highlands. That was implicit in the report, with its rejection of comprehensive security of tenure and rent revaluation. In private communication with Harcourt, Napier stated this explicitly. He did not believe that the 'three Fs' – fixity of tenure, free sale, and fair rent – were appropriate to the Highlands, and believed the scheme which he presented for a partnership between tenant and proprietor, based on leases and corporate townships would form a more useful alternative.[20] In short, Napier was aiming to create economic, rather than tenurial, security.

16 *PP*, 1884, XXXVI: *Report of Commission on Crofters*, p. 17

17 Ibid., pp. 17–22.

18 Ibid., pp. 121–34.

19 Ibid., pp. 22, 41.

20 Ibid., pp. 39, 51; BLO, MS Harcourt, dep. 115, fos. 7–10, Napier to Harcourt, 3 Apr. 1884.

II

Whilst the *Report of the Royal Commission* may have been a novel contribution to the debate on Highland land, its impact on policy was minimal. The nature of the scheme proposed by Napier, as well as the political divisions within the Commission, ensured that the government was not responsive to its contents. Nevertheless, for a time it did provide a focus for the debate, and it also had an impact on the course of the agitation. Initially, it led to a period of calm as the expectation of government action spread through the crofting community. But this hope was soon dashed, for no sign of government action was evident. The situation in Skye had reached a critical stage by the autumn of 1884. Under pressure from the strident sheriff principal of Inverness, William Ivory, the government agreed to send troops to the island to bolster the police's authority. The county authorities had also pressed for this, but were not keen to acquiesce in the Home Secretary's suggestion that they match the government's contribution by providing extra police for the operation.[21]

The essential problem was that the Commission's report had received a cool reception in private and in public. Both the Lord Advocate and the Home Secretary agreed that legislation would be needed to carry out the recommendations of the Commission. The government was reluctant to consider such an eventuality in 1884. It believed that it was within the power of the proprietors to undertake voluntary action to deal with some of the crofters' outstanding grievances: they could deal with insecurity of tenure by offering leases. Also, the government was not sanguine about the prospects of persuading crofters to emigrate in the current climate of high expectations of government action.[22] The Prime Minister agreed with Harcourt and J. B. Balfour about the recommendations. He regarded the report as 'neither wise nor acceptable', and went on directly to contradict Napier's view of the Highland land question by suggesting that proposals akin to those of the Irish land legislation of 1881 'could be introduced with advantage'.[23] The government was to spend the rest of 1884 attempting to persuade proprietors to initiate voluntary concessions.

Crofter impatience with the government over the report's implementation expressed itself through renewed agitation in the Highlands.[24] In Parliament, the crofters' supporters pressed the government to act on it. Harcourt replied to a motion put forward by Fraser-Mackintosh and MacFarlane by enlarging on his theme of the need for voluntary effort from the proprietors; Lochiel also contributed to the debate by pointing

21 HRA, R/13, Lochiel to Cantray, 3 Nov. 1884, 6 Nov. 1884, 4 Dec. 1884.

22 BLO, MS Harcourt, dep. 115, fo. 13, Memo by the Lord Advocate; fos. 15–44, Memo by Harcourt, 29 Jul. 1884.

23 BL, WEGP, MS Add. 44547, W. E. Gladstone to W. H. Gladstone, 14 Sep. 1884.

24 *Oban Times*, 3 May, 10 May 1884.

out the difficulties of drawing up an effective land bill. The issues of geographic definition and the problem of the cottars and squatters were serious obstacles to any legislation.[25] It was this debate which made it clear to the crofters that the government was determined to take no action along the lines suggested by the Napier Commissioners. It marked a new phase both in the argument over Highland policy and in the agitation in the Highlands.

Despite the political irrelevance of the Commission by the end of 1884, however, there was a considerable debate surrounding the ideas which it had proposed. Criticism of the report came from all quarters. For the crofters, Alexander MacKenzie, at that time editor of the *Celtic Magazine*, welcomed it as an admission of the validity of the crofters' grievances, and as a justification of the agitation; but he derided it as hopelessly inadequate, on the grounds that it offered incomplete security of tenure and no real mechanism for the wholesale extension of the crofters' land. He also opposed the idea of emigration as a valid option. This, of course, was predictable: the Crofters' movement was particularly keen to oppose any suggestion of emigration. If it went ahead, it posed a considerable threat to their own central contention that there was an abundance of available land in the Highlands.[26]

From a completely different perspective, the duke of Argyll was equally emphatic in his denunciation of the Commission's report. He condemned the analysis of the structure of land-holding as 'a strange reversal of the truth'. Napier had contended that there was a lack of variation in the size of holdings in the Highlands, with a certain number of very large holdings and a large number of very small holdings, but with very few of an intermediate size. The duke attacked Napier's methodology, criticising it for a crude selection of facts and for basing the conclusions on information from a small number of parishes. He further noted that the Commission had failed to take into account the county of Argyll, which contained the greatest variety of size of holdings. The central contentions of the duke's rebuttal, however, were twofold. First, he argued that Napier had made a fundamental error in his basic conception of the crofting problem: to regard the crofters as mere small farmers neglected the important part of their time which was taken up with wage labouring. This was a point which Sir John MacNeill had made in his survey of the Highlands for the government in 1851. The duke's point was that it was not peculiar that so many tenants had such small holdings, but that so many labourers had such large holdings. Secondly, Napier had argued that the case of the Highlander was worthy of special attention because he had had his land forcibly removed over the course of the preceding century, and that there was a valid case

[25] *PD*, 3rd ser., vol. 293, cols. 1730–1, 1751–7, 1758–60, 14 Nov 1884.

[26] A. MacKenzie, 'Report of the Royal Commission an analysis', *Celtic Magazine*, Jun 1884

for restoring it to him. The duke regarded this as a sentimental view. He was sharply critical of the kind of evidence which the crofter delegates had put before the Commission, and equally critical of Napier for allowing himself to be seduced by the picture of a pre-Clearance paradise in the Highlands. He argued that changes in the land-holding structure of the Highlands were not singular, but were part of a general progressive movement which was evident across Europe.[27] The duke's argument was the latest in a long line of writings which he had presented on the land issue. He had always stood out against the prevailing movement for tenant rights, and presented the running of his own estates as a model for improvement: his management of the island of Tiree, which included a concerted attempt to consolidate holdings, was an example of the way to modernity in the Highlands. He was scathing about the crofters' standard of agriculture and social development under classic crofting conditions. He had resigned from Gladstone's Cabinet in 1881 in protest at the Irish land legislation.[28] Not surprisingly, given his own position, he was a forthright defender of the inalienable right of the landlord to control his estates without interference.

Argyll's views are certainly worthy of attention. However, two factors should be borne in mind when considering them. First, his analysis rested heavily on conditions in the county of Argyll and, more particularly, on the management of his own estate. Secondly, the early 1880s were not a good time to emphasise the labouring element of crofting life. The fishing industry was in recession, and was responding with structural changes which would affect crofters' incomes from this source. Moreover, the duke misunderstood the relationship between crofting and wage earning. The amount of time spent in wage labouring was extensive compared to time spent on the croft; but the individuals involved regarded themselves as crofters, and wage labouring was undertaken in order that they could sustain that perception.[29] Also, the slump in the wider British economy had reduced the opportunity for crofters to gain employment, on even a temporary basis, in the industrial areas of Scotland. These economic considerations serve to emphasise the importance of land to the crofting community. It was land which would be at the centre of the debate, and at the forefront of the government's developing policy on the Highlands.

In the face of such diverse criticism of his proposals, it was left to Napier to take up the defence of his brainchild. He found this a solitary and thankless task. The government had rejected his report in private,

[27] G. D. Campbell, Duke of Argyll, 'A corrected picture of the Highlands', *Nineteenth Century*, xvi (1884).

[28] J. W. Mason, 'The duke of Argyll and the land question in late nineteenth-century Britain', *Victorian Studies*, xxi (1978).

[29] See chap. 3, below.

and had implicitly done so in public by moving on to a new strategy of attempting to entice landowners to offer voluntary concessions to crofters. Donald Cameron of Lochiel had condemned the report as 'hardly worth considering'.[30] Nevertheless, Napier was not slow to defend himself against the duke of Argyll's attack. He rejected the notion that the process of depopulation in the Highlands was part of a general and identifiable process. The Highlands were peculiar and special; restitution of land to the crofters was possible and relevant. In the Lowlands the depopulation had occurred through 'natural causes and arbitrary will'. In the Highlands, the question was still a live one: 'the two factors in the quarrel stand face to face; on the one side is the vacant land, on the other the craving multitude'. This was the point which ensured that the Highlands merited preferential treatment. Napier also rejected the duke's contention that the crofter should be seen primarily as a labourer. Characteristically, Napier took his argument from history. He suggested that the crofter was descended from the sub-tenants of the Highland tacksmen. Further, the land was central to the crofters' life, and a variety of agricultural activities were centred on it; this placed it apart from the allotment of the labourer. Psychologically, the crofter regarded himself as a tenant of the land, not as a wage labourer: 'the field, the humble homestead, the common hill form the permanent centre of his life'. Napier went on to conclude that the informal nature of the Commission, where the ordinary crofter could give evidence in the same forum as the proprietor and his factor, was a constructive contribution to social harmony in the Highlands. The article is instructive for the hint which Napier gave about his view on the political fate of his report. He was now arguing that the lack of unanimity in the Commission was one of its strengths; it could not be accused of being a captive of one party or another. This was in contrast to his private correspondence with Harcourt, in which he lamented the Commission's lack of harmony. Napier's defence of his proposals and of the original report was firmly rooted in the view of Highland history which he had acquired, or had confirmed, through the crofter evidence to the Commission. This encapsulated the proposition that an ideal, or at least commendable, social condition had been disturbed recently by the Clearances and ought to be restored.[31]

The exchange of views was important in the context of the question of whether the crofters should be treated as a special group worthy of preferential treatment. At the outset of the agitation, the government was reluctant to admit this. The creation of the Napier Commission and the choice of districts for it to examine, from Ardnamurchan to

[30] Achnacarry Castle Papers, Lochiel to Harcourt, 20 Dec 1884.

[31] Lord Napier, 'The Highland crofters: a vindication of the report of the Crofters' Commission', *Nineteenth Century*, xvii (1885), pp. 437–63. BLO, MS Harcourt, dep. 115, fo 7, Napier to Harcourt, 3 Apr 1884

Caithness, was an implicit admission that the crofters and the Highlands were a special case. But the government, in rejecting the Commission's report, was signalling that it did not wish to take that admission too far. By the end of 1884, it held the view that crofter legislation was something to be avoided. Gladstone, however, had hinted that this was not completely out of the question, when he privately raised the possibility of granting compensation for unexhausted improvements as an alternative to the Napier Commission's proposals.[32] Nevertheless, before this extreme was reached, the government was determined to find alternative solutions. By late 1884, its attempt to initiate proprietorial movement on the crofter question began to bear some fruit.

III

In January 1885 a conference of proprietors took place in Inverness. The prime mover in the events leading up to it was Donald Cameron of Lochiel. He was aware that the government had rejected the report of the Royal Commission, and was also well aware that the agitation had not ceased with the report's publication. At the same time, he believed that, as a response, the government was slowly moving towards the idea of legislation. Therefore, he was determined that the proprietors should evolve a coherent position on the areas where they would find government interference acceptable, and on other areas where they would prefer to act alone. The alternative would be a bill into which the proprietors had had no input, and which might act against their best interests.[33]

Lochiel was aided in the task of setting up the conference by the young Easter Ross landowner, R. C. Munro-Ferguson, who had recently been elected to Parliament for Ross and Cromarty as a Liberal. A preliminary meeting was held at Beaufort Castle, home of Lord Lovat, an avowed Conservative, prior to the convening of the main conference. Considerable pains were taken to persuade the government that there was a genuine desire amongst proprietors to come to terms with their tenants, and to give the impression that land legislation was impossible. The only possible bases for legislation were the Napier Commission Report, which had been rejected, and the Irish Land Act, which was not relevant to the Highlands because, amongst other reasons, the value of tenants' improvements was so low. The only other possibility would be for the government to buy land and establish crofting communities which, clearly, was a political non-starter in Scotland in the mid-1880s.[34]

32 BL, WEGP, MS Add. 44547, W. E. Gladstone to W. H. Gladstone, 14 Sep. 1884.

33 Donald Cameron of Lochiel, 'Speech to the 13th annual dinner of the Gaelic Society of Inverness', *TGSI*, xi (1884–5), pp. 106–12; HRA, KEP, Lochiel to Alexander MacDonald, 2 Dec. 1884.

34 Achnacarry Castle Papers, Lochiel to Harcourt, 20 Dec. 1884.

The landlord body was not united. There were divisions on the value of holding a conference, and, also, there is every indication of a forthright debate on the resolutions which had been prepared by Lochiel and Munro-Ferguson and refined at the preliminary meeting. Although this had been held at his home, Lord Lovat wrote privately to another Inverness landowner that he considered a conference 'injudicious': he feared that it would only provoke opposition and harden attitudes in the Crofters' movement.[35]

The proposals which the landlords adopted at the Inverness conference were threefold. They undertook to offer more land to crofters wherever possible. Secondly, leases of nineteen or thirty years, along with revised rents and compensation for improvements, were to be volunteered to crofters who were not in arrears of rent. Thirdly, they reminded the government that the Napier Commission had made a host of other recommendations – on fishing, transport, communications and emigration – which were far less controversial than those relating to land. It was in these areas that the proprietors envisaged a role for the government, as a provider of loans to crofters and proprietors which would aid the development of the Highlands. Certain landlords had already taken steps along these lines. The duke of Sutherland, in response to demands from his tenantry, had considered offering leases, arbitrated rents and low interest loans for improvements. But such schemes were overtaken by events, as the government attempted to legislate in 1885 and 1886.[36]

Some proprietors were sceptical about the relevance or necessity of these changes. Lochiel, in setting up the conference, had been critical of the small number of proprietors who, by such actions as rent increases, had provoked agitation and soiled the reputation of the generality of landowners who, in Lochiel's view, were conducting the management of their estates in a responsible manner. In the former category he included William Fraser, owner of the Kilmuir estate in North Skye. Fraser ranked high in the demonology of the Crofters' movement; close behind him was W. L. Winans, a North American who had purchased and rented broad swathes of land in central and west Inverness-shire to facilitate his indulgence in questionable sporting pursuits.[37] MacLeod of MacLeod was also a sceptic. Like many landowners, his view was heavily prejudiced by the condition of his own estate. He pointed out to Lochiel that the latter's resolutions were irrelevant: crofters' improvements were not worth any compensation; more land and leases would not help, as

35 HRA, R/13, Lovat to Cantray, 4 Dec. 1884; *Glasgow Herald*, 15 Jan. 1885; A. G. Gardiner, *The Life of Sir William Harcourt* (London, 1923), pp. 531–3.

36 'Conference of landlords at Inverness', *TGSI*, xi (1884–5), pp. 134–6; SCRO, Sutherland Estate Papers, D593 N/4/1/2, Memo by the duke of Sutherland, 19 Nov 1884.

37 HRA, KEP, AG INV 10/69, Lochiel to Alexander MacDonald, 2 Dec. 1884, BLO, MS Harcourt, dep. 115, fo. 73, Lochiel to Harcourt, 15 Nov 1884

crofters did not have the financial capability or the technical aptitude to manage a sizeable piece of land; and reduced rents would be superfluous, as existing crofter rents were already too low.[38] But, despite the criticisms of such men, they were still careful to send a representative to Inverness to ensure that they would be fully informed of the proceedings, and that their interests could be protected. In the case of Fraser, MacLeod, and the other major Skye proprietors, their affairs were handled by Alexander MacDonald, a Portree solicitor. He received instructions to be cautious and not to commit himself to any scheme. Fraser told him that peasant proprietorship would be preferable to wholesale intervention by the State, and MacLeod instructed him to remind the meeting of the good relations between crofters and estate management and the continuing contribution of the estate to the social welfare of the crofters.[39]

Reaction in the press to the resolutions of the Inverness conference was predictable. Newspapers which had traditionally been supportive of proprietors, such as the *Inverness Courier* and the *Northern Chronicle*, were impressed with the magnanimity of the landowners' offer to the crofters. Other newspapers which were more favourably disposed towards the crofters were distinctly unimpressed with its conditional nature; the *Celtic Magazine* condemned the resolutions as 'worthless' and 'at least two years out of date'.[40] Elements of the Scottish, as opposed to the Highland, press were able to take a more balanced view. The *Glasgow Herald*, while emphasising the conference's importance, was unsure how far the proposals would satisfy the crofters; it pointed to the lack of a land court and to the question of the provision of facilities for stocking larger holdings, which the proprietors wanted to leave in the hands of the government, as being potential problems.[41]

More significantly, the proposals which emerged from the Inverness conference fell far short of the published demands of the Crofters' movement. The London HLLRA had organised a meeting in Dingwall in August 1884, which adopted proposals that became known as the 'Dingwall Programme'. These included immediate legislation to deprive the landlord of the power of eviction, and the granting of the 'three Fs' to be administered by a Land Court. The proprietors were never likely to approach this level of political concession. But it was noted at the time that the Inverness conference was significant because it marked the first

[38] Dunvegan Castle Papers, 4/1381, MacLeod of MacLeod to Lochiel, 1 Dec. 1884.

[39] HRA, KEP, AG INV 10/31, William Fraser to Alexander MacDonald, 8 Jan. 1885; Dunvegan Castle Papers, 2/721, MacLeod of MacLeod to Alexander MacDonald, 9 Jan. 1885.

[40] *Inverness Courier*, 15 Jan. 1884; *Northern Chronicle*, 21 Jan. 1885; A. MacKenzie, 'Landlord resolutions at Inverness', *Celtic Magazine*, Mar. 1885, p. 113.

[41] *Glasgow Herald*, 15 Jan. 1885; J. Rae, 'The crofter problem', *Contemporary Review*, xlvii (1885), p. 196.

real concerted attempt by landowners to state their case.[42] Until early 1885, the Crofters' movement had been allowed to take, and hold, the initiative in the agitation.

The significance of the Inverness conference has been greatly underestimated by historians.[43] However, 1884 had seen little government action to deal substantively with the crofter question. The year had been dominated politically by the publication, and subsequent rejection, of the Napier Commission report. As has been noted, it was partly through government encouragement that the Inverness conference had been called in the first place. Lochiel had informed Harcourt of his proposals for it in December 1884, and after it, Harcourt sent the details of the proceedings to the Prime Minister. The Home Secretary explained that he had told Lochiel and the duke of Argyll that it was probably too late for voluntary action. On the other hand, he felt there was no point in granting more land by legislative means; this would not help the crofters if they could not find the money to stock the additional land, and the government was resolutely opposed to providing any money for them. It believed that loans to crofters to purchase stock could not be properly secured, due to the fluctuations in livestock prices. The practice of common grazing also did not help in this regard, as it made it difficult to establish the ownership of stock.[44] J. B. Balfour, the Lord Advocate, advised the government that legislation could be contemplated to grant security of tenure – which would necessitate the establishment of a mechanism for setting a fair rent. Further, since crofters had largely undertaken their own improvements, it was only equitable that they should be compensated for them; but this was not considered a very important concession, because of the low value of most crofter improvements.[45]

IV

By early 1885, it was clear that the government was committed to the idea of legislation for the crofters, along the lines detailed by the Lord Advocate in his letter to the Home Secretary. The motivations for this are unclear. Certainly, the government was worried about the agitation. However, it is important to appreciate that the crofters' demands were limited. They were not demanding the end of landlordism, but, rather, the redefinition of the landlord–tenant relationship. The granting of some extra land, security of tenure, fair rents and compensation for improvements – demands which could all be accommodated within the existing social structure – fell far short of the usurpation of the

42 *Northern Chronicle*, 21 Jan. 1885.
43 Hunter, *Crofting Community*, p. 153; MacPhail, *Crofters' War*, pp. 169–70.
44 PRO, CAB37/14/166–174, Confidential letters relating to the Skye Crofters.
45 CAB37/14/169, J. B. Balfour to Harcourt, 13 Jan. 1885

landlords' social position. The government was determined to attempt to restore law and order, although it was worried about the prospects of doing this without running the risk of 'increased agitation and excitement'.[46]

The government carefully weighed the submissions of the landlords following the Inverness conference. In private, as well as in public, it was dismissive of the role of the HLLRA, contending that the Association's views were far in advance of, and hence did not represent, the majority of crofters. The other major problem for the government in dealing with the Crofters' movement, certainly before the electoral successes of November and December 1885, was to identify a leader who could be regarded as truly representative of the movement. Hitherto, Charles Fraser-Mackintosh had been considered to be a respectable exponent of the crofters' case; but, as the agitation proceeded, doubts were entertained about his ability to convey the views of the generality of the crofters.[47]

The proprietors were certainly slow to produce a response to the agitation, but this was due to its limited nature. Only a small number of landowners were seriously affected by the crofters' actions, and therefore many landowners felt there was no need to develop a joint position because, as the agitation was either irrelevant to them or, at worst, a mere irritant, it was not perceived as a threat to their social position. They had to be prompted by the government and by men with a reputation for public service, such as Lochiel, before they convened at Inverness. Those who were affected by rent strikes and other tactics, such as Fraser of Kilmuir, received scant sympathy from other proprietors. 'Landlordism' was not, in fact, a monolithic force, and the stereotype of Highland proprietors as a 'vastly rich elite'[48] can be misleading. Certainly there were immensely wealthy men among the Highland proprietors. However, many landowners were as far removed in wealth and social position from the likes of the dukes of Argyll and Sutherland as the crofters were from them.

The threat of ill-considered government intervention was what the landlords feared most. It was this that stirred them into action. One of the most important elements in the discussion between government and proprietors over legislation was the question of the area which should be covered. The reluctance to regard the crofters as a special case went back to the earliest days of the agitation; there was a fear that if special land legislation was applied to a crofter area, however defined, it would inevitably be applied to the rest of Scotland at a future date. Both the landlords and the government were keen to avoid any unnecessary alterations in general tenurial relations in Scotland. This, in Lochiel's view, was one of the best arguments for voluntary action: it was more

[46] CAB37/14/170, Harcourt to Gladstone, 17 Jan. 1885.
[47] Achnacarry Castle Papers, Harcourt to Lochiel, 20 Jan. 1885.
[48] Grigor, *Crofters and the Land Question*, ii, pp. 18–19.

flexible and could be applied as the need arose. A second worry arose from the landlords' proposals. They had demanded action to relieve poverty and encourage development in the Highlands, through emigration and government expenditure; but the government did not see why the Highlands should be regarded as worthy of special treatment in this respect. As Harcourt stated:

> The objection ... is, that if they are good enough for the Highlands they are good enough for the United Kingdom, and there is no possible reason why the state should emigrate a pauper in Skye more than a pauper in Spitalfields.[49]

This was an academic point, as the government had no intention of legislating along those lines.

The Highlands could be defined in terms of a special system of land tenure, although this was not an easy task; indeed some Liberals, including the Ross and Cromarty MP, Munro-Ferguson, felt it to be impossible. Harcourt and Balfour were unclear on how to resolve this difficulty. Gladstone, however, did have a solution: he had formulated his Irish land legislation on a supposed historical basis of customary rights to land, and now he proposed to extend this principle to the Highlands. He argued that the people had a historic title to the land which had been usurped by the proprietors for material gain, regarding that as a 'wrong' which ought to be redressed, despite the passage of time since the Clearances. The rights of property in the Highlands were not absolute, he argued, but came with 'engagements' in the shape of this history.

> For it is, after all, this historical fact that constitutes the crofters' title to demand the interference of Parliament. It is not because they are poor, or because there are too many of them, or because they want more land to support their families, but because those whom they represent had rights of which they have been surreptitiously deprived to the injury of the community.[50]

The Prime Minister suggested that any new law could be applied to parishes with an established history of common pasturage during the previous century. When this definition became public, it led to complacency among proprietors in the fringes of the Highlands, such as Caithness, as they would not be affected by the bill.[51]

49 PRO, CAB37/14/170, Harcourt to Gladstone, 17 Jan. 1885; SRO, Balfour of Whittingehame Muniments, GD433/2/78/8, Lochiel to A. J. Balfour, 28 Jan. 1885; Achnacarry Castle Papers, Harcourt to Lochiel, 23 Jan. 1885; BLO, MS Harcourt, dep. 116, Lochiel to Harcourt, 26 Jan. 1885.

50 PRO, CAB37/14/173–4, Gladstone to Harcourt, 19 Jan. 1885.

51 NLS, Rosebery Papers, MS 10017, fos. 1–3, Munro-Ferguson to Rosebery, 9 Mar. 1885; Sinclair of Ulbster Papers, Thurso Estate Office, Letters to the Proprietor, 1880–7, fo. 593, G. Logan to Sir Tollemache Sinclair, 14 Mar 1885; Dewey, 'Celtic agrarian legislation'.

By the end of January, once the views of the proprietors had been digested and the agitation showed no signs of decreasing, the government began to consider the provisions of a crofter bill. The expectations of the Crofters' movement, fuelled by the 'Dingwall Programme', had risen to new heights. Elements in the government argued that a bill along moderate lines 'would at all events clear the air and show the people what they have a reasonable prospect of getting'.[52] This was based on the assumption that the crofters would be satisfied with far less than the demands of the HLLRA, which, in some ways, was a surprising assumption. But the government had already seriously underestimated the crofters' expectations in 1883 and 1884 when the Napier Commission was appointed and when it reported.

If there had ever been doubt about the rejection of Napier's proposals, this was confirmed when the bill was drawn up. By mid-February, Harcourt, with the assistance of Rosebery and J. B. Balfour, was ready to submit the bill to the Cabinet. He warned the Prime Minister that an announcement would have to be made as soon as possible as to the government's intentions.[53] When the Cabinet considered the draft Bill, there was some dissent. The marquess of Hartington, the Secretary for War, condemned the measure, which was based on security of tenure, rent revaluation and compensation for improvements, as being 'too much'. On the other hand, Joseph Chamberlain derided it as 'too little', which demonstrates the diversity of the Liberal Cabinet.[54] Chamberlain was well known for his anti-landlord views: at Inverness, in the course of the 1885 election campaign, he was to call for the institution of landlordism to be carefully examined, condemning the Highland landlords as 'irresponsible' and their conduct of estate management as a mixture of 'extortion and exaction'.[55]

By late March or early April, the bill had been refined and came before the Cabinet once again. Even at this late stage, discussion still centred on the geographical line within which it would operate. Gladstone's 'historicist' definition was finalised, and Harcourt was given the authority to present his bill to Parliament when the opportunity arose.[56] Rumours reached the Highlands of a moderate measure 'far short of the crofters expectations'.[57] However, it was not until the middle of May that the bill was presented to Parliament by the Lord Advocate.

52 BLO, MS Harcourt, dep. 116, fos. 55–6, J. B. Balfour to Harcourt, 22 Jan. 1885.
53 BL, WEGP, MS Add. 44199, fos. 181–2, Harcourt to Gladstone, 14 Jan. 1885; PRO, CAB41/19/9/60, Gladstone to Queen Victoria, 16 Feb. 1885.
54 BL, WEGP, MS Add. 44646, fo. 38, Notes of the Cabinet meeting of 16 Feb. 1885; A. B. Cooke and J. Vincent, *The Governing Passion: Cabinet Government and Party Politics in Britain, 1885–86* (Brighton, 1974), p. 198.
55 J. L. Garvin, *The Life of Joseph Chamberlain* (London, 1933), ii, pp. 68–9.
56 BL, WEGP, MS Add. 44646, fo. 71, Notes of a Cabinet meeting of 27 Mar. 1885; MS Add. 44547, fo. 193, Gladstone to Sir Henry Ponsonby, 1 Apr. 1885; MS Add. 44548, Gladstone to Harcourt, 16 Apr. 1885; Cooke and Vincent, *Governing Passion*, p. 225.
57 HRA, KEP, AG INV 10/31, William Fraser to Alexander MacDonald, 11 Mar. 1885.

Balfour spent much of his speech defending the concept of special legislation for the Highlands. He pointed out that, in the rest of Scotland, land was held by tenants who entered into free contracts with landowners. In the Highlands, historically, freedom of contract did not prevail. Other peculiarities included the smallness of the holdings, the practice of tenant improvements, and common pasturage. The 1885 Bill granted security of tenure to all crofters; valuators were to be appointed to fix rents; and compensation for improvements was to be made available. However, no compulsory provisions for granting more land to crofters were included. This was justified by the apparent willingness, as signified by the Inverness resolutions, of proprietors to give more land voluntarily to their tenants.[58]

Reaction to the bill was diverse. Perhaps the most common description of it was 'moderate', although in some cases this adjective was used more in criticism than approbation.[59] At the extremes, opinion was predictably polarised. Dedicated critics of the crofters' case, such as *The Scotsman* and the *Northern Chronicle*, attacked not only the details of the legislation, but also the very idea of legislating on behalf of special groups.[60] Conversely, supporters of the Crofters' movement, such as the *Oban Times* and the *Scottish Highlander*, described it variously as 'inadequate' and 'worthless'.[61] The Crofters' movement itself attacked the bill on the grounds that it was descended directly from the proposals which had been made by the proprietors in Inverness in January. The principal criticism was that the bill made insufficient provision for the settlement of the crofters' main grievance: the need for more land.[62]

In Parliament, the Conservatives were 'perplexed', to use Arthur Balfour's expression, to know how to respond. Balfour had been delegated by the Conservative Party, at the suggestion of some of the Highland proprietors, to co-ordinate the opposition to the bill. However, he was aware that outright opposition would not advance the Conservative cause in the Highlands. Further, there was the possibility that the bill would take the heat out of the agitation and make it easier, politically, for the government to enforce the law with vigour. All this went against the Conservative grain; their instincts were to oppose a bill which violated property rights and perpetuated crofting conditions.[63] These tactical considerations were also evident at the local level in the Highlands. The Commissioners of Supply in Inverness-shire discussed

58 *PD*, 3rd ser., vol. 298, cols. 844–62, 18 May 1885.

59 *Glasgow Herald*, 20 May 1885; *Inverness Courier*, 21 May 1885.

60 *The Scotsman*, 20 May 1885; *Northern Chronicle*, 21 May 1885.

61 *Oban Times*, 23 May 1885; *Scottish Highlander*, 24 Jul. 1885.

62 *Inverness Courier*, 26 May 1885; *Oban Times*, 23 May, 30 May 1885.

63 HRA, KEP, AG INV 10/31, William Fraser to Alexander MacDonald, 24 May 1885; *The Salisbury–Balfour Correspondence, 1869–1902*, ed. R. Harcourt-Williams (Hertfordshire Rec. Soc., 1988), p. 118, A. J. Balfour to Salisbury, 8 Jun. 1885; BL, AJBP, MS Add. 49800, fos. 7–8, duke of Argyll to Balfour, 5 Mar 1886; B. E. C. Dugdale, *Arthur James Balfour* (London, 1936), p. 108.

the possibility of sending a petition to the government in support of the bill. This horrified some proprietors in the county, such as Lord Lovat and Major Fraser of Kilmuir.[64] In the event, however, the bill did not reach the statute book. The Liberal government fell unexpectedly on 8 June. Irish nationalist MPs, dissatisfied with Liberal coercive measures in Ireland, supported the Conservatives on an amendment to the Budget, and brought Gladstone's second administration to a sudden end.

As a result, the Conservatives were forced reluctantly to enter a period of minority caretaker government. New electoral rolls had to be prepared for a general election – the first under the new franchise granted by the third Reform Act – which would be held in November and December 1885. There has been some speculation as to whether the Conservatives intended to bring in their own Crofters' Bill in this period. But, even if some thought were given to the subject, no substantive proposals emerged. The first Secretary for Scotland, the duke of Richmond and Gordon, was extremely reluctant to touch the question.[65]

V

The 1885 elections have been hailed by historians as the most significant the Highlands had ever seen. The Crofters' movement put up candidates in all the crofting counties and the Northern Burghs. Five Crofter MPs were returned, a result which caused much annoyance in Liberal as well as Conservative ranks. In Ross and Cromarty, the defeated Liberal, Munro-Ferguson, declared that he had been defeated by the votes of 'illiterates'. Leading Liberals were warned not to oppose Crofter candidates at future elections.[66]

Gladstone resumed office at the beginning of February 1886, with a majority that depended on the eighty-six Irish Nationalist MPs pledged to support him after his conversion to Home Rule. His short-lived third administration was dominated by Irish Home Rule and the Liberal split. However, a fresh Crofters' Bill was the main piece of Scottish legislation on the agenda. The new Scottish Secretary, G. O. Trevelyan, urged the Prime Minister to act quickly. The ground had been prepared by the preceding year's bill and there was every chance of getting the new bill through if room could be found for it on the parliamentary timetable;[67] the controversial issues, such as the geographic limits to the legislation,

64 HRA, KEP, AG INV 10/31. William Fraser to Alexander MacDonald, 28 May, 2 Jun. 1885.

65 Hatfield House Papers, 3M/E, fos. 234–7, Richmond and Gordon to Salisbury, 20 Dec., 26 Dec. 1885; Cooke and Vincent, *Governing Passion*, pp. 289–90.

66 MacPhail, *Crofters' War*, pp. 147–69; Hunter, *Crofting Community*, pp. 153–4; NLS, Rosebery Papers, MS 10017, fos. 13–15, Munro-Ferguson to Rosebery, 3 Dec., 26 Dec. 1885.

67 BL, WEGP, MS Add., 44494, fo. 117, Gladstone to J. B. Balfour, 3 Feb. 1886; MS Add. 44335, fo. 198, G. O. Trevelyan to Gladstone, 11 Mar. 1886.

had already been settled in 1885. This allowed the Cabinet to deal promptly with Trevelyan's bill, which was closely modelled on that of Harcourt and Balfour. It received its first reading on 25 February 1886, only three weeks after the formation of the government.[68]

By comparison with its predecessor, Trevelyan's bill appeared to muted comment. The only appreciable differences were the establishment of a permanent land court – instead of the Valuators of 1885 – and stronger provisions for enlargements to the grazing land of crofters. The latter innovation did not impress the pro-crofter press, which lamented the inadequacies of the bill, albeit to a lesser extent than in 1885.[69]

The Crofter MPs, of whom so much was expected, proved to be impotent in the debate on the new Crofters' Bill. They did have the reciprocal support of the Parnellites, but the latter were unlikely to indulge in any action which would endanger the vulnerable Liberal administration which held out the prospect of Home Rule for Ireland.[70] They were able to put pressure on the government to have the enlargement provisions of the bill strengthened, but this pressure was successfully resisted.[71] In general, the debates in 1886 were not so vigorous as those of the previous year; the issues had been well aired then, and there was now little appetite for a full rehearsal of the arguments. By the time the bill had passed its parliamentary stages and had received royal assent in June (just before the fall of the government), organs of the Crofters' movement were condemning it as useless. The Crofter MPs had arrived in Parliament a year too late to influence the content of crofter legislation.

The Crofters' Holdings (Scotland) Act of 1886 was modelled on the Irish Land Acts of 1870 and 1881. Crofters were defined as those year-to-year tenants (that is, those without a lease), paying rent of less than £30 and residing in a 'crofting parish'. Parishes within the seven crofting counties qualified as 'crofting parishes' if the existence of crofters with common grazing in the period since 1806 could be demonstrated. The Act granted security of tenure to all such crofters, subject to the conditions that they paid their rent on time, maintained their holdings and buildings to an acceptable standard, and did not subdivide or sublet their crofts. A Crofters' Commission was established to set fair rents and adjudicate on arrears; it was also to set the levels of compensation for unexhausted improvements when a crofter left his holding. In addition,

68 BL, WEGP, MS Add., 44647, fos. 3, 22, 26, Notes of Cabinet meetings, 15 Feb., 22 Feb., 25 Feb. 1886; PRO, CAB41/19/9, Gladstone to Queen Victoria, 16 Feb. 1886; CAB41/20/8, Gladstone to Queen Victoria, 25 Feb. 1886; Cooke and Vincent, *Governing Passion*, pp. 376–7.

69 *Glasgow Herald*, 27 Feb. 1886; *Inverness Courier*, 2 Mar. 1886; *Northern Chronicle*, 3 Mar. 1886; *Oban Times*, 6 Mar., 20 Mar., 10 Apr. 1886; *Scottish Highlander*, 4 Mar 1886.

70 A. O'Day, *Parnell and the First Home Rule Episode* (Dublin, 1986), p. 172.

71 *PD*, 3rd ser., vol. 302, cols. 1315–31, 25 Feb. 1886; Lubenow, *Parliamentary Politics*, pp. 196, 343–4; *Oban Times*, 15 May, 22 May, 19 Jun 1886.

the Act allowed a croft to pass at death to an heir at law, but a crofter could not assign his tenancy to any other individual. The enlargement provisions allowed a group of five crofters to apply to the land court for extra grazing land; such land had to be contiguous to their holding, and be under the same landlord. A host of conditions on the types of land available for enlargements ensured, however, that these provisions were largely redundant.

It is important to realise that the Act created crofters, not crofts. If an individual fulfilled all the necessary conditions on 25 June 1886, the day the Act received royal assent, he would be admitted to its protection; but if these conditions only became applicable at a later date, he could not be defined as a crofter. Crofter status could only be passed on to an heir at law, and not to any third party. Thus the Act created a highly static position: the crofting area was unlikely to expand under this regime and, indeed, it could very well contract.

One historian has described the reaction of the 'propertied classes' to the new Act as 'inevitable and unimportant ... shrieks of alarm'.[72] Certainly some outrage was evident. Mackintosh of Mackintosh described the legislation as 'detestable', and Fraser of Kilmuir declared that he would rather have his estates bought out completely than suffer the dual ownership which it proposed.[73] However, most were resigned to the bill's becoming law, as the events of 1885 had prepared them for the inevitability of a Crofter Act. Even such a resolute opponent of the concepts behind it as the duke of Argyll felt that its passing could help to restore normality on his estate.[74]

VI

It is clear from this examination of the making of the Crofters' Holdings (Scotland) Act that the politics behind it passed through a number of different phases, largely as a result of the crofters' agitation. The problem was first seen as essentially administrative, but it soon became a political issue. The government's initial view was that it was part of the general, nation-wide, problem of tenurial relations. It had to be persuaded that the crofter issue was a special case worthy of exceptional treatment. This was the crofters' biggest achievement, both in their contest with the landlords and in their campaign to influence the government. The most politically aware and sophisticated representative of the landowners, Cameron of Lochiel, was perpetually concerned about the problems to which this recognition would lead. Thus, the process by which the

[72] Hunter, *Crofting Community*, p. 162.

[73] SRO, GD176/2435/28, D. P. MacDonald to The Mackintosh, 9 Jun. 1886; HRA, KEP, AG INV 10/32, Fraser to Alexander MacDonald, 15 Apr. 1886.

[74] Dunvegan Castle Papers, 2/724, MacLeod of MacLeod to Alexander MacDonald, 2 Apr. 1886; BL, AJBP, MS Add. 49800, fo. 7, duke of Argyll to Balfour, 5 Mar. 1886; Inveraray Castle Papers, bundle 1594, duke of Argyll to factor, 25 May 1886.

government became convinced that the agitation concealed greater grievances, and that these could be dealt with only by legislation, is more complicated than a simple reaction to the lawlessness of the Crofters' War.

The government was well aware that neither the Crofters' movement, nor the landlords, represented a monolithic force. Most of 1884 was taken up with an attempt to discover what level of concession would satisfy the majority of the crofters, rather than to silence the vocal activists of the Crofters' movement. A further trend in this period was the search for sufficient voluntary concessions from the landowners to obviate legislation. The dialogue with respectable landlordism helped to isolate those proprietors, like Major Fraser of Kilmuir, who were considered to have contributed to the agitation by their harsh estate management. It is, therefore, difficult to see the Act of 1886 as merely the product of a two-dimensional conflict between a justly aggrieved crofting population and a set of vindictive proprietors. Instead, the Act was the product of a government calculation as to what was necessary and possible. The hiatus created by the fall of Gladstone's government in June 1885, the period of the Conservative caretaker administration and the subsequent re-election of the Liberals, did much to take the heat out of the question. As a result, the 1886 Bill had a rapid passage through Parliament. Even the arrival of the Crofter MPs could not deflect the government from its course.

The 1886 Act was to be the defining feature of the next forty years of Highland history. It created a static structure of land-holding, with only limited opportunity for the relief of congestion. It may have made eviction impossible, but this was a Pyrrhic victory. The forces which had generated Clearance had gone into reverse, and the exploitation of crofters' land for commercialised sporting pursuits was a muted threat. In fact, the Act and its legacy served only to perpetuate congestion. To understand its legacy properly, an investigation of the extent to which subsequent policy developments represented a refinement of, or a challenge to, the *status quo* is essential.

CHAPTER TWO

The Crofters' Commission, 1886–1912

Section 17 of the Crofters' Holdings (Scotland) Act, 1886, provided for the appointment of a Chairman and three Commissioners whose job it would be to administer the Act. Over the next twenty-five years, they travelled throughout the crofting counties, fixing fair rents, granting enlargements, awarding compensation for improvements, and dealing with the other legal and administrative points that were bound to arise in the working of an Act for which there was so little precedent.

According to the Act, one of the three Commissioners had to be a Gaelic speaker, and another an advocate of the Scottish Bar with at least ten years' standing.[1] The first Chairman of the Commission was David Brand, who was currently sheriff of Ayr. This was a classic Liberal appointment. Brand, the son of a Glasgow merchant, had no connections with the Highlands, whether familial, professional or intellectual; he had been an active Liberal, notably in Gladstone's 'Mid-Lothian Campaign' prior to the general election of 1880, and had served as an Advocate Depute in the second Gladstone ministry. The other appointments provided some balance, both in terms of Highland connections and knowledge of agriculture: Mr Peter MacIntyre, who provided the requisite knowledge of Gaelic, was a farmer from Easter Ross; William Hosack was a land valuator and agent currently practising in Oban; and William MacKenzie was a well-known figure in journalistic and Gaelic circles in Inverness, who was appointed principal clerk to the Commission.[2]

These appointments had been made, and the Commissioners had already met, by the time the Act received royal assent in June 1886. The haste may have been stimulated by an awareness that the Commission would soon face a huge workload, but there may also have been a political element in the decision. Because of the lack of precedent for their work, those persons appointed to the Commission would have an all-important say in determining its nature. This is not, however, to argue that the Commission was seen by the incoming Conservative government of July 1886 as partisan; indeed, throughout its existence

1 SRO, AF67/2, Draft letter from the Scottish Office to the Treasury, 17 May 1886; Treasury to the Scottish Office, 31 May 1886; Directions for letters to the Commissioners, 16 Jun. 1886.

2 *Scots Law Times*, 6 Jul. 1907; *The Times*, 23 Jan. 1908; *Ayrshire Post*, 24 Jan. 1908; *Ayr Advertiser*, 30 Jan. 1908; *Northern Chronicle*, 14 Jul. 1886.

the Commission in general, and Brand in particular, retained the confidence of governments of both parties.[3]

I

The first potentially controversial issue to face the Commission was the confirmation of crofting parishes under section 34 of the Act. The qualifications were the existence, in the eighty years prior to the Act, of year-to-year tenants paying less than £30 rent, and of holdings with a right of common pasturage. Difficulties were confined to the fringes of the crofting counties; the marquess of Breadalbane protested about the inclusion of the parishes of Kilbrandon and Kilchattan, Kilninver, and Kilmelford, while the earl of Cawdor questioned the decision concerning Ardersier and Petty.[4] The greatest controversy came from Orkney, where the island proprietors were violently opposed to their designation as crofting parishes. In all these cases, the dispute concerned the status of the crofters' right to common grazing. The Orkney proprietors argued that there was no right, 'merely a tolerance'. However, although the Secretary for Scotland agreed that no written agreements had existed in this or in many other cases, and that, therefore, no 'right' in legal terms could be recognised, he stated, nevertheless, that the usage under 'tolerance' would have to be accepted as a *de facto* right.[5]

The more active work of the Commission could not begin until a decision had been made about the location of the first sitting. If the government hoped that the Commission would have a calming influence in troubled areas, then clearly it would be sensible to give areas like Skye, Tiree, the Outer Hebrides, and western Sutherland immediate attention. But one drawback of this approach was that the government left itself open to accusations of rewarding lawlessness and ignoring the claims of crofters who had conducted themselves peaceably. That point was made with reference to Shetland, and more generally when the Commission spent time in Skye and Tiree in 1887.[6]

If, in the longer term, the Commission helped to pacify the Highlands, in the short term uncertainty about its movements fuelled more agitation.[7] There were competing claims for the Commission's early attention: from Skye, as a consequence of the intensity of the agitation

[3] BL, WEGP, MS Add. 44497, earl of Dalhousie (Secretary for Scotland) to WEG, 6 Jun. 1886.

[4] SRO, AF67/3, Davidson and Syme to A. J. B[alfour], 8 Sep. 1886; Tods, Murray and Jamieson, to Scottish Office, 11 Oct. 1886.

[5] SRO, AF67/3, Crofters' Commission to A. J. Balfour, 10 Oct. 1886; A. J. Balfour to Sir Francis Sandford, 7 Oct. 1886; BL, AJBP, MS Add. 49871/1, fo. 251, AJB to Sandford, 29 Oct. 1886; W. P. L. Thompson, *The Little General and the Rousay Crofters: Crisis on an Orkney Crofting Estate* (Edinburgh, 1982), chap. 13.

[6] *The Scotsman*, 9 Oct. 1886.

[7] MacPhail, *Crofters' War*, p. 175.

and the likelihood that proprietors would soon take legal action for the recovery of arrears; and from Caithness, because of the promptness of the applications. A consideration as simple as the weather may have precluded an autumn visit to Skye. In the event, the Commissioners began their work in eastern Sutherland; the low value of arrears and general absence of lawlessness there suggest that this area might have been low on the Commission's agenda. Some suspected the duke of Sutherland's influence with Lord Lothian, the then Secretary for Scotland, to have been the crucial factor.[8]

The Commission's early movements provide enough evidence to suggest that it had a 'policing' role as well as a judicial one. In March 1887 it began work in Skye, and then moved on to Tiree – two islands where military expeditions had been experienced in the course of the previous twelve months. Arthur Balfour, the Scottish Secretary in 1886–7, made it clear in a confidential memorandum to Alexander MacDonald, factor to Colonel Fraser of Kilmuir (who was considering legal action for the recovery of arrears), that, before taking such drastic action, it would be politic for them to wait until the Commission had adjudicated in the fair rent applications. He added that he could not see any circumstances in which the government would be likely to sanction the use of military forces to help with the recovery of rent. Balfour was well aware that military force could do little to deal with the rent issue, which was the most pressing consideration; only the Commission had the facilities for such a task. Sheriff Brand later pointed out that this had been one of the most important contributions of the Commission, describing its ability to bring 'tranquillity' in place of 'agitation and discontent'. William Ivory, the sheriff of Inverness, thought that even a simple announcement of the Commission's intention to visit a particular area would 'please the crofters and induce them to be quiet'.[9] The Commission had thus given the government wider scope in its policy towards the Highlands. Military force had been useful in the past, but in many ways it was a limited instrument of policy, tending to create resentment and alienation and certainly lacking the Commission's problem-solving capacities.

One problem, however, was that the Commission could not be in more than one place at a time. From 1886 to around 1892 its correspondence is replete with letters from a comprehensive selection of proprietors asking, demanding, and in some cases even pleading that the Commission should be sent to their estates forthwith. This is interesting in a historiographical sense. Contemporary writers described

[8] SRO, AF67/4, Brand to AJB, 13 Oct. 1886; *Scottish Highlander*, 12 Mar. 1891.

[9] SRO, AF67/4, MacLachlan and Reid (Portree Solicitors) to AJB, 14 Jan. 1887; AJB to Brand, 10 Nov. 1886; SRO, HH1/190, Ivory to AJB, 21 Jan. 1887; SRO, Ivory Papers, GD1/36/1/48/26, Confidential memo by AJB to Alexander MacDonald, 26 Jan. 1887; *PP*, 1896, xxxv: *Royal Commission on Land in Wales and Monmouthshire*, q. 77104.

the Commission as a scandalous usurpation of proprietorial rights: Reginald MacLeod lamented its 'despotic power' and called its cancellation of arrears 'confiscation'; Scott Moncrieff Penney described the sections of the Act referring to the Crofters' Commission as 'iniquitous', and pointed out that the Commission had the power to cancel debts which were due to the proprietor 'for the enjoyment of his property'.[10] But the various landowners who asked for the Commission to be sent to their estates were acting pragmatically. The demand for a visit by the Commission did not amount to an admission that rents were too high or the burden of arrears too heavy. Sir John Campbell-Orde, the proprietor of North Uist and one of the most prolific correspondents to the Commission, argued that the crofters on his estate were determined to pay nothing until the Commission had decided their fair rent: 'It is plain to me that in the great majority of cases, the applications are made with a view to get quit of the arrears, and the crofters have a distinct interest in letting them increase.' He attributed this tendency on the part of the crofters to the 'liberal' view of rents taken by the Commissioners in their Skye decisions. Some landowners felt that a possible way round this problem would be that the Commissioners' powers with regard to arrears should be limited to applying only to those areas which had arisen before the passing of the Act, because, 'As long as crofters are lead to understand and believe that their arrears will be struck off by the Commission, they will not pay'.[11] In Lewis, Lady Matheson's factor found that the crofters were 'resolved not to pay until the Commissioners come, and they say so openly'. The proprietor felt that 'were a single township even dealt with, the present discontent would be much allayed'. On the Cromartie estate in Ross-shire, the factor made a similar complaint to the Commission when requesting its presence on the estate. There can be no doubt that these proprietors, and Lady Matheson in particular, faced massive problems with arrears of rent. But demands were also being made by others who did not face the same kind of difficulties. Campbell of Jura, on whose estate there were only fourteen holdings to be dealt with, asked, in April 1888, if the Commissioners could be sent to the island. Demands were made on the Commission from proprietors in all the crofting counties. In effect, therefore, the Commission was in an impossible position: its movements, regardless of their nature, were sure to occasion displeasure from some quarter or other.[12]

[10] S. M. Penney, 'The Highlands and Islands under Commissioners', *Juridical Review*, xiii (1901), p. 427; R. MacLeod, 'The Crofters' Commission', *Blackwoods Magazine* 1889, p. 518; for a modern view emphasising landlord suspicion of the Commission, see Hunter, *Crofting Community*, p. 168.

[11] SRO, AF67/6, John Campbell-Orde to Skene, Edwards and Bilton, 20 Jun. 1887; HH1/200, Alexander MacDonald to Balfour, 31 Jan. 1887.

[12] SRO, Lothian Muniments, GD40/16/18/33, the Chamberlain, Stornoway to Lady Matheson, 20 Aug. 1888; GD40/16/18/31, letter on behalf of Lady Matheson to

One issue underlying this controversy concerned the influences being brought to bear on the Secretary for Scotland. Dugald MacDonald, the Aberdeen solicitor who represented the South Uist crofters before the Commission, stated quite bluntly that the crofters had gained the impression that the Secretary for Scotland's power to fix the sittings of the Commission was 'only a new form of landlord tyranny'. He also made wider allegations, pointing out that it was the proprietor, Lady Gordon Cathcart, who had made the fair rent application (as she was perfectly entitled to do). In this, and in the fact that the Commission had been sent to South Uist at a time when the majority of crofters were allegedly absent from their holdings and working in the fishing industry, he detected a landlord conspiracy. This latter allegation was proved to be unfounded when the vast majority of crofters attended the sittings of the Commission in person. Such charges did not impress the Commission, or the proprietor's agent, who condemned MacDonald as an agitator – or indeed the government, when they were raised in Parliament.[13] Nevertheless, applications by proprietors to fix fair rents tended to cause problems, leaving crofters with the feeling that they had not been consulted. Brand, however, was quite clear in his statements as to the proper criteria for deciding the Commission's visits, pointing out in 1887 that 'public interest must come above the wishes of individual landlords'.[14]

The evidence for direct proprietorial influence is circumstantial. However, the dukes of Argyll and Sutherland do appear to have been influential with Lord Lothian, the Secretary for Scotland. The Commission spent a good deal of time in Sutherland, and went to Tiree immediately after Lord Lothian received a letter from the duke of Argyll in June 1887 requesting such a visit. Argyll had attempted to induce the Commission to visit Tiree by using the facility for proprietors to apply for fair rents to be set, but Lothian's influence was probably the decisive consideration. Skene, Edwards and Bilton, agents for Lady Gordon Cathcart, also appeared to carry weight with the Scottish Office, as they were asked to provide the Secretary for Scotland with information as to the most convenient time for the Commission to visit South Uist and

Lothian, 1 Sep. 1888; GD305/2/1895, William Gunn to William MacKenzie, 28 Oct. 1889; AF67/9, William MacKenzie to Cochran-Patrick, 1 May 1888; AF67/10, MacLeod of MacLeod to William MacKenzie, 21 Aug. 1888; Dunvegan Castle Papers, 2/730, J. T. MacKenzie to William MacKenzie, 24 Apr. 1890.

13 SRO, AF67/10, D. C. MacDonald to Lothian, 3 Jul. 1887; AF67/7, Skene, Edwards and Bilton, to the Scottish Office, 8 Aug. 1887; *PD*, 3rd ser., vol. 319, col. 1700, 24 Aug. 1887; *Glasgow Herald*, 19 Jul. 1887.

14 SRO, Cromartie Papers, GD305/2/1004, Alexander Ross to William Gunn, 10 Apr. 1887; AF67/4, Minute of meeting of Coll crofters, 1 Dec. 1890; AF67/5, Brand to Sandford, 30 May 1887.

Barra.[15] On the other hand, less highly-connected proprietors were not so successful; for example, the many letters written by Sir John Campbell-Orde to the Commission failed to elicit such a direct response.

Every proprietor who wrote to the Commission seemed to think that his case was the most pressing. However, the most persistent and concerted pressure on the Commission came from an organised group of Skye proprietors. They were not dissuaded from their demands by the fact that the Commission had spent a considerable amount of time in Skye during 1887: in November 1887, they presented the Secretary for Scotland with a memorial which aired familiar arguments about deliberate withholding of rent on the part of crofters who had not yet had their fair rent fixed, and about the Commission's unfairness in leaving Skye without dealing with all the applications. They went on to argue that the government should be consistent in its attitudes to arrears of rent on the part of crofters, and to arrears of rates and other public burdens on the part of proprietors. The military expedition in the winter of 1886–7 had been concerned with collecting arrears of rates, and the proprietors pointed out that:

> It is a notorious fact that for the last three or four years landed proprietors in Skye received almost no rent from crofters, while at the same time they are forced, under threat of legal proceedings, to pay the rates, taxes and other public burdens, including interest on mortgages exigible from their estates, just as if they had recovered their rents in full.

In conclusion, they pointed out that the agitation had begun, and had been conducted with the greatest intensity and the greatest cost to proprietors, in Skye – which demonstrated that 'the crofter cases in the Island of Skye should be first disposed of.' In 1888, they renewed the pressure with appeals from a number of individual proprietors to Lord Lothian.[16]

These problems had been caused by an unforeseen side-effect of the policing role of the Crofters' Commission. For this policy to be effective, the Commission had to cover as wide an area as possible as quickly as possible. That meant that areas had to be left unfinished, as it was more important that the Commission should move on and establish its presence in the maximum number of areas. The pattern is clear from the Commission's early movements. But there was method in these meanderings: the Commission would have its greatest effect if it sat just

15 SRO, AF67/6, duke of Argyll to Lothian, 23 Jun. 1887; HH28/5/2/144, Cochran-Patrick to Skene, Edwards and Bilton, 13 Apr. 1889; Inveraray Castle Papers, bundle 1595, duke of Argyll to factor, 10 May, 14 May 1887.

16 SRO, AF67/8, Memorial of the landed proprietors of Skye, Nov. 1887; AF67/10, Alexander MacDonald to Lothian, 23 Oct. 1888; HRA, KEP, AG INV 10/32, Fraser to MacDonald, 29 Nov. 1886; Clan Donald Centre, Lord MacDonald Papers, bundle 4745, Alexander MacDonald to Secretary for Scotland, 12 Oct. 1888.

before a rent deadline, whereas if it missed such a deadline its effect would be blunted. For example, the Commissioners decided that, despite not having completed all the cases in North Uist in September 1887, it was more important that they should proceed to Caithness before the beginning of the Martinmas term, in November.[17] Further, by adjudicating in a proportion of the cases in each area, they would set a standard by which crofters and proprietors could come to private agreements; section 5 of the Act made specific provision for these. In many cases, however, such hoped-for agreement did not come about – though it did happen on the Skeabost estate in Skye,[18] and also in places like Lochaber and Strathpeffer. Private agreement was not so likely on estates where the agitation had been conducted with vigour, creating a climate of mistrust between the estate managements and the tenants.[19]

A second problem resulting from the tendency of the Commission to leave areas unfinished was the fact that it created two classes of tenants: those who had had their fair rents fixed, and those who had not. This situation caused some bitterness within the crofting community. It was reported that jealousy had arisen on the part of crofters who felt that they had not received such favourable attention from the Commissioners as others, and, further, that there would be difficulty in getting payment of rent from those crofters whose cases had not yet been heard by the Commission.[20]

It may be concluded at this point that the movements and activities of the Commission in the early years after the passing of the Act were governed by factors wider than simply ease of administration. The Commission was a component of public policy, and, as such, it was involved in what the Conservative government saw as its principal task with regard to the Highlands: that of keeping the peace and stifling the demands of the crofters for more reforms of the land laws. Other aspects of this policy included its attempted emigration schemes, programmes for the development of the Highlands through the extension of the communications' network, and the provision of employment through public works.

II

As with any new piece of legislation, the 1886 Act had teething troubles. One of these related to the time-lag between the application to the Commission by a crofter with arrears and the Commission's decision in

[17] SRO, AF67/8, William MacKenzie to Sandford, 27 Sep. 1887.

[18] AF67/9, William MacKenzie to Cochran-Patrick, 21 May 1888; *Crofters' Commission Annual Report, 1886–7*, p. xi.

[19] HRA, SEP, AG INV 11/5, Lachlan MacDonald to Alexander MacDonald, 25 Jul. 1887; SRO, GD305/2/1891/310, William Gunn to R. M. Brereton, 27 Apr. 1888; *Crofters' Commission Annual Report, 1893–4*, pp. 6–7.

[20] SRO, HH1/241, Sheriff Lidell to Ivory, 15 Jul. 1887; Police report, Staffin, Skye, 4 Jun. 1887.

his case. This had caused problems from an early date. In a case in Portree sheriff court in October 1886, it had been declared that a landlord had no powers to undertake proceedings for recovery of rent during this period. Sheriff Ivory felt this to have been an 'unfortunate decision'; he feared it would induce crofters not to pay rent until the Commissioners had sat. The case reached the Court of Session, where it was decided that although the Act protected a crofter from eviction in this period, it did not prevent the landlord from taking action to recover the debt.[21] Further problems were encountered over section 1, which laid out the statutory conditions which had to be fulfilled by crofters if they were to receive security of tenure. The sixth condition was that a crofter would lose the protection of the Act if he was declared a 'notour bankrupt'. Quite soon there were accusations that some landlords were using this provision deliberately to deprive crofters of the Act's protection, before the Commissioners had even had a chance to determine their fair rent. The tactic allegedly employed was that the proprietor would institute proceedings whereby a crofter's effects, including his stock, would be sold to raise money to settle his debt of overdue rent. This would have the double effect of putting him in a position where he was declared a 'notour bankrupt', and of making it difficult for him to continue working his holding. These accusations disturbed the government, which felt that such proceedings were contrary to the 'spirit and intention' of the Act.[22] Investigations by the Commission pointed to Caithness as the area experiencing most of the problems: in particular, the estates of Thrumster, Forse and Latheron. Events on these estates had led to the crofters becoming 'very indignant', and the government clearly saw the need to legislate.[23] However, there were other pressures on the government. Arthur Balfour, then Secretary for Scotland, summed up the situation neatly:

> To deprive landlords altogether of the power of recovering their rents and arrears during the two or three years which will probably elapse before the Crofters' Commission have completed their work would be manifestly unjust. At the same time to give them unrestricted power to deprive their crofters of all benefits from the Act may lead not only to great injustice, but also to considerable local disturbance and political difficulty.[24]

21 BL, AJBP, MS Add. 49800, fo. 161, Ivory to Balfour, 31 Oct. 1886; fo. 164, Balfour to Ivory, 2 Nov 1886; *Court of Session Cases*, 4th ser., xiv, pp. 181–90; *The Scotsman*, 8 Dec. 1886.

22 SRO, AF67/5, 'Resolution of Caithness farmers, crofters, farm servants and labourers, Thurso, 16 Mar. 1887'; GD40/16/8/75, Memo, with reference to amendment of the Crofters' Holdings (Scotland) Act, 18 Jul. 1887

23 SRO, GD40/16/8/46, Brand to Sandford, 14 Apr 1887; GD40/16/8/56, George Sutherland to William MacKenzie, 19 Apr. 1887.

24 GD40/16/8/62, Cabinet Paper by AJB, 11 Feb. 1887

The year 1887 saw an amending Act to give the Commission powers to sist [temporarily halt] proceedings for the sale of a crofter's effects for the recovery of arrears. The Commissioners were duty bound to consider the circumstances in which the arrears had arisen.[25] The hope was not only that the Commission would grant sists, and thereby prevent any local difficulties, but that it would quash, and be seen to quash, applications for sists from crofters who were deliberately withholding arrears. It was not only the government which espoused this position; Sheriff Brand advocated it strongly:

> A few instances of refusal by the Commissioners to sist proceedings for arrears which they were satisfied that the tenant ought to pay up, in whole, or in part, will tend to prevent the improper withholding of rents.[26]

The Crofters' Commission and the government were not simply responding to the demands of crofters.[27] The government was, in fact, using the Crofters' Commission as an authoritative body among proprietors, and crofters, to help in the re-establishment of 'normal' social relations in the Highlands.

If this policy was to be successful, the Commission had to proceed very quickly, and it soon became apparent that, as originally constituted, it was incapable of doing so. In its first year of operation, the Commission received 8,906 applications to fix fair rents, but only managed to deal with 1,767. By the time of the issue of its second annual report, it had a backlog of 7,621 fair rent applications.[28]

Under the Act, the Commission could sit as one court, with all three Commissioners present, or alternatively (under section 23), it could delegate its duties to two Commissioners. The value of this was that the hearing of evidence and the inspection of holdings could take place simultaneously. In Sutherland and Skye all three Commissioners sat in court; but, by the time they reached South Uist in the late summer and autumn of 1887, they found it necessary to use the provisions of section 23. However, even this was not sufficient to speed the Commission up to the required degree, and, as we have seen, it came under pressure from many proprietors. The government responded with an amending Act to cancel the clause in the 1886 Act which required that two Commissioners should form a quorum. This enabled each of the present Commissioners to sit in a court by himself, aided by two assessors.[29]

25 Hunter, *Crofting Community*, p. 167.

26 SRO, GD40/16/8/66, Memo by Secretary for Scotland on 'Double Object' behind bill to amend Crofters Act; GD40/16/8/58, Brand to Sandford, 3 May 1887.

27 Hunter, *Crofting Community*, p. 170.

28 *Crofters' Commission Annual Reports, 1886–7*, p. 105; *1887–8*, p. 179.

29 SRO, GD40/16/58/4, Lothian to Argyll, 29 Nov. 1888; GD40/16/55/36, 'Crofters' Commission alternative scheme', undated; GD40/16/24/13, Brand to W. C. Blackburn, 28 Nov. 1888.

III

Reaction to the Commission began even before it held its first sitting. Initial criticism came from a predictable source. The *Scottish Highlander*, the Inverness newspaper run by Alexander MacKenzie, and more a mouthpiece of the HLLRA than a newspaper of record, condemned the composition of the Commission as 'objectionable' and labelled the individual Commissioners 'landlord nominees'. However, when the Commissioners' initial decisions were made known, the attitude changed somewhat. The reductions of rent and the cancellation of arrears in Skye were held to be a justification of the agitation, and were generally welcomed. It is difficult to gauge the reactions of crofters to the Commission's decisions. The Commission itself felt that the fair rents fixed in Skye were giving 'every satisfaction', and the *Oban Times*, a paper with a similar perspective to MacKenzie's, followed the same line in its editorials.[30] However, the *Scottish Highlander* carried many reports of meetings of crofters where the Commission and all its works were condemned. The objectivity of these reports can be questioned: for instance, the *Scottish Highlander* of 14 July 1887 contained a report of a mass meeting of crofters and cottars at Kilpheder in South Uist, but when the local policeman at Lochboisdale made enquiries, he discovered that this 'mass meeting' was in fact attended by only a dozen people. Similar sources suggest that other meetings were exaggerated by the press.[31]

Prior to their initial decisions, no one was sure what form the Commission's decisions would take. Arthur Balfour did not feel, on the strength of reports he had received from the Highlands, that the crofters' rents were too high. But there is no doubt that the Commission was a major part of the crofters' expectations for justice, and its decisions were keenly watched all over the Highlands.[32] From the evidence of Ivory's intelligence-gathering network, it is possible to gauge the differing reactions. In Uist, the Commission did appear to have the desired calming influence. In Skye, where the agitation had been more intense and the expectations were possibly higher, the reaction was more mixed; it was reported that the rent collections conducted there, following the fixing of fair rents, were not an unqualified success.[33]

One factor which played a part in determining the differing reactions to the Commission was the nature of the hearings in that particular area.

[30] *Scottish Highlander*, 5 Aug., 19 Aug., 26 May 1887; *Oban Times*, 8 Jan., 9 Apr., 28 May 1887; SRO, AF67/7, William MacKenzie to Sandford, 27 Sep. 1887.

[31] SRO, HH1/245, Police report, Lochboisdale, South Uist, 23 Jul. 1887; HH1/253, Sheriff Hamilton, Portree, to Ivory, 15 Sep. 1887.

[32] BL, AJBP, MS Add. 49871/1, fo. 254, Balfour to Dunbar, 29 Oct. 1886; fo. 262, Balfour to Sandford, 1 Nov. 1886; SRO, AF67/401, Confidential reports on the Highlands by Malcolm MacNeill; HH1/180, Police report, Staffin, Skye, 11 Jan. 1887.

[33] SRO, HH1/260, Sheriff Webster, Lochmaddy, North Uist, to Ivory, 3 Nov. 1887; HH1/246, Ivory to Scottish Office, 17 Aug. 1887

The Commission was a highly informal court; neither the crofters nor the proprietor had to be represented by a lawyer, and, indeed, on some estates the presence of lawyers was resented by the estate management.[34] Part of the reason for the ambiguous reaction to the Commission in Skye was the presence of Alexander MacDonald, who acted for many of the proprietors. He attempted to show that the arrears were due not to inability to pay, but to the malign influence of agitators.[35] This line of reasoning was unhelpful, as it did not elicit the information required to fix a fair rent. However, when the Commission reached Caithness, it noted that the cases were disposed of much more quickly and without the confrontational attitude which had prevailed in other areas.[36] Skye was notable for the high intensity of the agitation throughout the 1880s, and the atmosphere of distrust between the estate managements and the crofters of that period carried over into the sittings of the Commission.

It would seem that the reactions of the crofters, although difficult to gauge, were ambiguous. The Commission's novelty engendered high expectations. Crofters expected it to treat groups of cases generally with uniform rent reductions, rather than – as happened – to adopt a sophisticated case-by-case approach.[37] As for proprietors, they mostly reacted to the Commission with equanimity; extreme reactions were very much the exception. In general, they did not question the Commission's legitimacy,[38] nor did they plague it with appeals, as their Irish counterparts had done with the land court set up under the Irish Land Act of 1881.[39] They often did, however, complain about details of the Commission's procedure – such as, for example, its tendency to leave areas unfinished, and the complications this caused for rent collections. In 1891, the factor for Lady Matheson communicated, in some detail, how the districts of Lewis not dealt with so far by the Commission had yet to pay, which was unjust to both the proprietor and the crofters, who had had their rents fixed in 1888 and had been paying regularly since then.

It is interesting to note that factors reacted much more strongly against the Commission. George Malcolm, factor on the Ellice estates

[34] *Royal Commission on Land in Wales*, q. 75983; SRO, GD305/2/566, Alexander Ross to William Matheson, 21 Jan. 1889.

[35] *Glasgow Herald*, 29 Mar. 1887, HRA, KEP, AG INV 10/7, Remarks by Alexander MacDonald to the Crofters' Commission.

[36] *Glasgow Herald*, 9 Dec. 1887.

[37] SRO, HH1/237, Inspector MacDonald, Portree, to Sheriff Skene, Portree, 2 Jun. 1887.

[38] *PP*, 1906, LV: *Report of the Departmental Committee appointed by the Board of Agriculture and Fisheries to inquire and report on the subject of Small Holdings in Great Britain*, q. 4541; see also letters from various proprietors in SRO, AF67/8, 9, 15.

[39] SRO, AF43/6/13, Memo on dual ownership; K. Buckley, 'The records of the Irish Land Commission as a source of historical evidence', *Irish Historical Studies*, viii (1952–3), pp. 31–2.

around Invergarry, and secretary of the Highland Property Association, was forthright in his opinions, condemning the Commission as 'autocratic'. William Gunn, factor on the Cromartie estates in Ross-shire, complained, in a lengthy diatribe to the Commission, that the reductions in the Coigach area of the estate were 'excessive to a degree'.[40] Factors had a more intimate knowledge of the circumstances of each individual tenant, and were more aware of some inevitably dishonest or unscrupulous tenants receiving favourable treatment from the Commission. Also, factors may have seen their own role on the estates being usurped. Previously, they would have been responsible for selecting deserving cases for rent reductions; after 1886, the Commission played that role.

IV

A frequent accusation made against the Commission was that its decisions were arbitrary. Certainly, in their fair rent decisions the Commissioners did not append any reasons to their final order; the sheer number of cases precluded such detailed explanations. This point was made both by contemporary writers, and by those involved in estate management who had been involved in cases before the Commission. One argued that 'it merely follows its own will regardless of all fixed law'.[41] Brand did not wish to see the establishment of fixed rules for dealing with the cancellation of arrears, because cases tended to 'vary greatly in their particular circumstances'.[42] In December 1886, Brand issued a statement on section 6 of the Act, which governed the fixing of fair rents. He intimated that the Commissioners would take a case-by-case approach and fix a rent which was fair for each holding at that particular time, rather than fair in terms of the wealth of the tenant or the proprietor. However, the task of coming to an accurate valuation of crofters' improvements, on which no rent was liable, was far from easy, as crofters had a tendency to exaggerate their value.[43] One consideration which did play a part in the Commission's findings with regard to fair rent was the current value of livestock. Many crofters claimed that their difficulties in paying rent stemmed from their inability to realise the value of their stock at market. However, there was a danger in this method; a fair rent fixed by the Commission was set for seven years. Critics were not slow to point out that, with fluctuations in prices, fair

40 *Royal Commission on Land in Wales*, q. 78041; SRO, GD305/2/1898/549, William Gunn to Peter MacIntyre, Dec. 1890.

41 MacLeod, 'Crofters' Commission', p. 523; SRO, GD176/2488, The Mackintosh to Allan MacDonald, 26 Apr. 1894; Dunvegan Castle Papers, 4/1390/1, MacLeod of MacLeod to William MacKenzie, 4 Jul 1889; 4/1390/2, MacLeod of MacLeod to Lothian, 6 Jul. 1889.

42 SRO, GD40/16/8/58, Brand to Sandford, 3 May 1887

43 *Royal Commission on Land in Wales*, q. 78709; *Glasgow Herald*, 21 Dec. 1886; SRO, GD305/2/1892/487, Alexander Ross to William Gunn, 31 Mar 1887; HRA, KEP, AG INV 10/32, Fraser to MacDonald, 14 Feb. 1887

rents could soon cease to be fair. But this argument was also used to counter the claim, often made by crofters, that reductions were demonstrative of previous rack-renting.[44]

Nevertheless, in the longer term, there was general satisfaction with the fair rents. After seven years had elapsed, crofters could apply to the Commission to have the rent revised. Few made use of this facility: in 1894–5, the first year of septennial revisions, there were only 333 applications out of several thousand potential cases.[45] With improvements in stock prices and the ongoing benefit of the Commission's initial rents and arrears decisions, the rent issue became less important as time passed. Although crofter agitation did not cease with the advent of the Commission, it acquired a different character.

Despite the accusations of inconsistency, and the basing of decisions on transient criteria like stock prices, there does appear to be a measure of consistency about the fair-rent decisions of the Commissioners. Over the years from 1886 to 1893, when very large numbers of fair-rent decisions were issued, the average rent reductions are quite constant, as shown in Table 1. The lower reductions for 1890–1 and 1892–3 can be explained by large numbers of cases in Sutherland, where reductions were small. But this is consistent in itself, because the reductions in Sutherland were always lower than elsewhere.

Table 1: *Average Rent Reductions, 1886–1892*[46]

Year	No. of Holdings	% Reduction
1886-87	1,767	30.8
1887-88	2,185	29.5
1888-89	3,425	29.1
1889-90	1,963	30.8
1890-91	2,339	24.3
1891-92	1,477	30.0
1892-93	1,012	21.9

A second argument used to counter the idea that the reductions were a uniquely just response to crofter demands, was to note that farming rents were also being reduced by proprietors.[47] Some estates were finding it difficult to let large sheep farms. That led either to a reduction in the sheep-farming area of an estate in favour of deer forests, or to proprietors making voluntary abatements in rent to large tenant

[44] *The Scotsman*, 4 Jan., 1 Jul. 1887.
[45] *Crofters' Commission Annual Report, 1894–5*, p. 37.
[46] Figures calculated from *Crofters' Commission Annual Reports, 1886–93*.
[47] *Glasgow Herald*, 8 Jun. 1887; *The Scotsman*, 4 Jan. 1887.

farmers.[48] This fact was held to prove that the crofters' grievances were not unique, and that they were suffering in a 'common cause'. It is interesting to note, in this regard, that the farmers of Wester Ross advocated the setting up of an independent tribunal, similar to the Crofters' Commission, to fix fair rents for farmers.[49]

When the Commission announced a percentage reduction in rent, the old rent that was quoted had itself often been voluntarily reduced by proprietors. It can be established, for example, that this happened on the Lochalsh estates of Sir Kenneth Matheson and on the Cromartie estate; and small leaseholders in Glen Urquhart, on the estate of the countess of Seafield, benefited from a revaluation carried out by her factor. The exercise was based on the current decisions of the Commission.[50]

A more comprehensive appraisal of the overall impact of the Commission can be gleaned from its annual reports, which provide a record of every fair-rent and septennial revision case upon which it adjudicated. The details they give are as follows: the old rent; the fair rent; the decrease; the percentage reduction; the amount of arrears; the amount to be paid; the amount cancelled; and the percentage cancelled. These are aggregated according to townships, then according to estates, and finally according to county. The first two aggregations are useful in providing local detail, but do not give a general picture. The county figures are problematic, as the counties themselves contained areas with little in common. Ross-shire, for example, stretched from the fertile farming area of the Black Isle and Easter Ross peninsulas to the overcrowded, marginal land of Lewis, while Inverness-shire contained similar diversity. It is necessary, therefore, to rework the fair-rent figures slightly, for the purpose of Tables 2 and 3 (overleaf). To this end, the seven crofting counties have been divided into ten areas, eight of which are dealt with in the tables. A number of the counties have sufficient homogeneity to be treated as single units; namely, Argyll, Caithness, Orkney, and Shetland (though Orkney and Shetland are outside the main scope of this study). The other areas either cross county boundaries or are contained within them. The Western Highlands and the Eastern Highlands fall into the former category, and the Inverness-shire Islands (Skye, Harris, and the Uists), Wester Ross and Lewis, North Sutherland, and the Central Highlands belong to the latter.[51]

48 Richards and Clough, *Cromartie*, p. 305; J. Hunter, 'Sheep and deer: Highland sheep farming, 1850–1900', *NS*, i (1973), p. 89; Gaskell, *Morvern*, p. 109; SRO, GD176/2674/46, The Mackintosh to Allan MacDonald, 10 Jan 1889.

49 *Glasgow Herald*, 8 Jun. 1887

50 *Scottish Highlander*, 10 May 1887.

51 SRO, AF67/15, Sir H. G. MacAndrew to Brand, 1 May 1891, SRO, GD305/2/1889/417, William Gunn to the duchess of Sutherland, Dec. 1886; 1895, XXXIX: *Royal Commission (Highlands and Islands, 1892)*, q. 13654.

Table 2: *Fair Rents and Arrears Decisions, 1886–1895*

Area	Holdings	% Reduction	% Cancellation
Caithness	995	32.7	55.8
North Sutherland	1,210	8.1	33.3
Wester Ross and Lewis	3,935	29.8	72.0
Inverness-shire Islands	3,411	30.6	71.2
Western Highlands	1,336	21.1	40.8
Eastern Highlands	1,465	19.4	49.7
Central Highlands	91	21.6	69.2
Argyll	440	31.7	62.8

Table 2 shows that, in the Commission's first ten years, the Hebrides (with Wester Ross) experienced both the highest reductions in rent and the highest cancellation of arrears. Moreover, these areas had not only the highest percentage reductions, but also the highest actual reductions as well; Lewis was particularly notable in this respect, with over £30,000 of arrears being cancelled. Caithness had a high reduction in rent, but a comparatively small cancellation of arrears. It was noted at the time of the Commission's first visit to Caithness, in late 1887, that the arrears were of recent origin.[52] Averages can conceal the truth, however; the figures for most of the Caithness estates were low, but the estate of Clyth contributed a large number of holdings, and had high figures in both categories. This is, presumably, due to rack-renting by the proprietor – which can also be found in a few other areas, such as the estate of Kilmuir in North Skye, and Iona and the Ross of Mull in Argyll.[53] The fact that these instances involved a high number of cases pushes up the level of rent reduction in their respective regions. More generally, even within these more meaningful territorial divisions, great diversity existed. In Wester Ross there were estates with high figures in both categories, such as Lochcarron, and estates with equally low counts, such as Gairloch. The low reductions on the latter estate disconcerted the Crofters' movement, which had always claimed that it was 'rack-rented'; it resorted to allegations of collusion between Sir Kenneth MacKenzie and the Commission.[54]

The general conclusion which can be drawn from this table is that it backs up Brand's initial rejection of a universal system of principles to govern fair-rent decisions. The most important boundary in these decisions is that between estates. Further, the Commission clearly

[52] *Glasgow Herald*, 9 Dec. 1887.

[53] E. M. MacArthur, *Iona: The Living Memory of a Crofting Community, 1750–1914* (Edinburgh, 1990), p. 131.

[54] *Scottish Highlander*, 14 Jun. 1888.

realised that it would be worthless reducing rents if arrears were not cancelled: a heavy burden of arrears would nullify the benefit of a fair rent. Thus, even in areas where the rent reductions were low, like Lochaber, the proportion of arrears cancelled was high.

Table 3: *Fair Rents and Arrears Decisions, 1896–1912*

Area	Holdings	% Reduction	% Cancellation
Caithness	22	14.2	68.7
North Sutherland	—		
Wester Ross and Lewis	21	10.3	60.6
Inverness-shire Islands	108	17.5	31.1
Western Highlands	14	18.2	40.8
Eastern Highlands	57	15.1	51.8
Central Highlands	12	21.6	69.2
Argyll	27	12.3	42.0

The later decline in the Commission's workload, and the fact that the rents and arrears problems were no longer so pressing after the mid-1890s, is demonstrated in Table 3. It is particularly significant to note – from the first column – that far fewer holdings were dealt with than in the Commission's first decade.

V

Although the fixing of fair rents and adjudication of arrears was the largest task facing the Commission, it did have other functions. The Act provided the Commission with powers to grant enlargements of crofts or common pasture. This provision was widely condemned as inadequate. The fact that there were no powers to create entirely new crofts was often lamented,[55] and it soon became apparent that the enlargement clauses were ineffective. In 1888 – with no enlargements having actually been made by then – the Commission issued a report on the matter. It was concluded that the major difficulty was section 13 of the Act, which laid down conditions governing the scope of available land; the Commissioners pointed out that there was 'no adequate means of enlarging holdings' within the scope of the Act. A second difficulty was the poverty and agricultural ineptitude of crofters; this caused problems under section 12(2), which required applicants to satisfy the Commissioners that they could pay a fair rent for the lands requested and would be able to stock and cultivate them properly.[56]

55 *Oban Times*, 10 Dec. 1887; for resolutions on this matter from various bodies, see SRO, AF67/8, 11–13, 16–18, 20, 24–5.

56 *PP*, 1888, LXXX. *Report by the Crofters Commission in Regard to Applications for*

There was much rhetoric on the iniquitous nature of deer forests, as the Crofters' movement attempted to draw attention to the issue of afforestation. In addition, dramatic stage-managed demonstrators, such as the Park Deer Forest raid in 1887, were employed to that end. Nevertheless, it is significant that only twenty applications were received to remove land out of a deer forest. This was a point used by the government to blunt the arguments of those who complained about them.[57] In general, of all applications for enlargements, 67% came before 1897, of which the bulk were made by 1892. Crofter interest in this facility obviously declined when it became evident that little could be gained from it.[58]

As argued above, the role of the Commission in its early years was highly politicised, and was a central component of the government's Highland policy. A number of authors have made the point that, immediately after the passing of the 1886 Act, major instances of disorder occurred.[59] The government dispatched a military force to Tiree when it became clear that the police were unable to handle the situation there, following a land raid. A military expedition had to be sent to Skye in late 1886, when local government was on the verge of collapse because of arrears of rates; deforcements occurred when steps were taken to recover arrears from crofters. The year 1887 also saw land raids in Assynt and Lewis, and the use of the military in an attempt to deal with them. Yet it must be stressed that, in all these cases, the disorder preceded the visit of the Commission to the area in question. As noted above, the disorder was a major reason for the nature of the Commission's movements. Further, the post 1886 agitation was focused not on rent, but on 'more land' for crofters – which the Commission was not so well equipped to deal with. While the Commission played an important role in quelling the agitation, other factors were relevant. After 1886, disorder was not perceived favourably by public opinion, since the grievances of the crofters were generally felt to have been settled in that year. Thus it was much easier, politically, for the government to deal with disorder. Nevertheless, the Commission did have a positive effect on the state of law and order in the Highlands. The position in 1912 was a considerable improvement on that of 1886, when the 'Queen's writ did not run'.

The high profile work of the Commission was not sustained as time passed. When conditions in the Highlands changed, its role changed accordingly;[60] In the early to mid-1890s, its workload began to fall. The

Enlargements of Holdings for the period from 25 June 1886 to 10 December 1888.

57 *PD*, 3rd ser., vol. 325, col. 1059, 1 May 1888.

58 *Crofters' Commission Annual Report, 1910–12*, p. xxvi.

59 Hunter, *Crofting Community*, p. 164; Grigor, 'Crofters and the Land Question'; MacPhail, *Crofters' War*, p. 173.

60 D. J. MacCuish, 'Ninety years of crofting legislation and administration', *TGSI*, l (1976–8), pp. 300–1.

number of fair rent applications received dwindled considerably after 1891, and around this date the Commission had reduced the large backlog of cases to more manageable proportions.[61] Applications for septennial revisions did not fill the gap in its work left by the decline of new applications for fair rent.

It was this situation which led some to suggest that the Commission no longer had a meaningful role to play, and that its functions could be transferred to the sheriff courts. This idea was resented by those involved in the crofters' cause. They argued that the Commission should be sustained because it held the trust of the crofters and because it was both more efficient (since it was composed of specialists), and cheaper than the sheriff courts. The Commission was also adapted to the needs of crofters in a way that the sheriff court was not. When a hearing was required, the Commission went to the actual area, and the evidence could be heard in Gaelic. All these considerations helped to establish its credibility in the eyes of the crofters. But one problem with the Commission was that it had no powers of enforcement, and had to rely on the powers of the sheriffs of the relevant counties to enforce the decisions. The Highland Land League advocated strengthening the Commission in this respect, and giving it responsibility for all issues related to crofting.[62]

Nevertheless, at this time, the Commission at this time was a body in search of a role. Successive governments used it in a consultative capacity. Sheriff Brand was the Chairman of the Royal Commission (Highlands and Islands) from 1892 to 1895. In the early 1900s, the Commission was employed by the government to write factual reports on the social condition of Lewis (in 1902) and Uist (in 1904). Brand was also an ex-officio member of the Congested Districts Board from its creation in 1897. The Commission carried out much liaison work with the Board in connection with the organisation of estates purchased by the Board; in particular, it spent much time, in 1904 and 1905, dealing with the estates of Glendale and Kilmuir in Skye. The Commission had a great deal of expertise to be tapped, after nearly twenty years' experience – whereas the Congested Districts Board was largely composed of ex-officio members and, apart from its Secretary, had only one full time employee – a factor – who had to divide his time between all the properties of the Board.[63]

Another important role for the Commission in the 1890s was the

[61] *Crofters' Commission Annual Reports, 1886–7*, p. 105; *1892–3*, p. 144, *1893–4*, p. 79.

[62] *Royal Commission on Land in Wales*, qq. 27038, 78041, 75921–7; SRO, AF67/9, Speech at Taynuilt by Rev. Malcolm MacCallum, Feb. 1894; Inveraray Castle Papers, bundle 906, George Malcolm to the duke of Argyll, 19 Apr. 1895.

[63] *PP*, 1902, LXXXIII: *Report to the Secretary for Scotland, by the Crofters Commission on the Social Condition of the People of the Lews as compared with twenty years ago*; SRO, AF67/19, Crofters' Commission Report on Uist, 1904, *Crofters' Commission Annual Report, 1903–4*, appendix K, *1904–5*, pp. x–xvii.

administration of the Crofters' Common Grazings Regulation Act of 1892. This was a permissive measure, which empowered the Commission, in conjunction with crofters, to draw up rules for the effective stewardship of common grazings. An amending Act was passed in 1908 giving the Commission power to fine those who broke the rules, and in 1910 an officer was appointed to aid the Commission to administer this legislation.[64] The problem of overstocking and poor agricultural practice had been one of the Commission's central concerns; its first report noted the harmful effects of continuous cropping. During their early sittings, the Commissioners attempted to impress upon crofters the self-defeating effects of overstocking.[65] This was a problem for estate managements too, which they found difficult to deal with prior to the 1892 Act.[66] However, it was a persistent problem: in their final report, the Commis-sioners referred to the mismanagement of common grazings as 'the greatest source of trouble in the Crofting area',[67] and they were well aware that this was a problem for proprietors as well. Certainly, crofting agriculture was not of the highest standard – but estate managements had a role to play here as well: most estates would have regulations governing soumings, drainage and other technical points, which it was up to the managers to enforce.[68]

Despite all this important liaison and technical work, the government felt, and Brand agreed, that, when William Hosack retired in 1902, the workload of the Commission was not sufficient to occupy the time of the Chairman and two full-time Commissioners. A part-time replacement for Hosack was appointed, therefore, on a reduced salary of £600.[69]

So far, it can be argued, there had been two phases to the work of the Commission: a highly politicised phase from 1886 to around 1894, followed by a technical and consultative phase from 1895 to 1906. There was, however, a third phase of the Commission, between 1906 and its eventual abolition in 1912. During this period the Commission was essentially living on borrowed time. Its abolition had been advocated in 1906 and would have been carried out then, had it not been for the external political circumstances which delayed land reform until 1911. The Liberal government was aware, from the outset, of the need to reform both the Crofters' Commission and the Congested Districts Board. From 1905, the Commission was effectively paralysed due to Brand's ill health, and this particularly affected appeals to the

64 SRO, AF67/30, Treasury to Scottish Office, 26 Apr. 1910.

65 *Crofters' Commission Annual Report, 1886–7*, p. ix; *Glasgow Herald*, 31 Mar. 1887.

66 SRO, GD305/2/1005, Alexander Ross to William Gunn, 13 May 1887; HRA, KEP, AG INV 10/7, Alexander MacDonald, remarks to the Commission.

67 *Crofters' Commission Annual Report, 1910–12*, p. xxv.

68 SRO, AF67/13, Crofters' Commission memo on grazing rights.

69 AF67/23, Balfour of Burleigh to Brand, 26 Mar. 1902; Brand to Balfour of Burleigh, 1 Apr. 1902.

Commission which had to be heard before all three Commissioners.[70] By the time of Brand's death in 1907, the situation which had pertained in 1902 (when Hosack retired) was amplified. As the work of the Commission had decreased even further since 1902, it was proposed that, instead of appointing a new Chairman, the senior Commissioner would be elevated to that position, and another Commissioner would be chosen. The Chairman's position could be terminated at any time after six months' notice, and alteration of duties would not constitute a claim for compensation or additional remuneration.[71]

It can be seen, then, that the Commission's role, as a component of public policy, changed over time, as conditions in the Highlands, and the political priorities of successive governments, were altered. But there was no real opportunity for the Commission to carve out a new role for itself. It had no real independence: the Secretary for Scotland could decide its movements, or ask it to carry out tasks which were not specifically allotted to it in the Act. In the context of internal governmental politics, the Commission had lost influence by the early 1900s, as the importance of its task declined.

VI

Studies of rural Scotland in the late nineteenth and early twentieth centuries have noted the decline in the power of the landowner.[72] It can be argued that the Crofters' Commission contributed significantly to this declining power; it ended the free market in rents and had a decided effect on estate management in the Highlands. Many argued that its existence was a disincentive to proprietors to commit expenditure on behalf of their crofting tenants.[73] The setting of a fair rent altered the relations between the landlord and his tenant. Before the adjudication, the proprietor might have allowed a certain leniency in the rent collection if he believed the crofters to be poverty stricken. However, once the crofter had applied to the Commission and the fair rent had been fixed, the relationship was placed on a different footing: a third party had intervened and given official sanction to the rent, and the obligation on the crofter to pay was heavier.[74]

The Commission's effect on a landlord was, in its own words, to reduce his interest in the holding 'to that of receiving the rent and

70 SRO, AF43/6/2, 'Memo regarding the land agitation and the legislation following thereon'.

71 SRO, AF67/28, Treasury Statement regarding the Crofters' Commission, 30 Jan. 1908'; Treasury to Scottish Office, 27 Apr. 1908.

72 T M Devine and R. H. Campbell, 'The rural experience', in W H. Fraser and R. J. Morris (eds.), *People and Society in Scotland*, vol. II· *1830–1914* (Edinburgh, 1990), p. 66.

73 *Royal Commission on Land in Wales*, qq. 78717, 5641.

74 Richards and Clough, *Cromartie*, p. 385, *The Scotsman*, 2 May 1888; *Northern Chronicle*, 5 Jan 1887

preventing the illegitimate or deteriorating use of the holding in question'; and the effect of the Act was to 'displace the estate management' on the issue of grazing rights.[75] Nevertheless, security of tenure brought benefits to the proprietor as well: the Commission did much to quell the agitation which had troubled landowners throughout the 1880s. Rents were more secure after the Act and the work of the Commission than they were before. Further, the obligation of the crofter to pay his rent and keep his holding in a good state of repair was enshrined in the Act and could be enforced by the Commission.

When the Highlands were in an unsettled state in the late 1880s and early 1890s, the Commission had a policing role to play and its work had a high profile within government policy. However, as time passed and priorities changed, the role of the Commission changed too. The principal role of the Crofters' Commission had been to administer the 1886 regime, but by the 1890s this was coming under attack. From 1892 to 1912 the Crofters' Commission continued its work, as the debate on Highland policy proceeded. The 1890s and early 1900s saw the Conservatives attempt, unsuccessfully, to interest the crofting community in the idea of purchasing their holdings. The Commission was conscripted to help in this task, in co-operation with the Congested Districts Board, which had been created to carry out this policy in 1897. After 1906, the new Liberal government reacted against this. When they returned to power, they were determined to develop and extend the tenure they had initiated in 1886. The reasons for this were multifarious, and not always strictly relevant to conditions in the crofting counties.[76] This was the political context within which the Commission, its crisis-management role completed, moved on to a more technical and consultative phase. But during this period it was consciously downgraded by the government, and was abolished in 1912 – though after 1912, its judicial role was maintained, and indeed extended both geographically and administratively, by the Scottish Land Court.

In their final report, the Commissioners stated that the biggest change they had seen in the Highlands was the improvement in housing consequent upon security of tenure. Their biggest regret was their inability to deal with the related problems of the cottars and subdivision, especially in Lewis, where these problems were particularly acute.[77] The Crofters' Commission had been a bold and innovative experiment in public policy. Both the Commission and the 1886 Act as a whole had been a special response to a particular emergency.[78] Nevertheless, during that emergency, the Commission was sufficiently balanced to

75 *Crofters' Commission Annual Report, 1899–1900*, p. 21; SRO, AF67/13, Crofters' Commission memo on grazing rights.
76 SRO, AF43/6/2, Memo on land legislation and administration.
77 *Crofters' Commission Annual Report, 1910–12*, p. xxvi.
78 *Departmental Committee on Small Holdings, 1906*, q. 4541.

acquire and retain the trust of crofters – a notable achievement in an era when the 'crofting community' viewed the machinery of government with some distrust. This positive light in which the Commission was viewed helped greatly to secure the legitimacy of the 1886 regime in the Highlands.[79]

79 MacPhail, 'Gunboats to the Hebrides', p. 544

CHAPTER THREE

Conservatives and Liberals: Variations in Highland Policies, 1886–1895

The agitation in the Highlands leading up to the 1886 Act did not immediately cease with its passage. Indeed, the government's efforts to quell the agitation intensified between the middle of 1886 and the middle of 1888. Furthermore, emigration, which, as a policy option for easing congestion, had been a constant theme in government thinking since the 1850s, reached new heights with a government-sponsored colonisation scheme. There were also new developments. Apart from the brief period of Salisbury's unelected caretaker government in late 1885, the country had been governed by the Liberals since 1880. But in 1886, following the split in that party and the ensuing general election of that year, the Conservatives began a period of domination. The new government outlined major policy initiatives for the Highlands which included projections of heavy expenditure on the communications infrastructure. Then, in 1892, the election of a Liberal government produced another change in approach. The technocratic policy of the Conservatives gave way to a more ideological concentration on the relationship of the crofters to the land.

The course of the agitation following the 1886 Act was different from that preceding it. Most noticeably, the geographic focus shifted. In 1882–6, Skye had been the centre of the trouble; from 1887 to 1890 that was to be found in Lewis. The political focus shifted also, as a result both of the new geographic focus and of the perceived defects of the 1886 Act. The problem in Lewis was not so much to do with improving the status of the crofter, as with the lack of status of the cottars, who were more numerous and more concentrated in Lewis than anywhere else in the Highlands. Indeed, the population of Lewis was still increasing in this period, when the population of the Highlands as a whole was falling. The failure of the Act to deal with the cottars' central demand, namely the provision of more land, could only serve to fuel the agitation in Lewis.[1]

[1] Hunter, *Crofting Community*, pp. 170–1; MacPhail, *Crofters' War*, pp. 199–201; Day, *Public Administration*, pp. 183–5; *Oban Times*, 26 Nov. 1887.

I

The first outbreak of lawlessness following the Act occurred on the island of Tiree. A vacant farm at Greenhill was raided as a protest against its being leased to a farmer who had risen from the ranks of the crofters, rather than being shared among the bulk of the crofters. The police proved to be incapable of dealing with the situation, and troops had to be called in. The original decision to use the army was taken by a Liberal government, in July 1886, but by August, when the troops were dispatched, the Conservatives had come into office. It was they who attracted opprobrium for using military force to make a few arrests in Tiree.[2]

If they had inherited the decision to use the army in Tiree, the Conservative government was quick to prove that it would not hesitate to make the same decision itself. This was demonstrated in September when, faced with the paralysis of local administration in Skye caused by non-payment of rates, Arthur Balfour, the Secretary for Scotland, sent a force of marines to the island to back up the civil authorities in their attempts to deal with the problem.[3] Balfour was keen to make the point that the arrears of the proprietors should be pursued as avidly as those of the crofters, and this issue was simplified by the rapid settlement of their debts by the proprietors.[4] Despite the Prime Minister's belief that things were 'proceeding charmingly', trouble arose on a number of occasions during the operation. Deforcements took place at Bornesketaig and Heribusta on the Kilmuir estate on 25 October, and on the following day at Garalapin near Portree. Those involved at Bornesketaig were sentenced to terms of imprisonment, but the others were treated more leniently.[5]

Further outbreaks of disorder took place in Assynt in western Sutherland. Deforcements of sheriff officers took place in April and May 1887, and land raids occurred both in Assynt and in Durness on the north coast. Once again, it required the services of a gunboat and a force of marines to arrest those involved. The difficulties in this case were accentuated by the remote location of the disturbances.[6] In December of the same year, more military activity was centred on Assynt in an attempt to arrest one of the original deforcers, who had taken to the hills

[2] Inveraray Castle Papers, bundle 907, Hugh MacDiarmid to the duke of Argyll, 14 Jun., 17 Jun. 1886; MacPhail, *Crofters' War*, pp. 189–90.

[3] SRO, HH1/1, Secretary for Scotland to Lord Advocate, 10 Sep. 1886.

[4] HH1/47, William Ivory to the Scottish Office, 5 Oct. 1886; HRA, KEP, AG INV 10/32, William Fraser to Alexander MacDonald, 28 Oct., 29 Nov 1886; AG INV 10/72, John MacKenzie to Alexander MacDonald, 23 Oct. 1886.

[5] Hunter, *Crofting Community*, pp. 168–9; MacPhail, *Crofters' War*, pp. 196–8; *Salisbury–Balfour Correspondence*, ed. Harcourt-Williams, pp. 162–3, Salisbury to Balfour, 22 Oct. 1886.

[6] SRO, GD40/16/4/25, Police report, Lochinver, 23 May 1887. GD40/16/4/27, R. M Brereton to Sandford, 27 May 1887

in May. The presence of marines in the district was said to have induced the people to adopt a more law-abiding attitude.[7]

Despite these incidents, the main focus of trouble during this period was in Lewis. The event which began a period of intense agitation in the island, lasting from November 1887 to the middle of 1888, was the raid on the Park Deer Forest. This was a major demonstration by the Crofters' movement, rather than a spontaneous outburst of defiance against the deer forest system. Again, it occasioned a military response from the government; but by the time the soldiers arrived, the raiders had quietly given themselves up. The raid attracted some lurid press coverage, with reports circulating of rifles imported from Ireland and vast numbers of deer slaughtered. The official record casts some doubt on these allegations, but there can certainly be no doubt that the raid achieved its principal objective: that of attracting attention to the plight of the cottars who participated in it.[8]

The importance of the raid in terms of the agitation's overall pattern was that, despite ritual condemnations from all quarters, the raiders were acquitted on a technicality. The majority of the press felt that this would only serve to encourage the agitation.[9] This conclusion would seem to be accurate. Crofters in the Point district of Lewis had made it clear, as early as December 1887, that they intended to occupy the farms of Galson and Aignish on 9 January 1888. Indeed, a deputation of crofters marched to the latter farm and informed the tenant of their intentions. The raids duly took place on the appointed day, and considerable trouble occurred at Aignish. The problems for the authorities stemmed not only from these high profile events, but also from a host of more minor incidents,[10] and the general state of affairs necessitated the retention of the military force in Lewis.

The effect of the Lewis agitation was to raise the temperature in other parts of the Highlands – particularly in Skye and the Uists. It should be noted, however, that in the latter case there were autonomous factors: in particular a threat by the estate-management in South Uist, Benbecula, and Barra that it would begin to enforce the prohibition on crofters from giving potato patches to cottars. This threat was spectacularly unpopular, and so serious were its potential consequences that it was

7 SRO, AF67/36, Sheriff Cheyne to Lothian, 3 Dec. 1887; AF67/37, Cheyne to Lothian, 29 Dec. 1887; AF67/38, Sheriff MacKenzie to Lothian, 7 Jan. 1888.

8 *The Scotsman*, 24 Nov. 1887; *Glasgow Herald*, 24 Nov., 28 Nov. 1887; *Scottish Highlander*, 1 Dec., 8 Dec. 1887; *Northern Chronicle*, 30 Nov. 1887; SRO, AF67/35, Cheyne to Lothian, 26 Nov. 1887; SRO, GD40/16/12/39–40, Charles Innes to Sandford, 20 Dec. 1887; Hatfield House Papers, 3M/E, fos. 106–7, Lothian to Salisbury, 22 Nov. 1887.

9 *Northern Chronicle*, 25 Jan. 1888; *The Scotsman*, 18 Jan. 1888; *Inverness Courier*, 17 Jan. 1888; *Glasgow Herald*, 18 Jan. 1888.

10 SRO, AF67/36, William MacKay to Cheyne, 6 Dec. 1887, and Police report, Ness, 8 Dec. 1887; AF67/37, Cheyne to Scottish Office, 26 Dec. 1887; AF67/40, Cheyne to Scottish Office, 22 Jan. 1888.

very quickly withdrawn. By the middle of the year, however, the authorities in the disturbed districts felt that the worst of the agitation had passed. They put the improvement down to a number of considerations, including the departure of most of the young men to the fishing industry, and that industry's improved returns. But the principal reason was held to be the salutary effect of the six-month sentences of imprisonment passed on the Aignish rioters; these were widely held to have cancelled out the deleterious effects of the acquittal of the Park raiders earlier in the year.[11]

The government believed that the dispatch of military forces to a disturbed area was the best way to induce tranquillity. The police force was not regarded as unbiased; indeed, the police constable in Stornoway felt that its members were 'universally detested'. The perception of the police as landlord instruments stemmed from the fact that the crofters did not contribute to the police rates. It was noticeable that troops were held in higher regard by the crofters, though whether this was due to the preponderant force which they represented or to respect for the 'Queen's Uniform' is a matter for speculation. There were, however, limitations to the utility of military force: it could only be a back-up to the police in the presence of a magistrate, for anything else would be tantamount to the declaration of martial law. Nevertheless, by 1886–8 the government had learned much about the deployment of troops in the Highlands. Its principal value was to counteract the impression that the police were inadequate to deal with sustained lawlessness, and to strengthen the law by having an apparently irresistible force behind it. Other more obscure advantages were suggested by Cameron of Lochiel, who pointed to the purchasing power of the soldiers as a boon to local traders, and hoped that the military presence would do its bit to reduce congestion by stimulating recruiting.[12] Military force, however, was only one of a number of responses available to the government. The Crofters' Commission and the military tended to complement each other; the Commission had more subtle capacities than the military option, but could operate efficiently only in areas where the agitation had passed its peak.

Those who were behind the Park Deer Forest raid in 1887 argued that one of their objectives had been to provide food for the exceptionally destitute inhabitants of the parish of Lochs; indeed, they justified the killing of the deer in those terms. The government was keen to find out

[11] AF67/95, Police report, Staffin, 14 Jan. 1888; AF67/96, Webster to Ivory, 2 Dec. 1888; Skene, Edwards and Bilton to Lothian, 4 Mar. 1888; AF67/97, Webster to Ivory, 1 Mar. 1888; AF67/98, Police report, Lochmaddy, 2 Apr. 1888; C. W. J. Withers, *Gaelic Scotland: The Transformation of a Language* (London, 1988), p. 381.

[12] SRO, GD40/16/12/63–8, Confidential memo for the Secretary for Scotland; SRO, AF67/42, Police report, Stornoway, 8 Mar. 1888; AF67/40, Cheyne to Scottish Office, 20 Jan. 1888; AF67/41, Cameron of Lochiel to Cochran-Patrick, 4 Feb. 1888; BL, AJBP, MS Add. 49801, fos. 27–45, Memo, 14 Sep. 1886; MacPhail, *Crofters' War*, pp. 193–4; D. M. Henderson, *The Highland Soldier: A Social Study of the Highland Regiments, 1820–1920* (Edinburgh, 1989), pp. 219–20.

how true these allegations were and asked for information from the local officials. The picture which emerged was of a population suffering from acute poverty, though officials were reluctant to use the term 'destitute' except to describe the most abject poverty, as it had unpleasant connotations of exceptional relief measures and threatened to demoralise the population concerned. While the harvest of 1887 had not been exceptionally bad, the financial returns from east-coast fishing were almost nil. Further financial problems resulted from low stock prices, due to the change in the structure of the livestock market caused by the growing importance of chilled and frozen meat from New Zealand and from North and South America.[13] With the development of a higher degree of consumerism in the Highlands in the second half of the nineteenth century, falling stock prices had obvious repercussions for the population's social condition; the products of the crofts were more commonly used for wintering stock than for human consumption. The conditions were especially bad in the east of the island, where the land was less fertile and the holdings smaller. The cottars were likely to be hardest hit by these developments, as they were highly dependent on the income they could make from fishing and other forms of labour. And the problems were not confined to Lewis. The inspector of poor in Kilmuir parish, north Skye, reported similar circumstances: a reasonable harvest, but low returns from the fishing and the sale of stock. Unfortunately, the consequences of the agitation tended to exacerbate the problem and make the solution much more difficult. The widespread non-payment of rents, whether through a conscious protest or inability to pay, meant that contributions to the Poor Relief Fund were low – an important factor in the situation in Lewis, about which the estate officials assiduously informed the Scottish Office. As time went on the operation of the Crofters' Commission would help; in 1887, however, the Commission was heavily tied up in Skye and the Uists, and did not reach Lewis until the summer of the following year.[14]

II

The year 1888 saw the Conservative government respond to the situation with two separate initiatives, whose nature demonstrated a preoccupation with the problems of Lewis. As a short term expedient, it awarded the Highlands a subsidy of £30,000 in relief of rates paid out of the Probate duties. A proportion of this money was awarded to the School Boards and the bulk of it was distributed according to

[13] R. Perren, 'The North American beef and cattle trade with Great Britain, 1870–1914', *Economic History Review*, xxiv (1971).

[14] SRO, AF67/68, Supt. Gordon, Stornoway, to Chief Constable, Inverness, 5 Dec. 1887; Board of Supervision to Scottish Office, 10 Dec., 12 Dec. 1887; William MacKay to Board of Supervision, 6 Dec. 1887; AF67/74, MacKay to Lothian, 12 Jun. 1889.

population, with the highest rated areas being favoured. This was not the only direct subsidy which the Highlands received: in 1889–92, they were given money totalling £48,000 in relief of local taxation under the Local Government (Scotland) Act of 1889. This money did not produce any long-term benefit to the Highlands, but it was vital in tiding over the crisis of the late 1880s and early 1890s. The money, however, was not a contribution from central government to the Highlands: it was a reallocation of revenue raised in Scotland and intended to be spent there.[15]

The second immediate governmental response to the problems encountered in Lewis was to intensify the information-gathering operation. For this purpose, Malcolm MacNeill of the Board of Supervision and Sheriff Fraser of Stornoway were commissioned to write a report on the condition of the cottar population in Lewis. MacNeill had already been employed in the Highlands by the government; he had been Secretary to the Napier Commission, and, in the wake of the 1886 Act, Arthur Balfour had sent him on a confidential Highland mission, to collect information on prevailing attitudes there. As for Fraser, he had been commended on his sensitive handling of the difficult situation in Lewis at the time of the Park raid and the disturbances at Aignish and Galson. Importantly, both men were native Gaelic speakers. The information gathered by them would not only be helpful in substantiating policy options, but the very existence of their Commission would help to convince the people of the island of the government's sincere concern for them. But, as was customary when the government showed any signs of involvement in the Highlands, siren voices warned that this Commission would have a demoralising influence and would be regarded as a reward for the agitation and an encouragement to its continuation.[16]

MacNeill and Fraser personally visited 108 houses in the parishes of Lochs and Stornoway, and their conclusions presented a picture of unremitting poverty, dire housing conditions and chronic congestion. One response was the accusation that they went to the areas where the conditions were worst in order to present as bleak a picture as possible; it was said that they would have found different conditions if they had visited the Atlantic coast of the island where the soil was more fertile and the holdings were larger than in Lochs, which was the most poverty-stricken parish in the island. But the reasons for the sorry state of affairs in Lochs were clearly presented, and substantiated the picture the government had acquired from its informal enquiries. Reduced incomes

15 Day, *Public Administration*, pp. 121–2; SRO, GD40/16/25/7–11, 'Memo on the Memorial of Proprietors in the Western Highlands of Scotland'; GD40/16/53/37–8, 'Statement on the amount assigned to Parliament for purposes special to the Highland crofting counties from April 1st 1887 to March 31st 1892'.

16 SRO, AF67/36, Cheyne to Lothian, 3 Dec. 1887; AF67/68, Lochiel to Lothian, 6 Dec. 1887

from the fishing industry and extremely low livestock prices were held to be the immediate causes of the recent poverty. Moreover, the problems in the economy were not merely cyclical, but structural, particularly with regard to fishing. The basis of the herring fishing industry altered fundamentally in 1884. Faced with a worldwide downturn in the industry, the curers were no longer willing to continue the arrangement whereby boats were contracted to them for the duration of the season, at a fixed price per cran of fish. Instead, fish began to be sold at a daily pier-head auction, with the fishermen receiving a share of the price. The effect was to expose the fishermen to any fluctuations in the market – and in the late 1880s the dominant market trend was downwards.[17]

Similarly, fundamental problems could be discerned in the structure of land-holding in the island. MacNeill and Fraser referred to the consequences of congestion, due to the subdivision of holdings. This was a theme to which several government agencies were to return in the succeeding years. It was the characteristic problem in Lewis, although it did exist elsewhere.[18] Several reasons can be suggested for this state of affairs: they include the relatively buoyant state of the economy in the years following 1850; and the proliferation of sources of income, which reduced dependency on the land and encouraged population levels which could not be sustained when the population was thrown back to dependence of land alone, as happened in the late 1880s. Moreover, the congestion was indirectly exacerbated by the agitation. Before 1886, most estates would have had specific provisions in their regulations prohibiting subdivision, but this prohibition was given legislative authority in the 1886 Crofters Act. That did not solve the problem: as we have seen, attempts to outlaw subdivision in the Uists led to such an outcry amongst cottars that it was not followed through. In this period of agitation, cottars in particular were alert to anything that could constitute a grievance; while, by the same token, estates were reluctant to take actions which could lead to any further agitation. The agitation had seen lines of conflict drawn between the cottars and crofters and the estate managements. As a result, the authority of the proprietors, and more pertinently of the factors, was diminished. Thus, the problem of enforcing the prohibition of subdivision was made worse. Concluding their thoughts on a sombre note, MacNeill and Fraser declared:

> It is our conviction ... that actual starvation in the Lews [Lewis] has only been averted during the present winter by the exceptional abundance of last season's crop, and will almost certainly occur before the crop of next season is available; your Lordship will judge whether the immense population here congregated can safely be

17 Day, *Public Administration*, p. 121.
18 Devine, *Great Highland Famine*, pp. 292–4.

permitted to rely on a chance so precarious in this climate as a continuance of favourable harvests.[19]

The official recognition of the island's peculiar problems was regarded as a vindication of their position by the Crofters' movement; but this did not regard the proposed solution so positively.[20] Given the depth of the problems recounted in the report, it is not surprising that the authors proposed a solution which they regarded as permanent rather than palliative: state-aided emigration. MacNeill and Fraser were pushing an open door in terms of this policy recommendation; the government was already some way towards developing a scheme for state-aided emigration by the time MacNeill and Fraser reported. The climate of opinion and comment at the time was heavily in favour of emigration, or colonisation, for the Highland crofters.[21]

From an early date, the government was making efforts to organise a scheme which was both politically and financially acceptable. By mid-1887, Lord Lothian, the Secretary for Scotland, had concluded that 'the first step towards the solution of this great problem is an attractive and well devised scheme of state-aided emigration'. He undertook ultimately unsuccessful negotiations with various Canadian land companies to organise a scheme of colonisation involving their lands and the government's money. However, interest was revived on the part of the government – though not of the land companies – by the agitation and destitution which characterised the later part of the year, and it proceeded to organise a scheme involving the Canadian government. Malcolm MacNeill was dispatched to Lewis and Harris in the spring of 1888 to undertake the task of selecting suitable families for emigration.[22]

There were a number of reasons for the adoption of the scheme, only some of which were made explicit. Publicly, three basic aims were enumerated: to relieve the congestion; to benefit the population; and to increase the size of holdings available to those who remained. The latter two objectives were to be achieved by reallocating the holdings left by the emigrants. MacNeill saw a number of advantages for those remaining behind: not only would they benefit from 'increased elbow room', but, he predicted, the emigrant would find success in Canada and so would be able to 'help his poor relations at home'.[23]

[19] *PP*, 1888, LXXX: *Report on the Condition of the Cottar Population of the Lews*

[20] *Oban Times*, 18 Feb., 5 May 1888.

[21] *Glasgow Herald*, 13 Dec. 1887; *Inverness Courier*, 13 Jan. 1888; *Northern Chronicle*, 30 Nov. 1887; *The Scotsman*, 5 Jan. 1888.

[22] SRO, GD40/16/27/72–3, Confidential memo *re* crofter emigration, 10 May 1887; *PP*, 1889, CCLXXIV: *Evidence and Report of the Select Committee on Colonisation*, R. W. Cochran-Patrick, q. 25.

[23] SRO, AF51/137, 'Draft letter forwarding lists of families intending to emigrate to factors of estates concerned, 25 Feb. 1889'; AF51/51, Memo by Malcolm MacNeill on vacated crofts, May 1988; William MacKay to William Dunbar, 25 May 1888; R. Matheson to Cochran-Patrick, 13 Jun. 1888; SRO, GD40/16/18/23, MacNeill to Lothian, 5 Sep. 1888.

There were a number of other factors in the government's thinking on this issue which it did not reveal so readily. The emigration scheme fitted into the government's priority task at the time, which was to eradicate the agitation at source. Lothian admitted that, given its slow progress, the Crofters' Commission was not likely to settle the agitation. Further, it was felt that the Crofters Act was only a remedial measure and, as such, was insufficient to deal with the fundamental problem, that of population congestion. Although the scheme contemplated at this juncture was limited in the number of families involved, it was hoped that it would be a successful experiment in colonisation, which in the future would provide a model for the undoubtedly larger scheme necessary if congestion was really to be tackled.[24] Lothian, in fact, saw the scheme of emigration as an alternative to reform of land tenure: it was to his mind a 'permanent' remedy, whereas land tenure reform merely raised expectations which were impossible to fulfil. He shared MacNeill's view that a much bigger scheme would have beneficial effects.[25]

Attitudes to the emigration scheme varied considerably. MacNeill found no difficulty in finding enough people to use up the £12,000 which was available for it, and asserted, in 1889, that there was a general feeling in favour of emigration in the districts which he had visited. Equally strong in their assertions to the contrary were the representatives of the Crofters' movement. However, nothing in the way of reliable evidence was marshalled by either side to support their assertions. Interestingly, Lothian had claimed in 1887 that he had the support of three of the Crofter MPs, as well as the Parnellites, for an earlier version of the emigration scheme.[26]

While MacNeill was in Lewis and Harris selecting families for emigration, he encountered some concrete evidence of the Land League's opposition to emigration. League members submitted fictitious applications, which, since it was MacNeill's policy to visit every applicant personally, resulted in a considerable waste of his time. He attempted to counter this by insisting that the applicants were chosen early, and were subjected to extra 'encouragement' by the estate management to ensure that there was no 'hesitation' when the time came. It was, of course, in the League's interests to attempt to create the impression of crofter opposition to emigration. If emigration was seen to be gaining ground among the crofters, it would counter their argument that there was

[24] GD40/16/27/72–3, Confidential memo *re* crofter emigration, 10 May 1887; SRO, AF51/5, Memo by Malcolm MacNeill, 3 Nov. 1886.

[25] Hatfield House Papers, 3M/E, fos. 75–6, Lothian to Salisbury, 21 Jul. 1887; ibid., fos. 136–41, Lothian to Salisbury, 6 Dec. 1887, 17 May 1888, 29 Apr. 1889; Hunter of Hunterston Papers, bundle 1, Lothian to Cochran-Patrick, 29 May 1888.

[26] *PP*, 1889, CCLXXIV: Malcolm MacNeill, q. 370; *PP*, 1890, CCCLIV: William Edwards, q. 3667, John Murdoch, q. 4249, Alexander MacKenzie, q. 4800, George Malcolm, q. 6505, Angus Sutherland, q. 6946; Hatfield House Papers, 3M/E, fo. 76, Lothian to Salisbury, 21 Jul. 1887.

sufficient land for them at home, and severely limit the League's ability to campaign effectively on that premise.[27]

The 1888 emigrants went out to Canada too late in the year to be able to begin cultivating their land, and had to live off their money until the spring of 1889. Subsequent investigations concluded that the £120 loans made available to them were insufficient. In view of these problems, the government had difficulty in recovering its money, and the two settlements, Killarney in Southern Manitoba and Saltcoats in the North-West Territories, were less than conspicuous successes.[28]

Other problems existed closer to home: notably maladministration by the Board set up to organise the scheme. It has been argued that it was the crofters' opposition which ensured that the scheme did not continue beyond 1889, and certainly opposition from the Land League was encountered. But how far this reflected broad-based opposition by the crofting population can be questioned. Further, the government's attitude to the opposition makes it unlikely that it would capitulate. MacNeill actually reported that he regarded the opposition of the League as an encouraging sign.[29] The fact that the Board spent all the money it had available by 1889, and the difficulties encountered in extracting repayments, were more important in bringing the scheme to an end than any positive response to the crofting community's demands.[30]

It was in many ways a novel scheme; the first time the State had become involved in the concept of emigration to this degree. It would have been surprising if some attempt had not been made to test the possibilities of emigration as a policy, given the number of times it had been recommended to the government and the clamour for it which continued in the media. But, from 1889, the Conservative government began to develop more diverse policies; though emigration remained on the agenda, it was at a lower level than before. And the Liberal government which took office in 1892 had different priorities; it was not well-disposed towards emigration. More generally, perhaps the main problem about the colonisation policy was that it was geographically limited. The areas of congestion in the Highlands to which it applied were restricted to portions of the Hebrides – mainly Lewis and Harris – and the West Coast. There were many other areas of the Highlands which the government had not really reached with any of its policy initiatives.

[27] SRO, GD40/16/18/47, MacNeill to Lothian, 23 Sep. 1887; SRO, AF51/97, Memo by Malcolm MacNeill; AF51/134, Myles Macinnes to Lothian, 6 Feb. 1889; Hunter of Hunterston Papers, bundle 21, MacNeill to Cochran-Patrick, 19 Feb. 1889.

[28] W Norton, 'Malcolm MacNeill and the emigrationist alternative to Highland land reform, 1886–1893', *SHR*, lxx (1991); Day, *Public Administration*, pp. 122–5; Hunter, *Crofting Community*, p. 178; *PP*, 1891, CLII: *Select Committee on Colonisation, Report*, p. xi; NLS, Rosebery Papers, MS 10063, fos. 93–6, Memo by Sir G. O. Trevelyan.

[29] SRO, AF51/97, MacNeill, Memo on the Land League.

[30] Hunter, *Crofting Community*, p. 178; S. MacDonald, 'Crofter colonisation in Canada, 1886–1892: the Scottish political background', *NS*, vii (1986–7), pp. 53–4; Norton, 'Malcolm MacNeill and the emigrationist alternative'

III

The government policy, developed over the years from 1888 to 1892, for the development of the country and the stimulation of the fishing industry by large-scale investment in the Highlands' infrastructure, has been hailed as a watershed in government thinking.[31] A link should not be made, however, between the demise of the policy of colonisation and the beginning of the policy of development, first manifested in the appointment of the 'West Highlands and Islands Commission' in 1889.[32] Further, the policy of development should not be seen as a victory for the crofting community; nor should it be seen as indicating a sudden belief on the part of the government in the viability of the crofting system. The harsh reality was that the initiative stemmed from concerted proprietorial demands, and it should be seen as part of the same process that had led to the attempt at the colonisation scheme.

In mid-1888, Lord Lothian received a lengthy memorial from a group of major Highland proprietors, whose analysis of the state of the Highlands was closely in tune with the government's. They perceived the problems to be chronic, and believed that the only solution was concerted government intervention in three areas: first, a programme of public works with the specific aim of developing the fishing industry; secondly, relief of congestion through emigration; and thirdly, an injection of money to subsidise ratepayers in heavily-burdened areas. The proprietors argued that the development was only likely to be successful if the population had first been reduced, and came to terms with their distaste for government intervention by arguing that it was not they, but the government, which had begun this process with the 1886 Act.[33]

Lothian responded positively to the proprietors' demands, arguing that it was desirable for the possibilities for developing the fishing industry to be examined, for the colonisation scheme to be continued and extended, and for some money to be found to reduce local taxation in the Highlands. The objectives were clear: in the short term, to relieve the prevalent destitution; and, in the longer term, to diversify the economy in the Highlands, in order to reduce the centrality of the crofting system.[34] This idea of weaning the people off the land, or, at best, of separating the disciplines of fishing and crofting, was an abiding

31 Hunter, *Crofting Community*, pp. 178–9.

32 Hunter of Hunterston Papers, bundle 3, W. Blackburn to Cochran-Patrick, 6 Dec. 1889.

33 SRO, GD40/16/25/2–5, Memorial of proprietors of landed estates in the Western Highlands and Islands of Scotland; HRA, Miscellaneous Papers, AG INV 14/7, Papers relating to Lord MacDonald's circular to West Highland proprietors, 6 Feb. 1888.

34 SRO, GD40/16/25/7–11, Cabinet Paper on the memorial of proprietors in the Western Highlands of Scotland, 27 Jul. 1888'; SRO, AF67/71, 'Memo on the various schemes suggested for the benefit of the fishing population of the Highlands and Islands by William Dunbar, 3 Jun. 1889'.

concern for the government. It was felt that the people, in trying to follow both, only succeeded in doing neither well enough to make a living.

Lothian visited the Highlands in 1889 to view the sites of the potential developments, and to meet the crofters in what was essentially a public relations exercise.[35] Consequent upon this experience, he appointed the 'West Highlands and Islands Commission'. This body made two reports; the first and more important, in 1890, concerned the Islands and the Western Seaboard, and the second, the following year, dealt with the northern coast and the Orkney and Shetland islands. Its main recommendations were: a railway to the West Coast (preferably with its terminus at Aultbea), and the extension of the existing railways from Stromeferry to Kyle of Lochalsh and from Banavie to Mallaig; the operation of a system of subsidies to steamers on the West Coast; and the development of a major harbour at Ness in Lewis, and of numerous other, smaller landing places. It also proposed expenditure on seemingly minor, but nevertheless vital items, such as lights for shipping, and telegraph facilities. Another improvement which was recommended was a road from Stornoway to Carloway on the west coast of Lewis,[36] which proved to be a long-running saga: the work was beset with problems (both contractual and technical), and the road was not completed until 1912.

The Commission believed that the fishing industry had been neglected, because of both the lack of facilities, and a 'want of energy' amongst the Highlanders which was perpetuated by the poor facilities. It also thought that emigration was a crucial component in the development of the Highland economy, and added another voice to those arguing that crofting and fishing could not be pursued simultaneously.[37] Lothian pressed the Treasury hard for the £150,000 which he felt was necessary to carry out these recommendations, and used some interesting arguments in his submissions to G. J. Goschen, the Chancellor of the Exchequer – arguments which confirm that the policy of development should be viewed in conjunction with that of emigration. He stated that the Highlands were a special case requiring government intervention, as local taxation was insufficient to cover the necessary expenditure; but that this expenditure would see the Highlands transformed to a condition where agitation was a thing of the past, and where prosperity would be generated through the increased income from the fishing industry. Above all, Lothian pointed out:

> In conclusion, I must add that my recent visit to the North West Districts has confirmed my conviction that, concurrently with any

[35] AF67/72, 'Lord Lothian's visit to the Highlands, 1889'; *The Scotsman*, 11 Jun., 12 Jun., 19 Jun. 1889.

[36] SRO, DD4/1-3; Day, *Public Administration*, p. 328.

[37] *PP*, 1890, XXVII: *Report of the Commission appointed to inquire into certain Matters affecting the interests of the population of the Western Highlands and Islands of Scotland.*

other scheme of assistance, it is absolutely necessary, for the permanent relief of the destitution and overcrowding in many of these districts, that a regular scheme of emigration should be carried out. Without this the problem is I think, insoluble.

One of the arguments which Lothian used in his attempts to extract money from the Treasury was to stress that the government had sanctioned expenditure for similar purposes in the west of Ireland.[38] As well as coercion and poor relief, Balfour had initiated large-scale development schemes, including railway building and the improvement of agriculture through the Irish Congested Districts Board, set up in 1892. These schemes have recently been criticised by historians on account of their lack of contribution to the prosperity of the region and the Anglo-centric political motivations behind them.[39]

In December 1890, the Treasury agreed to the expenditure of nearly £70,000 to cover the building of the roads and harbours, the steamboat subsidies, and the telegraphic extensions. The full amount of grant would not be finalised, however, until the controversial railway question was settled.[40] The issue as to which of the proposed railway schemes should qualify for government assistance was generating a considerable amount of debate, and was not settled in the lifetime of the government. In the event, none of the large projects contemplated – to Aultbea and elsewhere – was carried out, though, with the help of government loans, the two existing lines were extended to Mallaig and Kyle of Lochalsh respectively. The Conservative government was uncomfortable about subsidising a new railway which was never likely to be a viable, commercial proposition. Despite defence implications and statements about the national good, the only real justification for such a line would have been the development of the fishing industry, and with the agitation dying out by the early 1890s, the Highlands were given less priority by the government.

Despite large claims in its early years, the Conservative policy failed to produce many substantial results. Most of its initiatives were never followed through: the colonisation scheme did not proceed past the stage of experimentation, the ideas for the development of the Highlands did not come to full fruition. Railway development was limited and protracted, and specific projects like the Carloway Road and the Ness Harbour in Lewis proved problematic. This is not to argue that progress was not made in the building of harbours, subsidising of steamers and development of the telegraph system, with the latter being especially helpful to the fishing industry; but those were minor

[38] SRO, GD40/16/25/16, Lothian to Goschen, 10 Aug. 1889.

[39] A. Gailey, *Ireland and the Death of Kindness: The Experience of Constructive Unionism* (Cork, 1987).

[40] SRO, GD40/16/15–23, Lothian to Goschen, 10 Aug. 1889, Lothian to W. H. Smith, 18 Nov. 1889; GD40/16/25/32–4, Smith to Lothian, 19 Feb. 1891.

achievements compared to the intentions of the government in its early years. Thus the Conservative government did not preside over a lasting transformation in the state of the Highlands. In particular, the fishing industry never achieved the central economic role for the indigenous population for which Lord Lothian and others had hoped.[41]

A second way of concluding the assessment of this government's record is to note not only the structure of its intended policy, with the combination of emigration and development, but also the direction of that policy.[42] The government attempted to deal with the problems of the Highlands without any further alteration of the arrangements of land tenure. It was worried about being perceived as weak in the face of continuing demands from the Land League, and was concerned about creating undue expectations among the crofters. This confounds the notion that the Conservative government was highly responsive to the demands of crofters.[43]

Away from the debates in the government about Highland policy, the situation on the ground had changed by the early 1890s. The agitation had declined considerably, taking on the appearance of a guerrilla campaign. Instead of the large-scale land raids which had been characteristic of the agitation in 1887 and 1888, action was limited to small-scale intrusions.

The period 1888 to 1891 had seen three, relatively mild winters and no particular cry of destitution. Livestock prices had been better, and there was a slight upturn in the income from the fishing industry. However, bad weather in early 1891 exposed the vulnerability of social conditions. Destitution was reported in the parish of Loch Broom in Wester Ross and in Skye, and was of such a scale and intensity that the Poor Relief authorities had to request imports of meal and to contemplate beginning relief works.[44] The following winter saw further problems, and although the focus of the problem this time was Lewis, problems were also encountered in north Sutherland. The mild winters had seen a build-up of livestock beyond what could be wintered on the land when the weather deteriorated. Valuable seed and meal was then used to keep animals which should have been sold years before, and a shortage of food was the ultimate result. Poor agricultural practice, particularly in Lewis where rotation of crops was practically unknown, certainly did not lead to optimism in the government.[45] Many of the attitudes which the authorities displayed towards the relief of this

41 M. Gray, 'Crofting and fishing in the north-west Highlands, 1890–1914', *N.S.* i (1972).

42 *The Scotsman*, 11 Jun. 1889.

43 Hunter, *Crofting Community*, p. 167

44 SRO, AF67/77, Petitions on destitution in the Highlands, Feb., Mar. 1891. AF67/78, Report on destitution in Lochbroom, 19 Mar. 1891.

45 AF67/79, Chairman, Parochial Board, Tongue, to the Board of Supervision, Jan. 1892; AF67/80, Peterkin to the Board of Supervision, 25 Apr 1892; AF67/82, William Hosack to Under Secretary for Scotland, 11 May 1892

distress were reminiscent of the famine of the 1840s. The idea of the 'destitution test' – that is, pitching the wage levels for relief works lower than anything else available, to ensure that only the truly destitute would consider accepting them – remained relevant.[46]

The Conservative government of 1886 to 1892 had clearly demonstrated its priorities: to adopt a structured approach, involving colonisation to reduce congestion, to be followed by development to ensure that the remaining inhabitants would not impose on the government again. This policy would, in theory, lead to the obsolescence of emergency action to deal with recurring crises, be they in the shape of agitation or of destitution. But the reform of land tenure – the crofters' principal demand – was simply not on the government's agenda. This demonstrates that the government was responding to its traditional constituency, the proprietors. The policies pursued in 1886–92 reflected proprietors' demands, as enumerated in their memorial to the government in 1888.

The unpopularity of the general thrust of the policy, as much as dissatisfaction with the government's failure to fulfil the promises it had made, accounted for the success of the Crofter candidates at the general election of 1892. Caithness, Sutherland, and Ross and Cromarty were all retained. In Argyll, D. H. MacFarlane recaptured the seat he had lost in 1886 to Colonel Malcolm of Poltalloch, a Tory proprietor. In Inverness-shire the crofters' most highly respected and longest serving representative, Charles Fraser-Mackintosh, was defeated by Dr Charles MacGregor, a Land League candidate; this result reflected the unpopularity of Fraser-Mackintosh's opposition to Irish Home Rule.[47] The result was inexplicable to the Tory press and led them to reflect on the ungrateful nature of Highland electorates and the cheap promises of the Land League.[48] By 1892, the Crofter MPs had become synonymous with the Gladstonian Liberal Party. The Land League itself had changed. Its interests had become broader, espousing Disestablishment and Home Rule – which only served to cause divisions among its members who, although they agreed on Highland issues, did not necessarily share the same views on those wider questions. This had been reflected in poor performances in the county council and school board elections. Many felt the League was being run by a London-based clique, and efforts were made to bring its decision-making structure closer to home and to revamp its campaigning facilities. Despite this, the various embodiments of the Crofters' movement could not regain the eminence of the HLLRA in the mid-1880s.[49]

[46] AF67/77, Peterkin to Board of Supervision, 18 Feb. 1891; Devine, *Great Highland Famine*, pp. 130–1.

[47] J. Hunter, 'The politics of Highland land reform, 1873–1895', *SHR*, liii (1974), pp. 57–68; D. W. Crowley, 'The Crofters' Party, 1885–1892', *SHR*, xxxv (1956), pp. 122–6.

[48] *Northern Chronicle*, 20 Jul. 1892; *The Scotsman*, 8 Aug. 1892.

[49] *The Scotsman*, 22 Sep. 1893; *Scottish Highlander*, 17 Dec. 1891; Hunter, 'Politics of

IV

Gladstone's fourth administration, which took office in August 1892, engendered high expectations in the Highlands. Sir George Otto Trevelyan, once more Secretary for Scotland, had toured the Highlands in 1890. He now poured scorn on the Conservative policy, denounced the West Highland Commission as a fraud, and went on to promise that the new government would legislate on behalf of the cottars and leaseholders who had been excluded from the 1886 Act, and bring more land under crofting tenure. He was, however, vague on the precise mechanics of this proposed transformation.[50]

Trevelyan proved to be a weak Scottish Secretary in an administration with a slim majority and little standing in the country, especially after Gladstone's retirement in March 1894. One contemporary described his performance as 'lamentable'.[51] The first evidence of the new government's Highland policy was the appointment, in December 1892, of the 'Royal Commission (Highlands and Islands) 1892', which became popularly, and somewhat misleadingly, known as the 'Deer Forest Commission'. The fact that Highland policy was low on the agenda of another Liberal government dominated by Irish Home Rule is suggested by the fact that Trevelyan and Harcourt had to remind Gladstone that such a Commission had been discussed in Cabinet. Its purpose was to

> inquire whether any, and if any, what, land ... now occupied for the purposes of a deer forest, grouse moor, or other sporting purposes, or for grazing not in the occupation of crofters or other small tenants, is capable of being cultivated to profit or otherwise advantageously occupied by crofters or other small tenants.[52]

The government had declared that this Commission was not being appointed to advise on policy – it had already been decided to give more land to the crofters – but to identify the land which would be given.

The Commission received a universally bad press on its appointment, throughout its work, and on the publication of its report. The initial criticisms focused first on the vague nature of its remit, particularly the words 'otherwise advantageously occupied', which commentators struggled to interpret. Secondly, the personnel of the Commission were attacked on account of their lack of practical expertise in land valuation

Highland land reform'; Crowley, 'Crofters' Party'; M Keating and D. Blieman, *Labour and Scottish Nationalism* (London, 1979), pp. 46–7.

50 *The Scotsman*, 22 Sep., 23 Sep., 1 Oct., 3 Oct. 1890; *Scottish Highlander*, 25 Sep. 1890.

51 D. Brookes (ed.), *The Destruction of Lord Rosebery* (London, 1986), p. 155; BLO, MS Harcourt, dep. 92, fos. 107–8, Trevelyan to Harcourt, 27 Jun. 1892.

52 Ibid., dep. 92, fo. 42, Trevelyan to Harcourt, 22 Dec. 1892; fo. 127, Trevelyan to Harcourt, 28 Oct. 1892; *PP*, 1895, XXXIV: Remit of *The Royal Commission (Highlands and Islands, 1892)*.

and agriculture, and further on their political persuasion, which was largely inclined to the Land League. One Highland factor called the Commission members a 'sorry crew' and predicted a wholesale attack on the property rights of landowners. The Commission was chaired by David Brand, the widely respected Chairman of the Crofters' Commission, but it included several well-known Land League personalities, such as Angus Sutherland, MP for Sutherland, and the Rev. Malcolm MacCallum, Church of Scotland minister in Muckairn, Argyllshire: both of these were prominent in the Crofters' movement, and the latter was a brother of the equally prominent Rev. Donald MacCallum of Waternish and subsequently Lochs in Lewis. George Gordon, a land valuer from Elgin, was the only member with any relevant expertise. Voices associated with the Crofters' movement commented, prophetically, that the only effect of the Commission would be to delay legislation. The response of the proprietors was to convene in Inverness, under the chairmanship of Cameron of Lochiel, to lament the effect the Commission would have on the value of their land.[53]

Prior to the publication of its report, in April 1895, the Commission held sixty-four sittings, interviewed hundreds of witnesses, accumulated 1,500 pages of evidence, and inspected the relevant lands. From the outset, the evidence took the form of a sterile debate between representatives of the crofters and the proprietors. The former argued that old, arable land suitable for reoccupation existed in abundance, and produced aged crofters to list the names of old townships which had been cleared at various points throughout the century. The latter responded by denying the validity of hearsay evidence based on the all too fallible memories of old men, and by pointing out that even if old, arable land could be identified, it did not necessarily mean that it could be reoccupied profitably; standards of living had changed, and conditions tolerable in the 1830s would not be contemplated by the crofters of the 1890s. The proprietors also stated that grazing farms and deer forests would be destroyed as letting properties, to the detriment of prosperity in the Highlands, if they were given over to crofters. Proprietors and factors were assiduous in their defence of deer forests, arguing that they contained very little arable land at a suitable altitude for cultivation.[54]

In fact the Commission was a forum where the lines between the Crofters' movement and the proprietors were clearly drawn. The Land League delegated its full time official, Donald MacRae, to help the crofters prepare their evidence and to see that they were questioned fairly by the Commissioners. The landlords' organisation, the Highland

[53] *Glasgow Herald*, 17 Dec. 1892; *Inverness Courier*, 2 Dec., 23 Dec. 1892; *Northern Chronicle*, 28 Dec. 1892; *The Scotsman*, 16 Nov., 5 Dec. 1892; *Scottish Highlander*, 8 Dec. 1892; *Oban Times*, 1 Oct. 1892; SRO, GD305/2/1999/648, William Gunn to the earl of Cromartie.

[54] *Royal Commission, 1892*, qq. 2–7, 7676.

Property Association, was represented by George Malcolm, who, in his lengthy evidence, delivered a classic exposition of the proprietorial case. He utterly denied the validity of Land League assertions that land existed for the crofters and that they should have it forthwith. The Highland Property Association had circulated a questionnaire to proprietors prior to the sittings of the Commission, enquiring as to the effect, on the estate and the local economy, of taking land away from sporting and grazing purposes. Malcolm now presented a strong argument that the amount of arable land in the deer forests was small, currently utilised, and hence not available for crofters.[55] Others with an interest in deer forests were keen to make the same point, arguing that if the low-lying, good land was given to crofters, there would be no place to winter the deer.[56]

The defence of the deer forest system was often conducted through the argument that it provided much needed employment and investment in areas which would not otherwise receive such benefits. The validity of these arguments has been eroded by recent studies of the issue, which tend to suggest that the employment created was seasonal and minimal, probably compensating only for the jobs lost when the land went from sheep farm to deer forest. Certainly, from the point of view of those involved in the Crofters' movement, such expenditure did not strike at the root of the problem of land shortage. The enumeration of the fringe benefits of deer forests was always likely to sound unimpressive to those who viewed their very existence with contempt.[57]

The Commissioners made some attempt to investigate the potential of club, or collective, farms as an alternative method of putting small tenants back on the land. They were held to have various advantages, in terms of improved husbandry and the greater attention paid to stock-breeding. Nevertheless, there were disadvantages. It was felt by some that crofters had a propensity to quarrel, which would hinder proper management. Also, club stocks tended to favour the crofter with means, at the expense of his less fortunate neighbour, which could lead to problems. In the event, club farms were not attempted widely enough for any judgement to be made as to whether or not they provided any answers to the problems of the Highlands.[58]

The Commission was never united, with members absenting

[55] Ardtornish House Papers, George Malcolm to Walter Eliot, 20 Mar 1893, Sinclair of Ulbster Papers, Ledger, Letters to Sir J. G. T. Sinclair, 1888–1894, D. B. Keith to Sir J. G. T Sinclair, 16 Feb. 1893; SCRO, Sutherland Estate Papers, D593 N/4/1/1h, fo. 140, Minutes of meetings with factors at Stafford House, 16 Dec. 1892.

[56] *Oban Times*, 4 Feb., 25 Feb. 1893; SRO, Campbell of Jura Papers, GD64/3/128, Queries submitted by the HPA; Ardtornish House Papers, Queries submitted by the HPA; *Royal Commission, 1892*, qq. 1310, 9946, 49506.

[57] W. Orr, *Deer Forests, Landlords and Crofters* (Edinburgh, 1982), p. 102.

[58] *Royal Commission, 1892*, qq. 6524, 16638; SRO, GD176/2666, The Mackintosh to Allan MacDonald, 22 Jul. 1886.

themselves at various points during its sittings. There was also a definite political split. Those members sympathetic to the Land League were derided by one of their fellow Commissioners for bias in their perception of the evidence; they argued that wherever signs of former occupancy existed, new holdings could be created. There had been problems finding suitable people to sit on the Commission at the outset, due to the lack of financial recompense offered. Trevelyan attempted, without success, to get the Chancellor of the Exchequer, Sir William Harcourt, to grant more money for the Commissioners.[59]

The Commissioners scheduled 1,782,785 acres throughout the Highlands as suitable for occupation by crofters, either as grazing extensions to existing holdings or as new holdings. This was regarded as spoliation by much of the press. A more pertinent criticism of the Commission's recommendations is that they did not define any solution to the problem of shortage of land. Despite a large amount of debate on the subject in the evidence, the Commission made no recommendation as to the optimum size of holding. Other substantial issues, which received no mention in the report, included the crucial issue of money: if new holdings were to be created, who was to pay for the buildings, equipment, and stock which would be required? The only hint of thought about the implementation of policy was an addendum to the main report by three of the Commissioners. They advocated carrying out the recommendations through a land purchase scheme undertaken by a 'representative body' with regulations for the selection of tenants and the management of grazings.[60]

The total number of acres scheduled was divided into three sections: land suitable for new holdings with corresponding pasture; land which could be used for extending existing grazings; and portions of deer forests and sheep farms which were considered suitable for occupation as moderately sized holdings at an annual rent of more than £30. In the first category, the Commissioners identified 794,750 acres, in the second category, 439,188, and in the third, 548,847. It was, however, clear that crofters would be unable to take advantage of holdings in the latter category, since they lacked capital; but the government was unenthusiastic about providing money for the equipping and stocking of such holdings. In turn, the land in each category was divided into old arable and pasture; the vast majority in each category being pasture, not old arable. The Commissioners added that they considered deer forests to be unsuitable for cultivation. They devoted special attention to the island of Lewis, concluding that even if all the forest and farm lands were given over to crofters, those would be insufficient to effect a permanent remedy. Clearly, therefore, the recommendations of the Commission

[59] BLO, MS Harcourt, dep. 92, fo. 170, Trevelyan to Harcourt, 1 Sep. 1893; Dunvegan Castle Papers, 2/712/15/2, M. H. Shaw-Stewart to Reginald MacLeod, 23 Apr. 1893.

[60] Addenda to the *Report of the Royal Commission, 1892*.

were limited, and were certainly not a vindication of the demands of the Crofters' movement.[61]

The government, armed with the report of the Commission, was expected to legislate.[62] The year 1895 saw an attempt to do so, but the bill which was produced was a disappointment to the Crofters' movement and caused the resignation of the Liberal and Land League MP for Inverness-shire, Charles MacGregor. In the bill, no attempt was made to implement the Commission's report; instead, it was concerned with extending crofter tenure to other areas of rural Scotland and improving the enlargement provisions of the 1886 Act.[63] Arthur Balfour taunted the government with the charge that they were unprepared, in comparison with his own party, to take difficult decisions.[64] The arguments proved to be irrelevant, as the bill fell with the government in the early summer of 1895. Liberal failure was clearly reflected in the election results, in the Highlands and beyond. Inverness-shire had been taken by the Conservatives at the by-election following MacGregor's resignation. They held this seat at the general election and also gained Argyll and the two burgh seats. The national swing against the underachieving Liberals was part of the problem, but several indigenous Highland issues were involved. As well as the failure on the land reform issue, the government's espousal of the cause of disestablishment was unpopular among the adherents of the Free Church in the Highlands.[65]

V

The period between 1886 and 1895 had witnessed two distinct approaches to Highland issues. The Conservatives sought to temper radicalism with a tight grip on law and order, before going on to destroy its base with policies of emigration and development. They specifically avoided the issue of tenurial relations. This reflected a belief that the Liberals had gone far enough in 1886, and a veneration for private property. Further, had they indulged in land legislation, the perception that agitation had its rewards could have been fostered. The duke of Argyll melodramatically warned Lothian that the inevitable end to such legislation would be crofters 'quartered on the fields ... of Monteviot and Newbattle'. Therefore the Conservatives restricted themselves to reforms

61 *Report of the Royal Commission, 1892*; MacPhail, *Crofters' War*, p. 221, *Oban Times*, 6 Apr., 13 Apr., 27 Apr. 1895

62 NLS, Rosebery Papers, MS 10145, fo. 84, Memo by G. O. Trevelyan, 1894; *Scottish Highlander*, 14 Aug. 1894.

63 Brookes, *Rosebery*; I. G. C. Hutchison, *A Political History of Scotland, 1832–1924* (Edinburgh, 1986), pp. 204–5; P. Stansky, *Ambitions and Strategies. The Struggle for the Leadership of the Liberal Party in the 1890s* (Oxford, 1964), p. 164.

64 *PD*, 4th ser., vol. 34, col. 915, 11 Jun. 1895; *Oban Times*, 4 May, 15 Jun. 1895

65 *Oban Times*, 20 Jul., 17 Aug. 1895, H. Pelling, *The Social Geography of British Elections, 1885–1910* (London, 1965), p. 482, A. M. Blair, 'Land and language', *Guth na Bliadhna*, xiii (1916), pp. 204–6

of the Crofters' Commission in 1887 and 1888, displaying that tendency to administrative reform which characterised their domestic policy.[66]

Under pressure from proprietors, the Conservatives tried to stimulate the Highland economy through the development of the fishing industry. This policy, however, promised far more than it delivered. Its aim was to change the nature of crofting, to move it away from a dependency on the land financed by income from supplementary activities, towards greater concentration on either farming, fishing or labouring. The incomplete implementation of this policy and the changing political environment in the Highlands produced a change of approach, although not of objective, when the Conservatives returned to power in 1895.

The Liberal government's Highland policy was hampered by the priority given to Irish Home Rule and by the failure of the Scottish Secretary, Trevelyan, to counter this by advocating the need to deal with Scottish issues. Despite the apparent commitment of this government and its considerable reservoir of support in the Highlands, the Liberals failed to produce anything distinctive. However, atrophy in the Crofters' movement, and better economic conditions, meant that there was no resurgence of the agitation which had greeted similarly dashed expectations a decade earlier. They did at least manage to lay aside the shibboleth of emigration, and concentrated on extending the crofting system – a policy to which they would return after 1906.

The major, distinctive, element to emerge from the period was the creation of a climate of opinion in which land purchase could become an acceptable policy. By the early to mid-1890s, the proprietors seemed to favour this development. Notable landowners, such as Cameron of Lochiel and MacLeod of MacLeod, advocated it before the Royal Commission of 1892.[67] It was a policy of which the Conservatives had had experience in Ireland. There, as in Scotland, the objective was to free the proprietor from the limitations of 'dual ownership' rather than to expropriate him on the crofters' behalf.[68]

66 SRO, GD40/16/35/25, Argyll to Lothian, 27 Jan. 1888; M. Pugh, *The Making of Modern British Politics, 1867–1939* (Oxford, 1982), p. 59.

67 *The Scotsman*, 22 Oct. 1894; *Oban Times*, 13 May 1893; *Royal Commission, 1892*, qq. 5641, 51867.

68 Foster, *Modern Ireland*, p. 414.

CHAPTER FOUR

Conservative Government and the Congested Districts Board, 1897–1906

The Conservatives' land policy in the elections of 1895 and 1900 was twofold.[1] Their rhetoric was critical of the Liberal government, accusing it of having ignored the Highlands. More substantively, they promised a measure of land reform based on land purchase. This had been advocated by a minority of the 1892 Royal Commissioners. There was a definite Conservative analysis of the land question which led to the application of the concept of land purchase in Scotland, as in Ireland. Not only was there the aim of relieving existing proprietors of the burden of their crofting tenants, but also the aim of creating new proprietors. The duke of Argyll summarised this neatly in 1895, as: 'A measure which could provide facilities for the purchase of estates at low prices to be broken up might create a very desirable Conservative middle class of proprietors.'[2]

I

The year 1897 saw the passing of the Congested Districts (Scotland) Act, which provided for the creation of a Board to administer a fund of government money, which would be used for the benefit of certain parishes deemed 'congested'. These were to be defined by the members of the Board with reference to the parochial populations and valuations. The formula employed was that the valuation of holdings under £30 should not exceed £1 per head of population,[3] and this led to fifty-six parishes in the crofting counties being defined as congested. Andrew Graham Murray, the Lord Advocate,[4] told MPs that the objectives of the new Board

> included the aiding and developing of agriculture ... the provision of land for sub division among crofters and cottars for cultivation

[1] Hutchison, *Political History of Scotland*, pp. 204–5; Pelling, *Social Geography of British Elections*, pp. 378–86; Hunter, *Crofting Community*, pp. 182–3.

[2] Hatfield House Papers, 3M/E, duke of Argyll to Salisbury, 27 Jul. 1895; *Oban Times*, 26 Jun., 10 Jul. 1897.

[3] Day, *Public Administration*, p. 207.

[4] Murray conducted Scottish business in the Commons because the then Scottish Secretary, Lord Balfour of Burleigh, was a peer

and grazing; the aiding of migration of crofters and cottars to other districts and their settlement there.

In addition, the Board was to have responsibilities for developing the fishing and other industries, and for extending the road and communications network in the congested area.[5]

Before the Board had even set to work, a number of criticisms were directed at it, which concentrated on three aspects of the new legislation. First, the Board's lack of compulsory purchase powers was lamented. Most of the Highland MPs made this point in the Commons, pointing to Lewis as an area where this shortcoming would be cruelly exposed. Not only was it the epitome of congestion, but the whole island was in the hands of one proprietor who, in the absence of compulsory powers, could veto any action by the Board. This, however, was to miss the point; the government was interested in relieving congestion – but only in co-operation with the proprietors, not at their expense. Furthermore, it saw the Congested Districts Board [hereafter CDB] as an experiment and, as such, was reluctant to provide it with draconian powers.[6]

Secondly, the Board's constitution was attacked. It was to be composed of the Secretary and the Under Secretary for Scotland, and the Chairmen of the Crofters' Commission, the Fishery Board for Scotland, and the Local Government Board, plus not more than three other nominated members. Although some found these arrangements commendable from the point of view of economy, it was felt by others that the Board would largely be staffed by men in different parts of the country, who would be busy with other responsibilities and unable to give the CDB the time demanded by the problems facing it.[7] This fear proved to be well-founded, and was often voiced during the Board's existence. It was pointed out that for no single member was the work of the CDB the first claim on his time and money; the inevitable conclusion was that the Secretary for Scotland was 'in reality the CDB'. The fact that the complete membership of the Board rarely convened together for a meeting hampered its ability to react quickly to situations.[8]

The third criticism concerned the fund which the CDB was to administer. Although the government announced that it would amount to £35,000 in total, it was pointed out that this was not all new money for the Highlands. Following the report of the West Highlands' Commission, in 1891, there was an annual vote of money to carry out the purposes outlined by that Commission. This was to be discontinued.

5 *PD*, 4th ser., vol. 50, cols. 355–6.
6 *Oban Times*, 31 Jul. 1897; *PD*, 4th ser., vol. 50, cols. 472, 922–3, 924.
7 *Glasgow Herald*, 19 Jun. 1897; *Oban Times*, 18 Sep. 1897.
8 SRO, AF43/6/2, 'Memo regarding the land agitation in the Highlands and Islands since 1880, and the legislation following thereon'; F. F. Darling (ed.), *West Highland Survey* (Oxford, 1955), p. 12.

Lord Balfour of Burleigh explained that the £35,000 included £15,000 which had been set apart for the Highlands by the Agricultural Rating Act of 1896, and that the balance was in lieu of the former Highlands and Islands vote. Thus the financial aspects of the Act did not grant new money to the Highlands; rather, they consolidated the administration of existing sums. Importantly, the CDB was to be allowed to accumulate a surplus without prejudicing the amount of its next annual vote. This attracted criticism to the Board in its early years, when it built up a sizeable surplus; but that was highly convenient, as it allowed the CDB to purchase both Glendale and Kilmuir when they came on the market almost simultaneously.[9]

There were more general worries that the objective of 'aiding of migration' of the cottar population was doomed to failure, because of the people's reluctance to move. This was seen by some to stem from the association in the people's minds of migration, however beneficial, with Clearance. Such an association was never likely to prove helpful, and these worries proved to be prophetic, in the light of the CDB's efforts to relocate crofters during the next fifteen years.[10]

Like the Crofters' Commission, the CDB was operating without any real precedent. Although the Act of 1897 defined the scope of its operations, there were a number of grey areas. How it was to acquire land was one. Given its lack of compulsory purchase powers, the Board had to consider expedients such as advertising for land. This question led to a debate on the CDB's general policy for land acquisition. Some members felt that the CDB's land purchases were, or should be, limited to the crofting counties. However there was nothing in the Act which specifically stated this, and Malcolm MacNeill, Chairman of the Local Government Board and a man with very definite views on the Highlands, disagreed. He argued that, if the CDB restricted itself solely to the crofting counties, it would be limiting its own chances of success. He believed that there would be more scope for settlers to achieve prosperity beyond the crofting counties, where there was a more active labour market. The creation of more holdings in the Highlands, where there was little demand for labour, would perpetuate the conditions which had led to congestion in the first place. Unfortunately, a likely drawback to the application of this admirable thesis was the crofters' own hostility to the idea of moving outside the crofting counties, or indeed of moving anywhere. There would also be practical obstacles in the way of buying land in the Lowlands, where most agricultural territory was held under lease. Nevertheless, what was clear was that the land to be bought

9 *CDB Annual Report, 1897–98*, appendix I, 'Note on the works carried out under the vote for Highlands and Islands works and communications, 1891–1898'; *PD*, 4th ser., vol. 52, col. 53.

10 *Glasgow Herald*, 21 Jun. 1897; *Northern Chronicle*, 3 Jun. 1897

did not have to be in the congested area, but that the person to be aided had to come from one of the congested parishes.[11]

Given its lack of compulsory purchase powers, the Board could not take the initiative in the land market, but had to wait until a proprietor was willing to sell a piece of land. Accordingly, for the first few years of its existence, the CDB concentrated on its other objectives: principally, the aiding of agriculture and stock-breeding in the Highlands.

As far as arable agriculture was concerned, the CDB helped by providing a better quality of seed, introducing new methods of combating crop diseases, and attempting to encourage vegetable-growing in the congested districts. With respect to animal husbandry, it provided bulls, rams and stallions to crofting townships in an effort to improve the quality of livestock. This policy was successful to a degree, but its ultimate success was hampered by the fundamental problem facing the CDB: the crofters' lack of quality land and of capital. The former was needed to winter the CDB's animals when they were in the hands of crofters, and the latter to supply them with adequate foodstuffs. The consequence was a high rate of mortality among the sires loaned by the CDB. The problems faced were, of course, different in the various parts of the congested area. In Lewis the problems were chronic. The standard of livestock was very poor, because of long years of inbreeding, and even the new blood introduced by the CDB failed to raise the quality significantly. But it was in Lewis that congestion was most acute, which demonstrates the multifaceted nature of the problems faced by the CDB.[12]

The CDB noted, as did the Crofters' Commission, that the arrangement of common grazings, with the prevalence of overstocking and the absence of fencing, reduced the value of crofters' stock. The more stringent provisions of the 1908 Common Grazings Act went some way to dealing with this problem. However, the crofters themselves showed a reluctance to deal with the problem through their grazing committees. At every opportunity, the CDB tried to impress upon crofters the benefits to be obtained by the club stock system. In Kilmuir, which the CDB purchased in 1904, the Board was to see such problems exemplified. By 1910, six years after the purchase and two years after the passing of the new Grazings Act, the problems remained acute. Further attempts were made to interest the crofters in the advantages of the club stock system, this time with some success. One result was that some capital for the participants was generated; it also had practical advantages, in that the stock was more expertly managed. As a native of

[11] SRO, AF42/1332, Memos on the question of advertising for land, 1902; AF42/6435, Memo by R. R. MacGregor to Lord Pentland on the powers of the CDB, 16 Aug. 1909.

[12] *PP*, 1910, XXI: *Report of the Departmental Committee appointed by the Secretary for Scotland to inquire and report upon the work of the Congested Districts (Scotland) Commissioners for the Improvement of Livestock and Agriculture*; *CDB Annual Report, 1911–12*, pp. xii–xvi.

Kilmuir pointed out: 'The Club Stock is also a step towards co-operation, a principle which is so greatly needed in these parts, and should be encouraged in every possible way.'[13]

It was not only ignorance and lack of instruction which caused the low standard of agriculture in the congested districts. The shortage of good arable land made ideal agricultural practice, such as crop rotation, difficult, and also meant that stock was rarely wintered adequately. Congestion, with its symptomatic problems of sub-division and squatting, created the conditions where overstocking became rife, leading to deterioration of the common grazings. Above all, the lack of capital among crofters in the congested areas perpetuated these problems. The crofter was always being tempted to sell his best ewe-lambs for ready cash, rather than to keep them for breeding. But the CDB felt it was not within its power to provide crofters with loans to buy livestock; it was concerned that, with the fluctuating prices of stock, such loans could not be adequately secured. Thus the crofters and cottars in the congested areas rarely achieved the financial security to enable them to equip a holding properly, or to take a long-term view of their principal asset: their stock.[14]

In accounts of the CDB's work, there has been a tendency to compartmentalise its functions into neat categories: land settlement; agricultural improvement; improvement of communications; and so on. But the above survey of what the CDB did with respect to agricultural improvement demonstrates that such an exercise fails to convey the many inter-connections among the apparently diverse problems which faced the Board.[15]

II

Although no major opportunities for large-scale land purchases presented themselves to the CDB, it endeavoured not to neglect their duty to create new holdings. Thus the years 1898 and 1899 saw the completion of a smallholdings scheme on privately owned land in North Uist. In co-operation with Sir Arthur Campbell-Orde, the proprietor, thirty-four new holdings were created at Sollas and Grenitote, and the vacated land was redistributed. Care was taken to relieve the most crowded townships, and the protection of the Crofters Act was extended to the new tenants on the condition that they paid their rents and kept up to date with the repayment of the CDB's loan for the equipment of the holdings. A similar scheme was developed on the Atlantic shore of

[13] SRO, AF42/5034, Memo as to club stocks by Donald Gillies, farm manager, Kilmuir, 7 Jul. 1908; AF42/7936, Angus Mackintosh to R. R. MacGregor, 23 Dec. 1910; Orr, *Deer Forests*, pp. 76–83

[14] *CDB Annual Report, 1900–1*, appendix IV; SRO, CDB Files, AF42/783, William MacKenzie (Principal Clerk of the CC) to R. R. MacGregor (Secretary of the CDB), 21 Feb. 1901.

[15] Mather, 'Congested Districts Board', pp. 196–200.

Harris.[16] MacLeod of MacLeod prepared another on one of his farms in Skye, at Bay: he proposed to create five large crofts of £20 annual rent each, but complained to the CDB that there was little interest in his offer. The CDB thought that he had provided insufficient information, and that the offer of such large holdings was too ambitious; it offered to reshape the scheme and to help with details such as access roads.[17] The MacLeod scheme is of interest, due to the large size of the holdings on offer. The CDB had stated in its first report that it intended to create holdings which would provide a complete livelihood for the tenant, without the need for any ancillary occupation.[18] The failure of the initial Bay scheme to attract any takers was one of the first instances of how the CDB's preferred policy foundered on the lack of interest and the economic problems of the crofting community. Over the course of its existence, the outlook of the CDB seemed all too often to be at odds with that of the crofters.

During the first few years of its existence, the CDB was heavily criticised for its perceived failure to act. It was attacked for its inefficiency and for its lack of contact with the people – especially on the mainland, since most of its activities had been concentrated in the islands. By 1903, such criticism was being echoed within the Scottish Office itself.[19] However, the following year did see some progress. The Board was then engaged in serious negotiations to purchase the estates of Kilmuir and Glendale in Skye. In addition, the duke of Argyll offered them his Ross of Mull estate for £60,000 – an offer which it refused due to the impending purchases in Skye. These purchases were an important breakthrough for the CDB: it could at last claim to be fulfilling the objects for which it had been created, and, for a brief period, it enjoyed an enhanced reputation.[20]

At the same time, the years before 1904 had seen the Board encounter problems with the policy of migration. This became evident with its intervention in the township of Sconser, in Skye – the scene of some of the worst social conditions in the Highlands.[21] There had been an ongoing dispute between the crofters and Lord MacDonald over the township's right to keep sheep. The estate was concerned about the animals encroaching on the deer forest; the crofters complained that the

16 *CDB Annual Report*, 1897–8, p. ix; SRO, AF42/207, R. R. MacGregor to Sir Arthur Campbell-Orde, 7 Jun. 1898; J.B. Caird, 'The isle of Harris', *SGM*, lxvii (1951).

17 SRO, AF42/472, Norman M. MacLeod of MacLeod to R. R. MacGregor, Nov. 1899; AF42/512, Lord Balfour of Burleigh to MacLeod of MacLeod, 12 Jan. 1900; MacLeod of MacLeod to Balfour of Burleigh, 29 Jan. 1900.

18 *CDB Annual Report, 1897–8*, p. ix.

19 *PD*, 4th ser., vol. 109, cols. 1132–3; SRO, AF42/1782, Memo by Reginald MacLeod, 4 Sep. 1903.

20 AF42/1816, duke of Argyll to CDB, 22 Nov. 1903; R. R. MacGregor to the duke of Argyll, 8 Dec. 1903; *Glasgow Herald*, 4 May 1904; *Northern Chronicle*, 11 May 1904.

21 SRO, AF67/124, Memo by the Under Secretary for Scotland on the Sconser crofters, 17 Nov. 1900.

deer damaged their crops. When the Crofters' Commission had tried to enforce the 1891 Grazings Act in respect of the overstock of sheep, a deforcement occurred, and the township came to the prominent attention of the country and the government. The preferred solution of the estate management was to move the crofters to other lands at Suisnish and Borreraig.[22]

The Crofters' Commission held a special sitting at Sconser to attempt to persuade the crofters to accept the move. Sheriff Brand reminded them of the frequent outbreaks of fever in the township. He pointed out that they would have the right to keep sheep, would have more arable land, more and better hill pasture, and access to fishing grounds, and would be able to retain all their crofting rights at Suisnish and Borreraig. Nevertheless, all his attempts at persuasion were unsuccessful.[23]

Many reasons have been suggested for the failure of the crofters to take advantage of such an apparently generous offer. It was certainly the case that Suisnish and Borreraig were less accessible than Sconser, and that the coastline was rocky in the extreme, as the crofters claimed. Some of the Sconser people may have been unwilling to give up their ancillary employment as mountain guides for the nearby Sligachan Hotel. Furthermore, the attitude of the estate and the CDB, in making the offer public before the crofters knew the details, did not help to secure their co-operation. In addition, Suisnish and Borreraig had been the site of a notorious clearance in the early 1850s, and as a result the crofters regarded the lands as tainted. However, Dugald MacLachlan, the Portree solicitor acting for the Sconser crofters, made an important point when he informed Lord Balfour of the 'unspeakable tenacity with which people like them cling to their native locality'.[24]

This episode is important for the pointers it provides as to the likely success of the CDB's key policy of migration. The Board would be unable to do anything to relieve congestion on a meaningful scale if it could not persuade the people of the congested areas to migrate. Sconser, as J. P. Day has noted, was the 'first and only serious effort made by the Board to migrate the people' and it was a complete failure. If the CDB could not succeed in enticing crofters away from a fever-ridden congested township and into land which had been a substantial grazing property on very liberal conditions, there could be little hope for the policy of migration.[25] It represented a defeat for the CDB, which was

[22] Hunter, *Crofting Community*, p. 187; Orr, *Deer Forests*, pp. 130–1, *Oban Times*, 24 Feb., 22 Dec. 1900.

[23] SRO, AF43/54, 'Proposed migration of Sconser, Skye: statement of Sheriff Brand at the close of the Sconser Inquiry, 8 Dec. 1900'; Brand to CDB, 8 Dec 1900; *Oban Times*, 5 Jan. 1901

[24] AF43/54, D. MacLachlan to R. R. MacGregor, 16 Feb. 1901, D. MacLachlan to Lord Balfour of Burleigh, 18 Feb. 1901.

[25] Day, *Public Administration*, p. 211; For a perverse interpretation, see Grigor, 'Crofters and the Land Question', ii, p. 77

engaged in reasonable efforts to relieve congestion, poverty, and in the case of Sconser, squalor. One commentator argued that the CDB had been 'baulked by the backwardness and immobility of those whom they wished to help'. Moreover, it was a defeat which left the Board chastened and pessimistic.[26]

Existing evidence adds to the complexity of this question. There were in this period, and before, examples of crofters expressing a desire to migrate from their present holdings. In 1890, the Crofters' Commission had received a petition from the inhabitants of the district of Kyles Stockinish on the east coast of Harris, expressing a desire to move to the west coast of the island. The Commission, however, had no powers to give effect to such a move, regardless of its sympathy with the undoubted poverty of those involved. Later, in 1906, crofters and cottars from Bruernish in Lewis applied to the CDB to be relocated; but the CDB was of the opinion that 'it would be most unwise to increase the number of miserable 25/- holdings that are so plentiful in Lewis', and concluded that the benefit to be gained did not justify intervention.[27]

In 1900, the CDB acquired the option to buy one of the duke of Sutherland's best grazing farms, Syre in Strathnaver, for a sum of £10,000, to include the shooting rights. The Board considered that only 12,000 acres of the 30,000 acre farm were suitable for smallholdings. The principal obstacle in the way of this highly desirable transaction was familiar: the crofters did not have sufficient capital to take over the sheep-stock on the farm. Nevertheless, after some delay the land was purchased and some twenty-nine holdings were set up, with the tenants purchasing them from the CDB.[28] By 1907, however, the settlers were petitioning the government (by then Liberal), to be allowed to return to the position of tenants. They complained of the smallness of their holdings, the heavy purchase annuity and the high rating burdens consequent on ownership. There was also a political element to the demand, because the government was in the process of trying to pass the Small Landholders (Scotland) Bill which was predicated on the basis of tenancy and not ownership. The petition was repeated in 1909. On both occasions the government declined to entertain the requests of the settlers. But, in 1911, the CDB's annual report recorded that a third petition had been received. This time, the request was granted, and the Syre settlers returned to the status of tenants. By then, the Small Landholders (Scotland) Act had been passed, and the government was in a better position to grant such a request.[29]

26 *Glasgow Herald*, 9 Feb. 1901; 'The Congested Districts Board: its constitution and aims', *Juridical Review*, xiii (1901), p. 218.

27 SRO, AF67/14, Petition from the inhabitants of Kyles Stockinish, Harris, 23 Dec. 1890; AF42/3284, Matheson to MacGregor, 21 May 1906; Day, *Public Administration*, p. 211.

28 SCRO, D593 N/4/1/1h, fo. 200, Minutes of meeting with factors, Dunrobin Castle, 5 Jun. 1899; *Oban Times*, 24 Feb. 1900.

29 *CDB Annual Reports, 1899–1900*, pp. viii–xii; *1900–01*, p. viii; *1911–12*, p. viii; SRO,

The political context of these events will be discussed below in greater detail, with reference to the Board's activities in Skye and the southern Hebrides. It is important to note at this point, however, that the Syre crofters did not become unsettled until the change of government in 1906 and the consequent change of policy.[30] Without speculating on the impact of this on the people of Syre, we must record the experience there as a failure of the CDB's policy of land purchase.

On this evidence, the record of the CDB does not appear attractive. The experience at Bay had suggested that large, potentially self-sustaining holdings were beyond the means and desires of crofters; the events at Sconser had exposed major problems with the key policy of migration; and the history of the Syre settlement from 1902 to 1912 hints that crofter support for the concept of land purchase could easily be eroded in changing political circumstances. The problems with the policy of migration eventually led to a reassessment of the CDB's latitude in 1910. Because the policy of migration was inoperative by that time, any purchase outside the congested area, was of no use to the Board. Thus Seafield farm in Easter Ross, acquired that year, was useless, because it was located in the parish of Fearn which, under the 1897 formula, was not deemed to be congested; consequently, the CDB could not use its money to aid the inhabitants of that parish. The result of these and other considerations was that, in 1910, all the rest of the crofting parishes were declared to be congested. It was hoped that this would give the CDB 'much more of a free hand'.[31]

III

One of the main arenas of the CDB's activities was the southern Hebridean estates of Lady Gordon Cathcart. The area had achieved notoriety in the period of her infamous father-in-law, Colonel John Gordon of Cluny, following his acquisition of the estate from the MacNeills of Barra in the 1840s. Lady Gordon Cathcart was herself a proprietor of note, and although she rarely visited her extended island properties, she held very definite views as to their administration.

Lady Gordon Cathcart's estate management had long been criticised by the Crofters' movement. Such criticisms received a polite echo from the Crofters' Commission in 1902: it noted that, in comparison to Arthur Campbell-Orde's North Uist estate, no new holdings had been formed in South Uist since 1886, and commented on the 'deplorable state of congestion' and the fact that the estate always 'strenuously opposed'

AF42/735, Letters regarding Syre, Jan., Feb. 1901, AF42/4401, Petition from Syre settlers, 30 Dec. 1907; AF42/5940, Petition from Syre settlers, 24 Feb. 1909; MacGregor to A. C. Morton, MP, 2 Jun. 1909.

30 AF42/4601, William MacKenzie to MacGregor, Report of a visit to Syre, Jan. 1908.

31 AF42/7786, Memo on the congested area, 27 Oct. 1910; Day, *Public Administration*, p. 207

enlargement applications. Much of South Uist was plagued by cottars: by 1902, there were 227, with over £2,000 worth of livestock and all the attendant squalor.[32] Such facts led to the estate becoming the focus of a further phase of crofter agitation from 1901 to 1909. There does seem to have been a certain amount of loyalty and respect for Lady Gordon Cathcart herself, but whether or not this was merely good politics on the part of the crofters, who knew their demands for more land could only be met by her, is unclear. The Commission itself was well aware that the proprietor was the key actor, stating:

> The congestion on her ladyship's estates is ... very serious , and we may be permitted to express the hope that wiser counsels may lead to its removal by well considered assignments of land to crofters and others, without the application of any drastic remedy.[33]

Lady Gordon Cathcart also held substantial lands on the east coast of Scotland, and was keen to apply some of the lessons from that area to her Hebridean estates. In particular, she believed that the exclusive pursuit of crofting by the people was a recipe for disaster, and that the ideal method of containing congestion was to provide smallholdings for fishermen who would obtain their principal livelihood from the sea and not the land, as her east-coast tenants did. In pursuit of this, she had granted land in 1883 in the vicinity of Castlebay on Barra for small fishermen's holdings. But these settlements were less than conspicuous successes; their prosperity was heavily exposed to the many and varied fluctuations in the fishing industry.[34] The exercise was not repeated, and, by the turn of the century, the problem of congestion on Barra was chronic. The estate had found it almost impossible to combat the problems of squatting and subdivision. The tenants on Barra were becoming discontented, as they had been in the 1880s, and this achieved expression in September 1900 when cottars raided the farm of Northbay. They claimed that they had petitioned the proprietor for more land without success, and that the raid was the only course left open to them.

William and Murdoch McGillivray, who were tenants of the farm of Northbay, could not easily be fitted into the customary rhetoric against an alien farming class, as they had been born and brought up on the island. Indeed, Lady Gordon Cathcart's agents, the Edinburgh law firm of Skene, Edwards and Garson, described them as 'two men of the crofter class who have been energetic and prudent beyond their fellows'.[35] One unusual factor in this situation was the close personal

32 SRO, AF67/351, 'Report on the social condition of Uist', pp. lxxvii–lxxxiv.

33 Ibid., pp. cxxv.

34 M. C. Storrie, 'Two early resettlement schemes in Barra', *Scottish Studies*, vi (1962), pp. 71–83.

35 SRO, AF67/120, Police reports, Barra, 13 Sep., 15 Sep. 1900; Skene, Edwards and Garson to Scottish Office, 24 Sep. 1900.

relationship between Lord Balfour, the Scottish Secretary, and Lady Gordon Cathcart. This allowed Lord Balfour to make an enquiry, in January 1901, as to whether the proprietor would consider a proposal by the CDB to purchase land in Barra, to enable some attempt to be made to relieve the crofters of the cottar burden. He made it clear that the CDB would purchase the land at fair value and no risk would fall on the estate. Lady Gordon Cathcart's initial reaction was that such a course of action would only provide temporary relief, and in the long run would be 'suicidal'. However, by February, in view of the 'strongly and repeatedly expressed wish of the CDB' she agreed to sell 'with misgivings' the whole of the farms of Eoligarry, Greian and Cleat, Ardveenish and Northbay to the Board, at an asking price of £15,000.[36]

This arrangement was ideal in principle, as the lands formed a self-contained unit in the north of the island which could be easily divided and administered as a whole. But a problem arose when the MacGillivrays proved unwilling to vacate their farm to facilitate the deal. Their reasons were curiously reminiscent of crofter rhetoric: they argued that, as they had spent all their lives there, they were attached to the place and unwilling to leave it. They went on to demand other land in compensation if they were to be moved, or alternatively, they enquired whether Lady Gordon Cathcart would be willing to sell the lands in question to them. In the event the farm of Eoligarry was divided between the CDB and the MacGillivrays, and in addition the CDB bought the farm of Northbay, for a total purchase price of £7,500.[37]

The whole transaction was a highly unsettling influence on cottars throughout Barra. The news that the CDB was to purchase land in Barra created high expectations, but then rumours circulated that the CDB had been unsuccessful in its attempt. The cottars around Castlebay were disappointed that the CDB was not trying to buy lands on the adjacent island of Vatersay, which they had coveted ever since the Royal Commissioners of 1892 had identified them as suitable for occupation by crofters. This mixture of expectation, rumour, disappointment and delay led to further land raids at Eoligarry and Vatersay, in February and April 1901.[38]

Once the details had been concluded, the CDB divided the land into twenty-five crofter holdings and thirty-three smaller fishermen's holdings. The number of applicants exceeded the number of holdings,

[36] SRO, AF42/742, Balfour of Burleigh to Lady Gordon Cathcart, 16 Jan. 1901, Lady Gordon Cathcart to Balfour of Burleigh, 22 Jan. 1901, H. Cook to Balfour of Burleigh, 13 Feb. 1901; SEGP, deed box A8, Lady Gordon Cathcart, no. 3, bundle 13, Lady Gordon Cathcart to Balfour of Burleigh, 8 Feb. 1901, Cluny Castle Papers, bundle 17, Balfour of Burleigh to Lady Gordon Cathcart, 30 Jan. 1901.

[37] SRO, AF42/798, SEG to H. Cook, 28 Feb. 1901; AF42/808, SEG to Balfour of Burleigh, 7 Mar. 1901.

[38] AF42/838, J. A. Dewar, MP, to MacGregor, 3 Apr. 1901, MacGregor to Dewar, 4 Apr 1901, AF67/121–2, Police reports, Barra, Jan.–Apr 1901

and selection had to proceed on the basis of favouring cottars for the larger holdings, and making judgements about those with experience or interest in the fishing industry for the others. This arrangement in itself caused disappointment among the cottars: they had expected that 120 holdings would be created, and were disappointed that the CDB appeared to be favouring applicants with capital. The CDB, on the other hand, believed that capital was necessary for securing the loans which it was to advance for the construction of improved houses, and for paying for stock.[39] This provides another example of the familiar problem which the CDB faced. It was unable to reach out to the very poorest class in the congested districts, because this lacked capital. Essentially, any settlement provided by the CDB was a partnership: the CDB procured and passed on the land, and provided money for housing and other equipment; while the settler, who was most often a former landless cottar, had to provide all the items for which the CDB would not lend money – principally livestock, without which the holding would be worthless.[40]

The CDB was keen to see the settlement managed along efficient lines. It made clear to the new settlers the absolute importance of adhering to the soumings; no overstocking was to be tolerated. Sheriff Brand made a personal appearance at Castlebay to press home these and other points, including the requirement that all houses should be completed by April 1904, on pain of removal. The CDB appreciated the importance of ensuring that the cottar houses vacated by the settlers should be demolished. If this was not done, other cottars would take possession of them, and the cycle of squatting and congestion would begin again, nullifying the work on which the CDB had expended so much time and money. The government took this task so seriously that it claimed it was prepared to spend £100 to fight each case of seizure, in order to establish the principle.[41]

It is instructive to compare and contrast the history of the Barra settlement with the CDB's experience of their settlements in Sutherland, discussed in the previous section. The two settlements were purchased in the same period, but that in Barra was located in the very heart of the congested area.

One obvious similarity is that the years 1907–9 saw petitions from the settlers in Barra to return to the position of tenants, just as happened in Syre in Sutherland. Changing political circumstances, awareness of the proceedings on other CDB estates and an initial miscalculation, or lack of awareness of what was involved in the purchase scheme, combined to

39 *CDB Annual Report, 1901–2*, p. vii; SRO, AF67/123, Police report, Barra, 2 Oct. 1901.

40 P. M. Hobson, 'The parish of Barra', *SGM*, lxv (1949).

41 SRO, AF42/1238, CDB to Barra settlers, 22 May 1902; AF42/1712, 'Conference at Castlebay, 26 Jun. 1903'; Cluny Castle Papers, bundle 15, SEG to MacGregor, 15 Nov. 1902; SEG to R. MacDonald, 15 Nov. 1902.

produce this state of affairs.[42] On the other hand, something which was present in the Barra situation, but which was absent at Syre, was the ongoing problem of congestion in the immediate vicinity of the CDB settlement. This proved to be a problem with which the estate could not cope, and the CDB could see little way to ease the situation, as the cottars possessed insufficient means for them to be helped. Land raids recurred in the northern part of Barra in March 1909.[43]

The pattern of events would seem to confirm the worst fears of Lady Gordon Cathcart, when she warned the CDB that the settlement would not prove a successful experiment in dealing with the cottar question. She had cautioned, 'I am profoundly impressed with the view that it would be a social and economic mistake to add to the number of crofter holdings in Barra.' This warning was repeated on many other occasions in her frequent dealings with the CDB. She believed that the tendency for the children of crofters to stay at home indefinitely with no secure occupation was the source of the congestion on her estates. They settled on a portion of their parents' croft or squatted on the common grazing. They learnt no trade or skill, became imbued with the habits of indolence, and were generally a detrimental influence on all those around them. In her view, temporary migration to the east-coast fishing, or to agricultural or industrial work in the Lowlands, was insufficient. Such migration represented an attempt by Highlanders to strengthen their position on the land by increasing their income; it did not represent a rejection of crofting life. In this regard, she co-operated with the CDB in a scheme of industrial and domestic training for boys and girls from crofter families, in the hope that they would be drawn away from the congested areas. This was certainly a worthy scheme, but it was not conducted on a large enough scale for it to have a sufficient impact on the inhabitants of the congested areas, to reduce the problem of congestion.[44]

Towards the end of its existence, the CDB's policy of allowing its settlers to return to tenancy was certainly not consistent with its earlier actions, and could be interpreted as an admission of failure. It was now operating under a Liberal government committed to the idea of tenancy and hostile to the concept of land purchase, and, furthermore, which had made repeated legislative efforts to have the CDB abolished – efforts which were eventually successful with the passage of the Small

[42] SRO, AF42/2273, Report on Barra settlement, Nov., 1904; AF42/2719, MacGregor to H. Cook, 29 Dec. 1905; AF42/3686, Petition from settlers of Grean and Cliat, 15 Dec. 1908; AF42/7876, A. Mackintosh to Lord Pentland, 7 Jan 1911, AF67/371 Petition from settlers at Grean and Cliat, 13 Aug. 1909.

[43] SRO, AF42/5644, Report on Barra; AF42/5958, Scottish Office to Mackintosh, 6 Mar 1909.

[44] SEGP, deed box A8, Lady Gordon Cathcart, no. 3, bundle 13, Lady Gordon Cathcart to Balfour of Burleigh, 6 Dec. 1900; Cluny Castle Papers, bundle 30, SEG to Lady Gordon Cathcart, 4 Mar 1899

Landholders (Scotland) Act in 1911. Like the Crofters' Commission, after 1906 the CDB was living on borrowed time, and it believed that to pursue its former policy (which had now been superseded) would be anachronistic.[45]

There were also other, more practical, reasons why the settlers at Barra and Syre should be allowed to return to a tenancy arrangement. The two settlements were showing heavy arrears on the purchase annuities and other monies which had been advanced to them. By 1907, the Syre settlement was showing arrears of £439 12s 1d, out of a total amount due, up to that date, of £2,093 7s 1d. The figures for Barra were arrears of £313 19s 5d, from a total amount due of only £864 15s 4d.[46] Under the purchase scheme, there was little that could be done to rectify this situation. Forfeiture of the holding was the only course open to the CDB; whereas under the Crofters Act, the Crofters' Commission could be brought in to revise the rents and arrears. It was also felt that the CDB's insistence that the settlers build a stone and lime house immediately was too onerous; if the settlers were allowed to live temporarily in a house of the old type until they became established, more progress could be expected. In addition, the CDB was of the opinion that tenancy would lead to better management of the common grazings. Above all, by 1911 it was abundantly clear that the settlers, whether through inability or unwillingness, could not keep up with all the payments expected of them. This again substantiates the premise that the CDB's policy of purchase was difficult to apply in an area so short of capital as the congested districts.[47]

The CDB was later to become embroiled in controversy surrounding its activities in Kilmuir and Vatersay (see Chapter 5), but the purchase which could be described as a textbook operation was that of the Glendale estate in the north-east of Skye. This estate was purchased in 1903. Like Kilmuir and Barra, it had seen the heights of the crofters' agitation in the 1880s, and it had already attracted the attention of the CDB in 1898 and 1901. But on those occasions, it was felt that it contained no land which could be used for new crofter holdings – though it did include a substantial sheep farm which could be employed for extra grazing or for other purposes. Sheriff Brand thought that if the purchase was of the whole estate, it would not be much use to the Board: the crofters would probably be uninterested in becoming purchasers of their existing holdings; and, as he pointed out, the CDB had, at that time, no powers to act as landlords of existing holdings. Prophetically, he argued that to contemplate such a role for the CDB would be to 'enter upon a sea of embarrassment'. However, political pressure was so great that the CDB could not afford to pass up such an

45 *CDB Annual Report, 1906–7*, p. v.
46 Ibid., appendices IV and V.
47 SRO, AF42/7876, Mackintosh to Lord Pentland, 7 Jan. 1911.

opportunity, and so the estate was purchased in December 1903, for £15,000.[48] The lands purchased amounted to 20,000 acres, of which about half was in the possession of crofters, and the remainder was used as grazing for a stock of 2,200 blackface sheep. It was clearly a desirable property with good ground and a fine flock of sheep, and it was important that it should be utilised as part of the scheme.[49]

After meeting the tenants at Glendale, it was decided that the CDB should offer each of them the opportunity of purchasing the holding he already rented, plus a share in the grazing farm which would be operated as a club farm. It was reported that the people 'appeared thoroughly to understand the advantages of the purchase system'. The scheme was completed in 1907, when 131 crofters became owner-occupiers, holding shares in the club farm which in 1906 had yielded the sum of £3 7s 4d to each participant.[50]

The subsequent history of the Glendale settlement is different from the others which have been considered. The purchase scheme was clearly conceived from the outset, and the process of acquiring the estate and selling the holdings to the crofters was expedited quickly and efficiently. There were none of the complications with stock, as found at Syre, or with competing purchasers, as found in Barra. A further distinction between Glendale and Barra was that in the former case the CDB was dealing with established crofters, not landless cottars. This is not to claim that the people of Glendale were unduly prosperous; the customary insanitary dwellings existed there as well. Nevertheless, the number of cottars on the estate was small. The main point is that the consensus of the crofters and the Board was established from an early date; perhaps the lessons of Sconser had been learned with regard to keeping the crofters scrupulously and exclusively informed.[51] It has been argued that the distinctive feature which made the purchase scheme attractive in Glendale was that it 'was the undisputed stronghold of antilandlordism'.[52] What was more important was the lack of an entrenched tradition of squatting and subdivision on the estate and, in addition, the existence of a profit-making scheme adjacent to the holdings, namely the club farm livestock. The development of other CDB schemes had been hampered by the paucity of crofters' capital and the burdens imposed on the cottars; but at Glendale the profits from the sheep-stock did at least provide a small income which could help pay off the purchase annuity. These points help to explain why the Glendale

48 AF42/226, Report on Glendale estate, 29 Apr. 1898; AF42/804, MacLeod of MacLeod to MacGregor, 23 Apr. 1901; Memo by Brand on Glendale, 15 Mar 1901

49 *Crofters' Commission Annual Report, 1903–4*, appendix K.

50 *CDB Annual Report, 1903–4*, p. ix; SRO, AF42/1851, Meeting at Glendale, 14 Dec. 1903; AF42/4108, Mackintosh to MacGregor, 4 Sep. 1907.

51 *CDB Annual Report, 1903–4*, p. ix; SRO, AF42/2574, Mackintosh to MacGregor, 29 May 1905; Day, *Public Administration*, p. 215.

52 Hunter, *Crofting Community*, p. 186.

settlers remained as owners when others returned to the position of tenancy.[53]

IV

The island of Lewis was the epitome of all the evils the CDB was supposed to combat: congestion, subdivision, poor agricultural practice and bad housing conditions. When the CDB was formed, it was confidently predicted that, through its lack of compulsory purchase powers, it would have no impact there; and the island's proprietor, Major Matheson, was held up as a prime example of an obstructive landlord who would not co-operate with the Board. The problems on Lewis were quantitatively and qualitatively different. It had accounted for almost the whole of the increase in the crofting counties' rural population over the nineteenth century, though from the 1890s the rate of increase did show some signs of slowing down. If 227 cottars had been considered problematic in South Uist, the scale of the congestion on Lewis can be gauged from the estimated figure of over 1,000 cottars. There was also a structural aspect to the problem: there was simply insufficient land to settle cottars and create new holdings. Thus, according to the Crofters' Commission, migration or emigration were the only possible solutions.[54] Nevertheless, there were over 70,000 acres of deer forest and well over 50,000 acres of farmland on the island. But much of the deer forest land was unsuitable for occupation; the Deer Forest Commission could only find 35,000 acres – almost entirely pasture – to schedule for the extension of crofting.[55]

The endemic congestion on Lewis strained the capacity of the local authority to provide services, and made it extremely difficult to raise the revenue for them to do so. The smallness and low rateable value of most of the holdings contributed to this problem. However, it was exacerbated by the number of squatters and cottars whose property did not appear on the valuation roll. They paid no rates, but received many of the services paid for by ratepayers.[56] In 1902, therefore, the CDB set up a local committee to examine the conditions of the various industries, social conditions, and structure of land occupation. Major Matheson responded by pointing out that he was not unsympathetic to the idea of such a committee making some recommendations, but that it should remember that it was his property that was being dealt with. His outlook was similar to that of Lady Gordon Cathcart, and there is evidence that he was directly influenced by her thoughts. He argued in December 1902:

53 SRO, AF42/4108, Mackintosh to MacGregor, 4 Sep. 1907.

54 *PP*, 1902, LXXXIII: *Report by the Crofters Commission on the Social Condition of the People of the Lews.*

55 *PP*, 1895, XXXIX: *Royal Commission (Highlands and Islands, 1892), Report.*

56 *PP*, 1906, CIV: *Reports to the Local Government Board on the Burden of Existing Rates and the General Financial Position of the Outer Hebrides.*

My own opinion is very decided, that an extension of the crofting system by making new crofts is a mistake. If one or two farms could be divided not into crofts (which means fishing and crofting) but into self sustaining holdings, that is little farms on which a man could live without fishing, of say 20 or 30 or even 40 acres, there would be some good done.[57]

By 1903, Matheson had come to the conclusion that self-sustaining holdings 'are not a success in the Hebrides'. He encountered similar obstacles to the CDB in this regard: landless cottars did not have the capital, expertise or motivation to make the transition to such holdings. However, Matheson did offer the farms of Aignish and Mangersta, where, in co-operation with the CDB, forty-five crofts were formed. Also, twenty-nine fishermen's holdings were established at Battery Park near Stornoway.[58] However, these efforts were insufficient to prevent land raids taking place at Croir on Bernera in 1901, and at Dalbeg in 1909. In addition, the settlement at Battery Park was a failure, as, by 1911, the settlers were asking for new holdings elsewhere; they pointed to the smallness of their holdings, and to the fact that the prosperity of the local fishing industry had been destroyed by the advent of steam trawling.[59]

It is evident that the CDB's failure to make a substantial impact on the problems in Lewis is due to more complex forces than simple proprietorial opposition. The very scale and depth of the congestion ensured that the usual problem faced by the Board – lack of capital in the cottar community – was magnified in Lewis. The CDB also had to contend with a connected physical and social problem. There was a distinct lack of available land in Lewis for the extension of crofter holdings. Certainly there were farms which, theoretically, could have been divided; but to do so on a large scale would not have been wise. Such farms were a repository of agricultural knowledge, invaluable in a predominantly crofting community. However, the social aspect of this problem should not be neglected. The CDB could have purchased land elsewhere in the Highlands for receiving migrants from Lewis; indeed, they considered using the farm of Seafield in Easter Ross, purchased in 1910, for this purpose. In reality, the much publicised, and undoubtedly real, reluctance of the crofters to migrate militated against such an undertaking. And before 1910, the problem was exacerbated by the difficulty of finding somewhere to relocate them to. The consequences of trying to settle them on the Board's land in Skye were too great for the CDB to

57 *CDB Annual Report, 1903–4*, appendix IV, SRO, AF42/1519, Matheson to Balfour of Burleigh, 12 Dec. 1902; Cluny Castle Papers, bundle 30, SEG to Lady Gordon Cathcart, 4 Mar. 1899.

58 *CDB Annual Report, 1911–12*, p. vii; SRO, AF42/1738, Report on the farm of Aignish, Lewis, 16 Jul. 1903; Matheson to MacGregor, 1 Oct. 1903

59 SRO, AF67/54, 'Raid at Crior, Bernera, Lewis, 11 May 1901'; AF67/140, Police report, Carloway, Lewis, 29 Apr. 1909; AF42/8418, Petition from Battery Park settlers, 4 Apr. 1911.

contemplate, given the disturbed state of these areas from 1906 to 1910.[60] Thus simplistic accusations about the CDB's inadequacy to breach proprietorial indifference or crofters' opposition to their plans seriously underestimate the multifaceted nature of the problems of the congested areas. The complexity was such as to bring the problems to the verge of intractability, given the conception of the problem by the Conservative government which had established the CDB.

V

In conclusion, it is useful to compare the Scottish CDB with its Irish counterpart, which dated from 1891. There were similarities in that the Irish Board was also largely composed of supernumerary officials. It had, however, a much larger income than the Scottish Board, receiving £41,000 per annum initially, which eventually rose to £231,000 after 1909; the Scottish figure remained static at £35,000. The powers of the Irish Board steadily increased, too. Under the 1891 Act, it was intended to aid and develop agriculture only, and throughout its existence, down to 1923, this remained an important facet of its work: inspectors and instructors were sent out to help improve agricultural practice in the congested areas. The success rate was considered to be high, especially in the poorest areas like Connemara; the same could not be said for the Scottish Board's influence in Lewis, perhaps the poorest area for which it had responsibility. There was a qualitative difference with the Scottish situation, in that, in Ireland, the policy debate was largely settled on the side of land purchase at an early date. In 1909, the Birrell Act made the Irish CDB a corporate body with compulsory powers of purchase. In Scotland after 1906, on the other hand, the terms of the debate changed and the Scottish CDB operated with the knowledge that its abolition was imminent; the objective for which it was constituted had been superseded. But perhaps the principle difference was that in Ireland the policy of migration was successful, whereas in Scotland the crofters could not be persuaded to migrate or purchase. The Irish Board had greater powers to cajole, and eventually compel, landlords to sell land, than the Scottish Board had.[61] In addition, the Irish Board's efforts were aided by the fact that it persuaded the smallholders to espouse the doctrine of co-operation – though, despite Irish opinion that the crofters would benefit greatly from co-operation and were well suited to its practice, this line of policy was never consolidated.[62]

[60] AF42/5068, Angus Sutherland to MacGregor, 10 Jun. 1908.

[61] L. P. Curtis, *Coercion and Conciliation in Ireland, 1880–1892* (Princeton, 1963), chap xv; W. L. Micks, *An Account of the Constitution, Administration and Dissolution of the Congested Districts Board for Ireland, 1891–1923* (Dublin 1925); 'The Congested Districts Board', *Scottish Law Review*, xxii (1906), p. 311.

[62] SRO, AF42/3963, Report by R. Anderson, Irish Agricultural Co-operation Society, 10 Jan. 1907.

To return to Scotland, the evidence of the Scottish CDB's first phase of operation under Conservative governments shows that its record is not wholly convincing. In particular, its key policy of migration was unsuccessful. This reduced the Board's impact in the most congested districts of the Highlands, principally Lewis, where relief could not be found close at hand. The Board also found that the strength of the crofting economy, particularly the chronic lack of capital among crofters, proved an obstacle to its purchase proposals. Lands were purchased, but through a combination of economic and political calculation, the crofters declined fully to grasp the opportunity before them. Glendale was the exception to this trend: the distinctive structure of this property, and the opportunities presented there for capital returns, allowed it to develop differently from other settlements in Barra and Sutherland.

The Board, nevertheless, does deserve some general credit for its important attempts to raise the quality of stock and the standard of agriculture in the Highlands. Here as well, however, it came up against the undercapitalised nature of the crofting economy. This prevented crofters from undertaking long-term development programmes for stock, which would involve an initial loss of revenue. Clearly, the CDB faced a general problem across the whole range of its efforts.

The CDB has been accused of acting 'opportunistically or responsively rather than on the basis of a grand design or development strategy'.[63] This point has some validity, but it sits uneasily beside the view that 'the 1897 Act was the first integrated development plan in the Highlands and Islands'.[64] A grand design may have been inappropriate, as the Board encountered a multitude of differing local conditions. Also, the CDB's objectives were as much political as social or economic. The implicit aim of creating a class of small proprietors was probably over-ambitious, given the funding available to the Board; nevertheless, an awareness of the political context of the CDB's operations is fundamental. But its political aim remained unfulfilled. Not only was this a failure of scale, but it was also one of ideology, with crofter interest in purchase failing to develop. The full implications of the ideological element of this failure became apparent at the general election of 1906, when the Liberals swept the crofting counties.

63 Mather, 'Congested Districts Board', p. 203
64 Kaye, 'Use of the countryside', p. 91

CHAPTER FIVE

Liberal Government and the Congested Districts Board, 1906–1912

The advent of a radical Liberal government in 1906 was a turning point in the history of the CDB. The new Prime Minister, Henry Campbell-Bannerman, appointed his close political associate of many years standing, John Sinclair [later Lord Pentland], to the office of Secretary for Scotland. The new government expressed a vague, but apparently radical, commitment to a measure of land reform early in its life: a bill was produced in 1906 which rejected the idea of land purchase and espoused a strengthened and extended version of the dual ownership principle which had lain behind the Crofters' Holdings (Scotland) Act of 1886. This created a potential inconsistency, however: while the government was trying to legislate according to one particular principle, it had inherited an institution and responsibilities with entirely different objectives. The inconsistency was accentuated when serious difficulties were encountered in passing the Small Landholders (Scotland) Bill. Because of the problems of obstruction from the House of Lords, and the government's inability to adapt to changed circumstances and demands from the crofting counties, this measure did not receive royal assent until 1911.

I

The CDB had acquired the celebrated estate of Kilmuir in North Skye in 1904. Known as the 'granary of Skye', it was recognised as agriculturally one of the best on the island. But, under the proprietorship of Colonel William Fraser from 1855 to 1892, it had become notorious for rack renting, and in the 1880s it had seen the heights of the 'Crofters' War'. The CDB paid £80,000 for the estate, which extended to 45,337 acres. Four thousand acres on the estate were in the possession of some 450 crofters, and the remainder included eight farms of varying sizes, six of which were under leases which expired during the period from 1906 to 1911.[1]

The CDB's land manager, Angus Mackintosh, was in favour of drawing up a comprehensive plan for the whole estate at the outset,

[1] *CDB Annual Reports, 1903–4*, pp. x–xi; *1905–6*, p. xiii; SRO, AF42/1870, Henry Cook (Solicitor to the CDB) to R. R. MacGregor (Secretary to the CDB), 11 Feb. 1904.

rather than conducting divisions in a piecemeal fashion as the various farm leases fell in. Most of the farms were used principally for grazing, with very little land being suitable for cultivation. Furthermore, it was noted that the crofters' holdings were chronically short of grazing land. Mackintosh therefore presented a scheme for the extension of the crofters' grazings, using the suitable portions of the farms as they became available. In addition, the farms of Monkstadt and Flodigarry were to be broken up, to create twenty-five new crofters' holdings.[2]

However, major problems had to be faced. The first was what to do about the outstanding arrears, which amounted to £4,463 19s 7d. The outlook for their recovery was not promising. Most of those who were hopelessly in arrears were aged or otherwise disadvantaged people, and it would serve no constructive purpose to pauperise them by turning them out of their holdings. As for those in arrears who could be expected to pay some money, it was felt that if they refused, it would multiply the Board's problems. The only method of recovering such debts was to have the assets of the indebted crofter sold by order of the sheriff court – an action which would cripple the crofter's economic prospects. The only viable course of action was for the Crofters' Commission to undertake a complete revaluation of the whole estate. The Commission had visited Kilmuir in 1887, and if the reduced rents and arrears ordered to be paid then had been firmly pressed for by the estate management, the bulk of the outstanding money would probably have been recovered. The prevailing opinion on the estate – that no crofter would be called upon to pay his arrears – was difficult to combat without causing hostility towards the CDB: clearly not a situation which would help the Board so early in its proprietorship.[3] These difficulties were yet another manifestation of the problem which had faced the CDB so often already: the crofter's vulnerability created by his lack of capital.

This was essentially the position which had been reached when the government changed in December 1905. More months were lost with the general election and the proper establishment of the Liberal government in January and February 1906. However, the principal cause of the increasingly noticeable delay in arranging matters in Kilmuir was the attitude of the crofters to the idea of purchasing their holdings. The delay led MPs from Highland constituencies to put pressure on the government to show some progress at Kilmuir, which added to the CDB's exasperation with the crofters' lukewarm attitude to the purchase scheme.[4]

The next stage was to begin a concerted effort to persuade the crofters

[2] AF42/2476, Preliminary report on the Kilmuir estate, 3 Apr 1904; AF42/3013, Report on the farm of Flodigarry, Skye, 29 Jan 1905, AF42/3014, Report on the farm of Monkstadt, 29 Jan. 1905.

[3] AF42/3011, Report by the Crofters' Commission on the matter of arrears on the Kilmuir estate.

[4] AF42/3257, MacGregor to Brand, 11 May 1906.

of the advantages of the purchase scheme. There would certainly come a time when this effort was abandoned, but, initially at least, the attempt was made, despite the Small Landholders (Scotland) Bill, which was published in the autumn of 1906 and which itself repudiated purchase.

The first argument used by the crofters to circumvent the purchase scheme was to claim that their rents were too high; this was important because the purchase terms offered were calculated on a specified number of years' purchase of the rental. The claim was generally considered to have some validity, and the CDB pointed out that it would not stand in the way if the crofters applied to the Commission to have the rents revalued. Indeed, the existence of substantial arrears ensured that such an application would ease one of the Board's difficulties. By March 1906, only seventeen of the 450 crofters on the estate had indicated a willingness to purchase their holdings. In the summer of 1906, the Commission adjudicated on 350 fair rent applications from Kilmuir and gave effect to the reorganisation of the estate. These rearrangements resulted in the conversion of nearly 3000 acres into croft lands, and large reductions of rent across the estate.[5]

However, even this did not meet with universal approval. Some crofters complained that the Commission had increased their rents – though they overlooked the fact that the Commission had also increased the acreage of common grazing available to them.[6] The CDB's support for rent reduction in Kilmuir should be seen in the context of the campaign to persuade the crofters to purchase their holdings. Given the widespread perception in Kilmuir that the rents were too high, and the fact that only seventeen crofters had responded positively to the initial offer of purchase, there was little else that the CDB could do but consent to a revaluation. It clearly hoped it would have the effect of making the purchase scheme look more attractive, as well as make a small contribution to improving the crofters' economic position.

From mid-1906 to May 1908, the campaign to have the Kilmuir crofters purchase their holdings reached its peak. By late 1907, it had been agreed that the lotting out of the remaining portions of the farms (that is, those not required for the extension of the common grazings of townships), an operation which would create seventy-eight new holdings, would have to be delayed until the estate's ultimate fate was decided. Responsibility for that decision lay firmly with the Kilmuir crofting community. The CDB was determined that the purchase scheme should be taken up by the crofters as a whole, rather than individually here and there. The reason for this delay was not made

5 *Crofters' Commission Annual Report, 1905–6*, pp. xiii–xvii; *CDB Annual Report, 1905–6*, p. xiii; SRO, AF42/3369, Recommendations as to Kilmuir by Angus Sutherland, 28 Jul. 1906.

6 AF42/3756, Petition from the crofters of Breckry, Kilmuir, 28 Feb. 1907; Minute by Angus Mackintosh, 6 Mar. 1907.

clear to the crofters, which led to a number of threats being made to take forcible possession of common grazing lands at Cuidrach, Monkstadt and Duntulm, on the east side of the estate.[7]

The reasons advanced by the crofters for rejecting or postponing the purchase of their holdings were clearly articulated. They would only buy if the purchase annuity plus the owners' rates was less than the fair rent – which could be achieved only if the Board was willing to bear a loss on the transaction.[8] But the impression should not be given that purchasers were unprotected: they would have the protection of their purchase agreement and, so long as they kept up with the payments, they would be secure. Significantly, it should be noted that the protection of the 1886 Act was conditional on the prompt and correct payment of rent. At the end of the defined period, the holding would belong to the occupier and he would be free of some of the limitations of the 1886 Act. For example, under that Act a crofter could not assign his holding, and it could only pass to his heir-at-law in the event of his death; as an owner-occupier, on the other hand, he would be able to let it out, or will it, to anybody of his choosing. In a statement delivered at a meeting with the Kilmuir crofters in June 1905, Sheriff Brand laid out the advantages of purchase with his usual clarity. He made the following crucial point:

> you would not be under the terms and provisions of any Act of Parliament, however liberal, but would be proprietors of the soil on which you live, as much proprietors as any other proprietor in the Isle of Skye.[9]

It is evident that the option of purchase offered opportunities as well as burdens.

Initially, the sticking-point was the perception of over-renting. But once the Crofters' Commission had dealt with this problem in 1906, the crofters were resourceful in developing further arguments to counter the CDB's position. Crofters were worried by the rating of their houses, and by other burdens consequent upon ownership.[10] The CDB was initially of the opinion that if those difficulties could be cleared up, most of the crofters would purchase. There were, however, further problems. Many felt that the number of years' purchase of the holdings was too high. It was not only that many crofters could never hope to live to see the day when they would be proprietors, but also that the amount of

7 AF42/4383, Mackintosh to MacGregor, 26 Dec. 1907; AF42/4693, Petition from the Earlish crofters to the CDB, 27 Feb. 1908; AF42/4866, Petition from the Totescore crofters to the CDB, 28 Mar. 1908; MacGregor to Sinclair, 1 Apr. 1908; AF42/4921, Petition from the crofters of Heribusta and Peingown, 7 Apr. 1908.

8 Day, *Public Administration*, p. 213; Hunter, *Crofting Community*, p. 186.

9 SRO, AF42/2780, Report of meetings held by the CDB with the people of Kilmuir in Jun. 1908.

10 Day, *Public Administration*, p. 211; M. D. MacSween, 'Settlement in Trotternish, Isle of Skye, 1700–1958' (Glasgow University B. Litt. thesis, 1959), pp. 173–4.

money which twenty years' purchase represented was thought to be too high for the land on offer. (It should be noted that although one source describes the calculation of the prices of holdings as twenty years' purchase, the payment of the annuities to the CDB would extend over a period of fifty years.) This argument had its supporters in the CDB. Its secretary, R. R. MacGregor, pointed out that, on this basis, the purchase of the estate by the crofters would bring in significantly more than the Board had paid for it in 1904. His colleagues felt that sixteen or seventeen years would be the highest price which would not compromise the scheme's success.[11]

In the early months of 1908, the government made an attempt to discover authoritatively the feelings about purchase on the estate. In December 1907, the CDB had sent out a statement to every crofter, detailing the conditions of the purchase offer and inviting replies before the end of February 1908. Only eighteen positive replies were received, but there had been 363 non-replies; one problem for the Board was how to interpret these non-replies. It is impossible to know whether the eighteen positive respondents represented the same group as the seventeen crofters who had indicated a desire to purchase in 1905. But what certainly is clear is that, in the period between the two surveys, support for the concept of purchase was not widespread in Kilmuir. Angus Sutherland was not exaggerating when he argued 'this does not look encouraging'. He felt, however, that the outcome was not a categorical refusal to purchase; on the other hand, his CDB colleague Reginald MacLeod (Under Secretary for Scotland and the future twenty-sixth chief of Clan MacLeod) disagreed in the strongest terms. MacLeod was well aware that the prevailing opinion in Skye was suspicious of purchase, despite what he called the 'golden terms' being offered to the Kilmuir crofters, whom he described as 'foolish ... ill advised and ignorant'.[12]

The prevailing political climate, its effect on the Highlands, and events elsewhere in the crofting counties all afford some clues as to which of these interpretations was the more valid. The Liberal government was attempting to pass the Small Landholders (Scotland) Bill. Its efforts in the years 1906 to 1908 were particularly vigorous. The bill had been introduced three times; it had been withdrawn voluntarily in 1906, but in 1907 and 1908 it passed the Commons, only to be rejected by the House of Lords. It was eventually taken up by a private member in 1911 and passed with government support; there was by then a different political atmosphere from that of the early attempts, following the Parliament Act of that year which restricted the powers of

[11] SRO, AF42/4429, Mackintosh to MacGregor, 6 Jan. 1908; AF42/6950, Minute by MacGregor, 30 Jan. 1906; Minute by Brand, 3 Feb. 1906; Minute by Angus Mackintosh, 11 Apr. 1906.

[12] *CDB Annual Report, 1907–8*, appendix III; SRO, AF42/4740, 'Kilmuir Purchase Scheme: statement of replies received, 9 Mar. 1908'; Minute by Angus Sutherland, 10 Mar. 1908; AF42/4903, Memo by Reginald MacLeod as to Kilmuir, 3 Apr. 1908.

the Upper House. The bill provided for a new improved version of the protected tenancy arrangements of the 1886 Act; and also for the abolition of the Crofters' Commission and the Congested Districts Board, and their replacement with a Board of Agriculture for Scotland and a Scottish Land Court.

The crofters in Kilmuir were now confronted with the situation whereby a government institution was attempting to persuade them to follow a particular line of policy, namely land purchase; while simultaneously, the government was attempting to legislate along the very different policy lines of dual ownership. Clearly, here was an ambiguity for crofters to exploit. In this context, the date of the introduction of the original Small Landholders (Scotland) Bill, in 1906, is actually more significant than the date of the passing of the eventual Act in 1911. The crofters knew from 1906 that, if they could remain as tenants, the idea of purchase and the CDB could well be things of the past. This fact was fully appreciated by the CDB, whose land manager pointed out at the beginning of 1908:

> They hoped to see the Bill passed into law last year and they are sanguine that it will be passed this year. In these circumstances there will, I fear, be a tendency to delay coming to a decision and to mark time to await the fate of the bill.[13]

The situation at Kilmuir was also affected by the ongoing events on the southern Hebridean estates of Lady Gordon Cathcart. It should be noted here (prior to discussing these events below) that, after buying a small portion of land on Vatersay (a small island adjacent to Castlebay, Barra), the CDB had responded to repeated land raids by Barra cottars by entering into a highly public debate with the proprietor. In this, the government position was that the proprietor was responsible for the condition of her estate, and that the best way of remedying it was to co-operate with the government in settling crofter tenants on the island.

Thus, from two sources, the crofters of Kilmuir could see the policy of purchase disintegrating. The government's strategy was a repudiation of that policy. On an estate renowned for political awareness and activism, the Kilmuir crofters needed no instruction to convince them that the chances of the purchase scheme being followed through were diminishing as time passed.

Some members of the CDB were in favour of responding to the crofters with a varied series of final threats to cajole them into purchase. Reginald MacLeod was of the opinion that, if the present crofters would not purchase, the new holdings should be sold to suitable holders from elsewhere on the island and even outwith Skye; this, he felt, would be a 'valuable object lesson'. Angus Sutherland was in favour of sending a

[13] AF42/4429, Mackintosh to MacGregor, 6 Jan. 1908.

circular to the Kilmuir crofters including 'all the arguments we think necessary to induce them'. Angus Mackintosh, with his superior local knowledge, argued that the CDB could threaten to sell the estate altogether if the crofters refused to purchase, but warned of potential trouble 'if outsiders are brought in'. Generally, the government cautioned that any developments for the benefit of the Kilmuir crofters would be retarded if they broke the law; this, however, did not look very convincing in the light of the government's positive response to the Vatersay raids.[14] A major difficulty for the Board was that legal opinion up to then had led it to believe that it could not act permanently as proprietors under the provisions of the 1897 Act. However, law officers such as the Lord Advocate were essentially political appointees, and as amenable as other members of the government to prevailing political trends. It is not surprising, then, to find in the CDB's report for 1908–9 the statement that:

> We were advised by the Lord Advocate and the Solicitor General that the provision of land by the Board for subdivision among, or enlargement of, the holdings of crofters and cottars in the congested districts need not proceed exclusively by sale to such crofters and cottars.[15]

This legal advice had cleared the way for the proceedings of mid-1908.

The fruits of the decision of May to allow the crofters of Kilmuir to continue as tenants can be seen in the earlier months of that year. The Scottish Secretary, Sinclair, had written confidentially in March, 'it must be borne in mind that if the tenants will not purchase, the method of crofter tenancy will probably have to be adopted'.[16] In May 1908 he wrote formally to the Kilmuir crofters, pointing out that the legal position of the CDB as proprietors was ambiguous. If the Small Landholders Bill had been passed, the statutory position of the government to hold land would have been clarified; but, in the absence of new legislation, it was proposed to offer tenancies under the 1886 Act, as opposed to terms for purchase, to all the existing crofters on the estate. Although Sinclair added that this did not necessarily mean that the purchase scheme would be abandoned or that the government would retain the estate, his letter, in tandem with the events in Vatersay and the continuing efforts to pass the Land Bill, meant that the political signal had been sent. The crofters now considered that they had seen off the purchase scheme.[17]

[14] AF42/4693, Memo by Reginald MacLeod, 27 Feb. 1908; AF42/4740, Minute by Angus Mackintosh, 10 Mar. 1908; AF42/4429, Mackintosh to MacGregor, 6 Jan. 1908; AF42/4855, Scottish Office to Kilmuir crofters, 3 Apr. 1908.

[15] *CDB Annual Report, 1908–9*, p. vii.

[16] SRO, AF42/4703, Minute by Sinclair, 14 Mar. 1908.

[17] *CDB Annual Report, 1908–9*, p. viii; SRO, AF42/5019, John Sinclair to Kilmuir crofters, 14 Mar. 1908.

This could be seen as a victory for the crofters, in that tenancy was their preferred position and the one which prevailed. However, the decision to opt for tenancy should also be seen in the context of the failure of the other CDB settlements to sustain the burdens of ownership, difficulties of which the well-informed Kilmuir crofters would have been aware. They may have reached this position on the basis of this evidence, rather than on ideological grounds. At any rate, what is certain is the fact that the Liberal government from 1906 onwards was well disposed to the idea of tenancy; it is this fact as much as any other which secured the crofters' victory. Furthermore, by the early years of 1908, it was clear that some sort of decision on the future of the estate would have to be taken. The government had owned it since 1904, and had been given a detailed plan for its rearrangement in a fashion that would reduce congestion. It would have been an abdication of the CDB's objectives, even in its less active second phase, if it had continued to mark time; indeed the delay in acting had brought the crofters to the brink of renewed lawlessness. Individual members of the CDB were pressing for action to be taken on the subdivision of the farms and the lotting out of the proposed seventy-eight new holdings, and, significantly, this was begun as soon as the *de facto* decision to abandon purchase in Kilmuir was taken.[18] Thus it is evident that considerations other than the power of the crofters' arguments were weighing on the government as it took this decision.

II

Before returning to Kilmuir to examine the developments between 1908 and the CDB's abolition in 1912, it is necessary to examine what was happening in the southern Hebrides, and particularly Vatersay, which has been referred to above. The events at Kilmuir and Vatersay, and indeed at Westminster, had important implications for each other. The CDB had already tangled with Vatersay's owner, the redoubtable Lady Gordon Cathcart, at the turn of the century, in the course of persuading her to sell land on Barra. The events surrounding Vatersay, which were to run until 1910, began shortly afterwards, in 1901.

The island of Vatersay was arranged as a sheep farm extending to 3,400 acres, rented at £400, and was separated from Castlebay, the main settlement on Barra, by a narrow channel. It had only a small amount of land suitable for cultivation, and had been scheduled as a grazing subject by the Deer Forest commissioners in 1895.[19] This was considered by the crofters as a mark of legitimacy for their claims to have new holdings set up on the island. Furthermore, in September 1897, a special committee

18 AF42/4742, MacGregor to Sutherland, 9 Mar. 1908, AF42/4903, Memo by Reginald MacLeod, 3 Apr. 1908.

19 AF42/1254, 'Negotiations to buy potato ground at Vatersay, May 1902'.

of Inverness County Council had decreed that, amongst other lands in Barra and North Uist, Vatersay should be leased for allotments under the Allotments Act of 1892. The committee had inspected the land and recommended that four-acre plots be leased for a trial period of ten years; but it had no powers under the Act to force the proprietor to follow a course of action of which she manifestly disapproved. Consequently, although no action was taken on this recommendation, the crofters regarded it as a confirmation of the righteousness of their claim, and the delay as a further grievance.[20] Further force was added to their arguments by the fact that the tenant farmer on Vatersay had given potato ground to cottars from the Castlebay area. In the early Spring of 1902, however, the cottars were surprised to find that the farmer wished to terminate this arrangement; so at this point they took matters into their own hands, raided land on Vatersay and proceeded to prepare it for cultivation.[21]

This put the CDB in an extremely difficult position. It had no real power to take the initiative in a matter of this kind. As the land was under lease, the proprietor had no real power either. However, the estate management did recognise the validity of the cottars' position, commenting:

> It must also be kept in view that this is not a case of a mob taking possession of land with which they had no previous connection. There undoubtedly has been a usage of long standing by which the cottars were allowed potato ground on Vatersay.[22]

There was the worry, shared by the Conservative government of the day and the estate management, that the precedent of making arrangements for cottars who had broken the law would encourage others to do likewise. On the other hand, this had to be balanced against the likelihood of destitution if the cottars did not receive land to grow their staple crop. Initially, the terms offered by the tenant were prohibitive and the scheme had to be laid to rest for the 1902 season. Negotiations were resumed in the autumn of 1902, against a background of cottar determination to seize more ground on Vatersay 'no matter the consequence' if they did not get potato ground. The proprietor was keen to sell the land to the CDB, as opposed to entering into a letting agreement with the raiders. This was both more profitable and more attractive to the estate management, whose strategy was to have fewer rather than more crofters on the estate.[23] Therefore, in November 1902,

20 *PP*, 1908, XCVI: Return of the *Report of a Special Committee of the County Council of Inverness upon Applications for Allotments in North Uist and Barra made in September 1897, together with any relative papers*.

21 SRO, AF67/130, Police reports, Barra, 19 Mar., 25 Mar. 1908.

22 Cluny Castle Papers, bundle 15, SEG to Lady Gordon Cathcart, 1 Apr. 1902; SRO, AF42/1549, Memo on Vatersay, 19 Jan. 1903.

23 SRO, AF67/130, Police report, Barra, 28 Oct. 1902; Cluny Castle Papers, bundle 15,

Hugh MacDiarmid, the duke of Argyll's factor on Tiree, was sent to Vatersay to report on the quality of the ground and to recommend a price. He stated that ground on the easternmost point of the island at Creagmhor and Uinessan was suitable for growing potatoes, and that £575 was a fair price. The estate management accepted this figure, but went to great lengths to point out how moderate it was in comparison with similar transactions on the east coast of Scotland.[24] This was a familiar refrain of the Gordon Cathcart estate management, but was of doubtful validity, especially in view of the different conditions and quality of land in the two areas. In addition, Hebridean cottars were likely to be much more dependent on potato land for their survival than east-coast fishermen, who would have more capital at their disposal and were closer to centres of population where supplies could be purchased. In the event, sixty acres were secured on condition that they be used only for potatoes, not pasture or settlement. In the spring of the following year, it was noted that there were fifty families at work on the land. Most of these people were fishermen who had house sites, but no land, in the vicinity of Castlebay.[25]

Although in the longer term this transaction was to prove unsatisfactory, it is noteworthy for the ease with which it was carried out. There had been the experience of the sale of lands in Barra, which had built up trust between the CDB and Lady Gordon Cathcart. The amity, political and personal, between Lord Balfour and the proprietor undoubtedly helped. However, the principal fact which facilitated the transaction was that it fitted in with Lady Gordon Cathcart's analysis of the way forward for the Highlands. The agreement was not for new crofter holdings, but for cultivation plots to be used by fishermen. This was in line with her ideas for steadily reducing the dependence of the people on the land. Of course, while the crofters had strong precedents for their claims to land on Vatersay, it was their raid that had concentrated the minds of the estate management and the government on the problem. Nevertheless, although crofter action did play a part in stimulating developments, it was the similarity between the views of the government and those of the proprietor which was the deciding factor in defining the nature of the purchase. Before this intervention was established, it is significant that the farm tenant of Vatersay refused to co-operate with the crofters.

Despite the acquisition of this land, 'the peace thus achieved proved transient'.[26] Over the next two years complaints were made about the

SEG to Ranald MacDonald, 16 Oct. 1902; SEG to Lady Gordon Cathcart, 17 Oct. 1902.

24 SRO, AF42/1549, Memo on Vatersay, 19 Jan. 1903; Cluny Castle Papers, bundle 15, SEG to Ranald MacDonald, 1 Nov. 1902; MacDonald to SEG, 4 Nov. 1902.

25 SRO, AF42/1594, Rev. D. Chisolm, Castlebay, Barra to CDB, 2 Mar., 13 Mar. 1903; AF42/3914, Reginald MacLeod to John Wilson, 7 May 1907; *CDB Annual Report, 1902–3*, p. ix.

26 Hunter, *Crofting Community*, p. 190.

quality of the land and the conditions upon which it had been let. Land raids recurred in the spring of 1905 – at which point the CDB made it clear to the cottars that such actions would prevent the Board from aiding them. Significantly, the CDB was slowly coming to the conclusion that the land which it had purchased was 'useless' for growing potatoes. A second agricultural expert had examined the land in 1906 and had directly contradicted MacDiarmid's opinion. Lady Gordon Cathcart was therefore approached with an enquiry as to whether she could make more land available to the CDB. Her solicitors responded negatively, and went on to say that, in their opinion, the failure to grow potatoes on the land was 'due not to any inherent incapacity of the soil but to the inability of the people to work it properly'.[27]

The land raid was repeated in February of 1906, prompting the comment by the chief constable of the county police force that 'this is a sort of annual proceeding at this season'. In contrast, *The Scotsman* commented that the Vatersay raid could be 'the portent and prelude to another Hebridean crofters' storm'. The intervention of the proprietor secured a further twenty acres of the farm, which were let to the CDB at a rate of 10s an acre for the period of two years. The implication, when this was communicated to the CDB, was that the government was now duty bound to afford the protection of the criminal law to the proprietor, in an effort to prevent any further land raids. This surprised the government, which had always regarded trespass as a civil matter, and which considered as such that it was up to the proprietor to initiate proceedings.[28]

The CDB has been criticised in this matter for giving the impression by its actions that it was encouraging land raids and other illegal acts.[29] Certainly, the cycle of raid and CDB intervention established at Vatersay did seem to coincide with illegal acts elsewhere in the Highlands. It is, however, difficult to see how else it could have acted. If the CDB, as the only body capable of intervention had not acted, it would have been criticised for ignoring distress and congestion, and for not facing up to its responsibilities. The estate management had shown no real inclination to act independently, preferring to work in conjunction with the CDB, which would helpfully bear some of the expense of dealing with such situations. In theory, it may have been judicious for the CDB to stand firm in the face of threatened and actual raids, but reality, and

[27] Day, *Public Administration*, p. 216; SRO, AF67/132, Police report, Barra, 22 Feb. 1905; AF42/2412, E. K. Carmichael to MacGregor, 14 Mar. 1905; CDB to SEG, 17 Mar., 28 Mar. 1905.

[28] SRO, AF67/132, Police report, Chief Constable, Inverness, 7 Feb. 1902; AF42/3129, SEG to Sinclair, 14 Mar. 1906; *The Scotsman*, 8 Feb. 1906; *Oban Times*, 17 Feb. 1906; *PP*, 1908, LXXXVIII: *Correspondence with reference to the seizure and occupation of the Island of Vatersay, 1908*, p. 91 [hereafter *Vatersay Corresp.*], SEG to the Under Secretary for Scotland, 27 Jun. 1906.

[29] Day, *Public Administration*, p. 217; Hunter, *Crofting Community*, pp. 190–1.

the fact that such raids indicated a degree of distress, compelled the CDB to act.

III

The remainder of 1906, and the early months of 1907, saw the situation at Vatersay deteriorate seriously. By May 1907 the cottars had taken their cattle to the island, were cultivating the land, and had erected huts on it.[30] This led to some vigorous debates, which characterised the period from the middle of 1907 to February 1909, when the CDB purchased the island. One such took place between the new Liberal government and the representatives of Lady Gordon Cathcart, on the issues of who should take responsibility for the Vatersay raiders, and how the law should be upheld. This developed into a broader debate on the island's future, with the estate arguing, in line with its long-held views, that the government should purchase Vatersay if it wished to extend crofting. On the other hand the government argued, in accordance with the policy on which it was trying to legislate, that the proprietor should retain the crofters as tenants, and should establish new holdings in co-operation with government agencies. Further, there was a debate within the Scottish Office itself, between the Secretary for Scotland, John Sinclair, and the Under Secretary, Reginald MacLeod, which developed along similar lines.

The first issue which emerged in these debates was that of law and order. The government firmly believed that, if the estate wanted to deal with the problems of the raiders, it should pursue them in the civil courts. The estate believed this to be an abdication of the government's responsibility to provide protection to a landowner whose property rights had been injured. Reginald MacLeod, in the Scottish Office, noted that the cottars had disregarded the conditions of the lease of the potato ground, and had been grazing their stock on it. He felt that the CDB's habit of responding to lawlessness in a conciliatory fashion had contributed to this, and that the moment was opportune for the CDB to demonstrate that it would no longer tolerate such behaviour.[31] The Secretary for Scotland was on a different wavelength. Sinclair argued that the way out of the difficulties in Vatersay was for the estate to co-operate with the CDB in setting up a new crofter settlement on the island. But, in addition to the well-known general opposition of Lady Gordon Cathcart to such a course of action, there were specific difficulties with Vatersay. As well as the problem about accepting the raiders as tenants, there were doubts about the adequacy of the water

[30] SRO, AF67/132, Police report, Barra, 9 Feb. 1906.

[31] Cluny Castle Papers, bundle 79, SEG to Ranald MacDonald, 16 Mar. 1906; *Vatersay Corresp.*, Reginald MacLeod to SEG, 9 Jul. 1906; SRO, AF42/4127, Minute by the Under Secretary for Scotland, 25 Apr 1906.

and fuel supplies on the island. Also, there were none of the necessary facilities for a settlement, such as a school, church or shop. Furthermore, it was pointed out to the Board that the farm of Vatersay was held under lease until 1926. Lady Gordon Cathcart's solicitors presented the government with a stark choice:

> either they must take effective action for putting down the present lawless movement and protecting the tenant of Vatersay in the peaceable enjoyment of his farm, or they must purchase the farm, make terms with the tenant for renouncing his tenancy, and deal with the farm and the squatters now on it in such way as they may consider proper.[32]

Clearly, if a settlement was to evolve on Lady Gordon Cathcart's terms, the CDB was going to incur a great deal of expenditure in compensating the tenant. The rating burden for the settlers would be crippling if the parish had to provide all the necessary facilities. Sinclair confided to the Lord Advocate, Thomas Shaw, in September 1907 that he was against purchase, 'on the merits and because of the example'.[33]

As has been noted, the Conservative government was able to work in co-operation with Lady Gordon Cathcart and her estate management with the minimum of public controversy. Not so the Liberals. There was a certain amount of political antipathy on the part of the estate management towards the new government; Sinclair had been condemned by them as 'a man with no administrative experience', and the Lord Advocate as 'an extreme radical' and 'hostile to landowners'.[34] Shaw, in particular, seemed to go out of his way to exacerbate the situation. Relations between the government and the estate worsened in August 1907, when the Vatersay situation was discussed in Parliament, and Shaw described the raid in the following downbeat manner:

> These poor tenants of Barra stepped across to the island of Vatersay and on the shore they planted a few potatoes, hoping to return in the spring to reap what little crop there was ... they were interfering with no human soul.

This enraged Lady Gordon Cathcart, and she demanded an apology from the Lord Advocate. One was provided, but proved to be insufficient, and the dispute festered on, to the detriment of the prompt settlement of the problems on Vatersay. Indeed, the proprietor was so bitter about the episode that she went to the trouble of having the correspondence privately published, with her own introduction.[35]

[32] *Vatersay Corresp.*, SEG to Under Secretary for Scotland, 9 Sep. 1907.
[33] SRO, AD59/8, Sinclair to Shaw, 26 Sep. 1907.
[34] Cluny Castle Papers, bundle 79, SEG to Ranald MacDonald, 16 Mar. 1906.
[35] *PD*, 4th ser., vol. 179, col. 1894; *Vatersay Corresp.*, Lady Gordon Cathcart to Shaw, 7 Sep., 13 Aug. 1907; Shaw to Lady Gordon Cathcart, 23 Aug., 12 Sep. 1907.

The estate management had begun to think that the government was favourably disposed to the position of the raiders, who were increasing in number all the time. In mid-1907 the sheriff of Inverness, John Wilson, visited Vatersay and reported his impressions. He took care to attempt to persuade the raiders to desist from illegal actions, and managed to convince the estate management to drop a civil action against them. But his report was not well received by the estate, as it appeared that Wilson had sought his information only among the raiders, and had not approached the estate officials. In reporting the raiders' views, he inadvertently gave the impression that he had some sympathy with them.[36]

The remainder of the period up to the eventual sale of the estate to the CDB in February 1909 was characterised by a rearguard action by the government to prevent such an eventuality, and by consistent attempts by the estate to complicate any scheme for setting up new holdings under the proprietorship of Lady Gordon Cathcart.

The estate's initial demand was that the CDB should compensate the tenant of Vatersay for the breach of his lease. The government was extremely reluctant to agree to this request, on the grounds both of the cost and of the fact that it was not at all sure that it wished to be saddled with responsibility for the whole farm. Conversely, the estate's position on this point, trenchantly put by Lady Gordon Cathcart, was that it had no wish to disturb the tenant, and was only doing so to help the CDB:

> The Secretary for Scotland has taken the extraordinary position that the government are not responsible for the conditions existing in these islands, that the only mode of dealing with these conditions is to yield to the violence of a handful of raiders and that it devolves upon me to pay compensation to the tenant in order to induce him to give up his lease and allow the farm, which he is managing successfully as a grazing, to be divided up into crofts which cannot be managed successfully, and to be handed over to those who have taken and retained violent possession, not only in defiance of the rights of the proprietor and tenant, but in defiance of the interdict of the supreme court.[37]

The next condition the estate made was that the government would guarantee that the remainder of the farm of Vatersay was not raided, if it only used part of it for the settlement. But the estate then exacerbated

[36] SRO, AF42/3914, Reginald MacLeod to John Wilson, 7 May 1907; AF42/5141, Statement by Lady Gordon Cathcart with reference to Vatersay; *Vatersay Corresp.*, Report with reference to Vatersay, 23 May 1907.

[37] *Vatersay Corresp.*, Reginald MacLeod to SEG, 14 Nov. 1907; SRO, AF67/135, SEG to the Under Secretary for Scotland, 3 Dec. 1907; SEG Papers, deed box A8, Lady Gordon Cathcart, no. 3, bundle 18, Introduction by Lady Gordon Cathcart to a pamphlet entitled, *Correspondence between Lady Gordon Cathcart and the Secretary for Scotland and the Lord Advocate*; *The Scotsman*, 4 Mar 1908

the situation in June 1908, when it took civil action against ten of the 150 raiders now on the island. They were duly sentenced to eight weeks' imprisonment. This put the government in an extremely difficult position, as it had consistently argued that the estate should follow that course. It was left with no option but to concede the point that it was responsible for compensating the tenant; indeed it had been given an incentive to follow this course by Lady Gordon Cathcart, who offered to apply to the court to have the raiders released if it did so.[38] This concession did not satiate the estate's desire to force its own analysis of the situation on the government. Following the release of the raiders, who were welcomed home as heroes, the government was faced with a new demand: namely, that it should guarantee and cover any loss to the estate through non-payment of rent by the proposed new settlers. The government thought this to be unreasonable, but the estate stuck to this position until October, when the government was forced to capitulate ignominiously to the estate's initial demand, and purchase the island outright. *The Scotsman* commented, 'in deciding to purchase Vatersay Lord Pentland [Sinclair] has taken the course which he obstinately refused to consider for more than a year'.[39] The transaction was eventually completed in February 1909, with £6,250 changing hands.[40]

The Small Landholders (Scotland) Bill cast a significant shadow over the proceedings. There was no doubt in the minds of Lady Gordon Cathcart's agents that it was this, above everything else, that influenced Sinclair so strongly against purchase. Indeed, Sinclair himself admitted that the objective in Vatersay was to try a dry run of the arrangements in the bill. So, as in Kilmuir, the government was reluctant to be seen to be financing further purchases when its preferred policy was to set up crofter settlements under the existing proprietors. In the case of Vatersay, it made no attempt to sell the holdings to the settlers, preferring to allow them to hold under the Crofters Act.[41] If the Small Landholders Bill had been passed, that would have given the government much needed authority in its negotiations with Lady Gordon Cathcart; moreover, the framework provided would have prevented the estate from introducing new and escalating demands at crucial points in the negotiations.

The Vatersay affair provides a good example of the continuing power of proprietors over government policy. The events in Vatersay have

[38] SRO, AF67/137, Under Secretary for Scotland to SEG, 14 Jul. 1908; SRO, AF42/5871, 'Narrative of proceedings leading up to the purchase of Vatersay, 19 Feb. 1909'.

[39] SRO, AF67/137, SEG to the Under Secretary for Scotland, 30 Jul. 1908; AF42/5344, Sinclair to H. Cook, 20 Oct. 1908.

[40] AF42/5871, 'Vatersay proceedings, 19 Feb. 1909'; AF42/6137, Donald Shaw to the Under Secretary for Scotland, 30 Apr. 1909; Hunter, *Crofting Community*, p. 191.

[41] SRO, AF42/5344, SEG to H. Cook, 16 Oct. 1908; AF42/5871, 'Vatersay proceedings, 19 Feb. 1909'; Minute by Angus Sutherland, 1 Mar. 1909; MacGregor to Sutherland, 3 Mar. 1909; AF42/5991, Notes of a conference held in Edinburgh, 13 Mar. 1909.

been interpreted most often as a victory for the direct action tactics of those who raided the island. There is certainly some substance in this, in that it focused attention on the situation and secured an extension of the crofting system on the Gordon Cathcart estates, against the wishes of the proprietor. However, the Liberal government was in sympathy with the raiders' objectives, if not their tactics. And the course of the negotiations in 1907 and 1908 was heavily in favour of the proprietor and her interests: the government was moved from its advocacy of a dual ownership arrangement for Vatersay, and was forced to take the whole island off the hands of the proprietor at a cost of over £6,000 to the CDB. Indeed, the government did not prevail at any of the crucial points of the negotiation until it came to the settlement of the purchase price. Almost from the beginning of the negotiations, the Scottish Secretary was well aware that he was fighting a losing battle; he confided to the Lord Advocate in September 1907 that 'ultimately purchase may be forced upon us'.[42]

Although Sinclair claimed that the dispute over Vatersay was 'a miserably small business and a sordid bit of work', its importance goes beyond the narrow geographical confines within which it took place. Reginald MacLeod was well aware of this wider importance when he remarked, 'responsibility is the key to the whole difficulty'. MacLeod was convinced privately that a settlement on Vatersay, although sanctioned by the Deer Forest Commission, would be a 'retrograde step'.[43] The debate can, in fact, be interpreted as a microcosm of the wider debate over Highland policy which had been going on since the early 1880s. This debate had left such rival landmarks as the statutes of 1886 and 1897 – with the former based on tenancy, and the latter on purchase. The proprietor was reluctant to establish new tenants under the 1886 Act. Although in the case of Vatersay this would have been done at the public expense, it still exposed her to a number of financial penalties. First, there would be a loss of rent, even assuming that the crofters paid regularly and in full: Vatersay had yielded a rent of £330 as a farm, whereas its crofters, once settled, were to pay only £157.[44] Then there was the question of rates. Setting up a crofter settlement imposed increases in public burdens, through the provision of sanitary and educational facilities, which would fall mostly on the proprietor. There were also considerations of social cost from the proprietor's perspective. Lady Gordon Cathcart, like many proprietors, believed that crofting only served to breed a congested and discontented population. Thus, for all these reasons, the option of purchase was attractive to her; she would no longer have any responsibility for the problems of the island, all of

[42] SRO, AD59/8, Sinclair to Shaw, 26 Sep. 1907.

[43] Ibid.; AF67/137, Memo by Reginald MacLeod to Sinclair, 13 Jul 1908; AF67/135, Minute by Reginald MacLeod, 7 Nov. 1907.

[44] SRO, AF42/5369, Report on Vatersay; Day, *Public Administration*, p. 220.

which would be transferred to the government. Sinclair, whose lack of experience in Highland matters was exposed in the debates over Vatersay, had the greatest difficulty understanding this and had to have it explained in specially simplified language by Reginald MacLeod.[45] But eventually, MacLeod resigned his post in the Scottish Office to fight Inverness-shire for the Conservatives in the general election of January 1910. His private doubts about the 'dishonesty' of the Liberal policy of encouraging crofter tenancies became public during the campaign, when he argued, 'I am in favour of people becoming owners of the land they cultivate.'[46] It was these arguments, which had been voiced by landowners in the early 1890s, which had moved the Conservatives in the direction of land purchase as their preferred policy for the Highlands.

One final issue was highlighted by the Vatersay affair: the relationship between the CDB's actions and the outbreaks of agitation. It had been an oft-repeated accusation that the CDB was responsive to such acts in a manner which would only serve to encourage their repetition. Lady Gordon Cathcart was reluctant to accept any of the raiders as tenants and was concerned that the liberation of the Vatersay raiders, in July 1908, would be regarded as a victory for illegality – a point echoed by the Conservative press. Indeed, their release was followed by a number of incidents throughout the Highlands: in August, cottars at Bruernish in Barra threatened a land raid; in February 1909, cottars from Lochboisdale in South Uist raided the farm of Glendale; and in March there was a raid at Ardmhor on Barra. Reginald MacLeod communicated proprietorial concern over this issue to the Scottish Secretary.[47] In allocating the holdings at Vatersay, the CDB was at pains to point out that an applicant's chances were neither improved nor made worse by his status as a raider; the most important criterion for the Board was agricultural ability. It is interesting to note that the ringleaders in the land raids of 1905 and 1906 actually refused holdings! They manufactured a grievance out of the CDB's method of allocating the sixty holdings on offer on Vatersay; arguing that the CDB had discriminated against the raiders in their allocation of holdings – a grievance not shared by the other applicants.[48]

The island of Vatersay continued to pose difficulties for the government and the CDB, even after the decision to purchase had been

45 SRO, AF67/137, Minute by Reginald MacLeod, 13 Jul. 1908.

46 Inveraray Castle Papers, bundle 314, Reginald MacLeod to the duke of Argyll, 9 Jan. 1907; *Northern Chronicle*, 12 Jan. 1910.

47 SRO, AF67/137, 'Threat of land raid in Barra'; AF67/138, Police report, Lochmaddy, 9 Feb. 1909; AF67/141, Police reports, Barra, 4 Mar., 19 Mar. 1909; AF67/163, Reginald MacLeod, 31 Oct. 1908; *Northern Chronicle*, 16 Jun. 1909; *The Scotsman*, 29 Jan. 1908.

48 SRO, AF42/6209, Report on Vatersay, 19 May 1909; AF42/6582, Minute by Pentland on Vatersay, 7 Oct. 1909; SRO, AF67/370, D. Shaw to Pentland, 5 Jul. 1909.

taken. Once that point was reached, the Crofters' Commission was duly dispatched to survey the farm and assess its suitability for holdings. It also had to deal with the difficult problem of rent. The current rent of the farm was £350. The Commission recommended £330 for the total rent of the crofting townships, but showed an awareness of the problem, commenting, 'it is not unlikely that the class of tenants proposed to be settled in Vatersay cannot afford to pay that rent'. Further problems surrounded the livestock which the raiders had taken over to the island with them. The island was unquestionably overstocked, and the Board realised that it would be impossible to remove the crofters' stock. So, in a somewhat self-defeating exercise, it decided to sell the existing high-quality sheep-stock.[49]

In the event, there were eighty-five applicants for the sixty holdings on offer. They were informed that the estate had been purchased with the object of relieving congestion in Barra and that nobody would be accepted or rejected simply because they had been involved in the raids. As noted above, the ringleaders of the raids rejected the holdings they were offered This posed no difficulty for the CDB, indeed it played into the Board's hands. Grateful to be rid of such troublesome incendiaries, it declared them trespassers on CDB land, and gave them a short time to leave; they responded by attempting, unsuccessfully, to stir up a dispute with the Scottish Office about the terms of the agreements they had been offered.[50] Yet, by September 1910, the CDB was still not in a position to demand any rent from the settlers, who had neither reaped crops, sold stock, nor earned any money from fishing. It was these sort of considerations which had initially prompted Lady Gordon Cathcart to urge purchase on the CDB . The fact that the CDB had paid £6,000 for the inheritance of these difficulties was no doubt a source of great satisfaction to her.[51]

IV

From the 'settlement' of the Vatersay difficulties, the focus of the Board's activities returned to Kilmuir. As has been discussed above, the Liberals had abandoned efforts to persuade the crofters to purchase their holdings. This was not the end of difficulties in this troublesome part of the Highlands.

During the early months of 1910, after most of the restructuring of

[49] SRO, AF42/5369, Report on Vatersay; AF42/5911, Angus Mackintosh to H Cook, 24 Feb. 1909.

[50] AF42/6209, Report on Vatersay, 19 May 1909; AF42/6768, Shaw to CDB, 24 Nov. 1909; AF67/370, Shaw to Pentland, 5 Jul. 1909; MacGregor to Shaw, 30 Jun 1909; Shaw to MacGregor, 1 Jul. 1909; Mackintosh to Pentland, 5 Oct. 1909.

[51] SRO, AF42/7634, Mackintosh to CDB, 4 Sep. 1910; J. Cameron, *The Old and the New Hebrides from the Days of the Great Clearances to the Pentland Act of 1912* (Kirkcaldy, 1912), pp. 132–3

the Kilmuir estate had been carried out, the Board received a flurry of threats from the crofters. Those at Heribusta threatened to raid the farm of Duntulm in the extreme north of the estate. In more menacing terms, the crofters of Idrigill indicated their designs on the neighbouring farm of Scuddaburgh.[52] They had long coveted this farm and were aggrieved, in early 1910, when the Crofters' Commission awarded them only 397 acres of it, on the argument that the crofters had neither the capital nor the skill to justify the award of the remaining sixty-three acres of arable land. Despite the fact that the CDB, in its position as proprietor, obtained interdicts to prevent a raid, such an event took place in late April 1910.[53]

The CDB believed that it had to stand by the Commission's decision, and not yield to the crofters' demands for an independent valuation of the farm. Further raids took place in June 1910, and the government began to make much more resolute noises about the necessity of stamping out lawlessness now that it was its own property that was being raided. However, it found out just how difficult it was to apply the civil law in such remote areas, when an attempt was made to serve writs on the raiders. The police refused to arrest, or even to point out, the guilty parties; and local CDB officials, fearful for their own safety, refused to become involved. The result was that Angus Mackintosh, the CDB's land manager, had to perform the task. He did so, but felt that the action destroyed his reputation in Kilmuir. The attempt to serve the writs was singularly unsuccessful: Mackintosh and the sheriff officers were attacked by the men, women and children of the township, and were sent packing in the general direction of Portree.[54]

After a meeting between Lord Pentland and the Idrigill crofters in the Free Church in Uig, the issue was settled by giving the disputed sixty-three acres to the Idrigill crofters to farm communally. A proposal had been made to form four large holdings on the land but, in Pentland's words 'jealousy was too much for it'. Pentland expected, and received, criticism for his carefully arranged solution, with *The Scotsman* condemning it as 'socialistic'.[55]

This period is notable for the number of land raids which occurred, so it is important to note the similarities and contrasts between them. The raids on Vatersay were the most prominent, principally because of the attitude of permanence taken by the raiders. They were also large-scale events, with 130 people being on the island by October 1908, who not

52 SRO, AF42/7047, Heribusta crofters to CDB, 5 Mar. 1910; AF42/7195, Idrigill crofters to CDB, 11 Apr. 1910.

53 *Crofters' Commission Annual Report, 1909–10*, p. 50; *CDB Annual Report, 1910–11*, p. vii; SRO, AF42/7282, Scottish Office to Idrigill crofters, 7 May 1910.

54 AF42/7371, Mackintosh to CDB, 7 Jun. 1910; Scottish Office to CDB, 8 Jun. 1910; AF42/7570, H. Cook to MacGregor, 28 Aug. 1910; AF42/7574, Mackintosh to CDB, 23 Aug. 1910; SRO, AF67/369, 'Scuddaburgh land raid'.

55 SRO, AF42/7652, Pentland to MacGregor, 24 Sep. 1910; *The Scotsman*, 23 Sep. 1910.

only brought their livestock with them, but also erected wooden houses to live in. This made the Vatersay raiders very difficult to dislodge. They had gone further than any other previous raiders in physically staking a claim to the land they coveted.[56] The challenge made by the raiders was to the estate, not to the government, which they perceived as being supportive of their cause, with Lord Pentland being held in particular reverence. Previous land raids in the 1880s had certainly been anti-landlord, but they had also been characterised by anti-government sentiment as well. And the land raids which occurred in South Uist can be characterised more accurately as demonstrations rather than challenges. Those involved did not take up permanent residence on the land in question, but withdrew when they felt their protest had been registered.[57]

The various threats, and the actual raid, on Scuddaburgh farm in 1910, however, are different from either of the above. First, they took place on an estate owned by the government, and the CDB acted like other proprietors in attempting to protect its property through recourse to civil law. The drawbacks of such procedures were made evident through these experiences. The raid is also notable because of the vehemence of those involved. This would seem to sit uneasily alongside the limited nature of the grievance: the desire for sixty-three acres of arable land. There would seem to be little doubt that Scuddaburgh held an importance to the Idrigill crofters well beyond the mere acreage – as their reaction to the sheriff officers clearly demonstrates. Perhaps the fact that the CDB was the proprietor had raised unduly high expectations for the receipt of land. This would go some way to explaining the depth of the reaction to the Commission's decision to hold back the arable land from the crofters.

A noticeable factor common to both Vatersay and Scuddaburgh was that, although participation in the raids was high in the respective communities involved, there was a hard core of ringleaders in both cases. The extent to which these men fuelled the sense of grievance in the other crofters is debatable, but it is clear that they had an exaggerated sense of it themselves. It has already been seen how the Vatersay ringleaders' sense of grievance outlasted that of their fellow raiders, to their own detriment. And it was said of one of the Scuddaburgh ringleaders, 'the others seem to think that they have only to follow him to get everything they want on their own terms'.[58]

Finally, it should be stressed that, in this period at least, land raids were not a direct challenge to the institution of landlordism. Rather,

[56] SRO, AF42/5344, SEG to H. Cook, 16 Oct 1908; AF42/5318, Scottish Office Engineering Dept to CDB (this file contains photographs of the wooden huts which the raiders built on Vatersay); Grigor, 'Crofters and the Land Question', ii, p. 88.

[57] Hunter, *Crofting Community*, p. 192.

[58] SRO, AF42/7829, Minute by Angus Sutherland, 7 Jan 1911

they were a tactic employed to extract limited gains – like the establishment of a few fishermen's holdings on Vatersay, or access to sixty-three acres of arable land in Scuddaburgh.

V

The overriding importance of the CDB's political context is clear. It was constituted by a Conservative government with a political aim in mind. Then, when a Liberal government ensued in 1906, the Board's outlook changed accordingly. Its impending abolition played an important part in this process, and it was placed in an uncomfortable position by the political difficulties of the Liberal government in the period 1906–11, which meant that its constitution was at odds with the preferred policy of that government. At the same time, the Liberals displayed a distinct lack of understanding over the Board's dealings with Highland proprietors like Lady Gordon Cathcart. Also, the events at Kilmuir demonstrated the basic unpopularity of the concept of land purchase among crofters. On the other hand, the events at Vatersay demonstrated proprietorial disapproval for the Liberal policy which they felt to be an unsatisfactory compromise as to responsibilities. In general, therefore, the CDB could hardly please anyone, and its reputation was certainly not enhanced in these years.

The two major parties attempted to implement different policies in the Highlands, and used the Board accordingly. A quantitative analysis of the CDB's performance is rendered meaningless by this change in policy, and by what was in effect the substantial overlap between the two periods: for example, the estate of Kilmuir was purchased under the Conservative government, although the estate's reorganisation straddled the election of 1906. Nevertheless, the important point to note is the differing political performance of the Board in the two periods, and how it was employed to implement first the Conservative policy of land purchase and then the Liberal policy of protected tenancy.

It has been said of the Irish CDB, that its land purchase operations 'completely changed the face of the congested districts'.[59] No such claim can be advanced for the Scottish Board. Its funding was insufficient and its effective working life too short. The Conservative aim, articulated at its creation, of ending the classic crofting system of bi-employments was certainly a failure. Up to 1904, no large estates were bought, and after 1906 its efforts were restricted for political reasons. The Board themselves commented in 1907: 'that to proceed further with schemes for settlement under the provisions of the Act of 1897, which the government desired to supplant by a new process would lead to no useful public result'.[60]

59 Micks, *Account of the CDB for Ireland*, p. 151.
60 *CDB Annual Report, 1906–7*, p. v.

If the Small Landholders Bill had been passed into law at an earlier date, this would have given the CDB a much easier task in dealing with its responsibilities in Kilmuir, and more authority in its negotiations in Vatersay. Instead, the latter dispute became symbolic of the general stalemate on Highland policy which existed from 1906 to 1912. Above all, it is an indication of how the CDB was absorbed by the politics of the government which it served. Had everything else been equal, the Board would have been reluctant to spend so much time and effort in creating sixty very small holdings in less than ideal circumstances. As it was, these disputes clearly demonstrate the tension between the contending policies of purchase and the extension of crofting tenancies. And they also highlight the continuing power of proprietors to influence government policy more than twenty years after the Crofters' Holdings Act.

CHAPTER SIX

The Small Landholders (Scotland) Bill, 1906–1911

In December 1905, during the general election campaign, Prime Minister Henry Campbell-Bannerman had declared that he wished to make land 'less of a pleasure ground for the rich and more of a treasure house for the nation'. This was a somewhat vague commitment, but a commitment nevertheless, to land reform. On the strength of this, as well as other factors, the Liberals reversed the Conservative and Liberal Unionist advance in the crofting counties which had been evident at the general election of 1900. Liberal Unionist defeats in Argyll and Sutherland and a Conservative defeat in Inverness-shire ensured a clean sweep of the Highland constituencies for the Liberals. This was emphatically a 'Liberal' victory, with none of the successful candidates describing themselves as 'Crofter' or even 'Liberal/Crofter' candidates. This was the logical culmination of the process which had begun in the mid-1890s, with the Highland Land League entering the wider political arena and moving closer to the Liberal Party, losing its identity and unity in the process.[1]

The antecedents of the Small Landholders (Scotland) Bill are important and instructive. In 1903 John Sinclair had received a lengthy memorandum from the widely respected Chairman of the Crofters' Commission, David Brand, who enumerated the benefits which nearly two decades of administration of the Crofters Act had brought to the Highlands, and advocated extending the Act in a number of particulars. Parishes in other counties where crofting conditions existed should be admitted to the Act (as Sir G. O. Trevelyan's abortive Crofters Bill of 1895 had attempted to do). In addition, leaseholders should be given protection under the Act, and the Congested Districts Board should be invested with compulsory powers of land acquisition to ease its task of relieving congestion. Brand argued strongly that the Crofters' Commission and the CDB should retain their separate existences, as they had different functions to perform. And, most importantly, he felt that the enlargement provisions of the Crofters Act were too limited, and that the conditions, such as the need for a group of five crofters to apply together for an enlargement of their lands, should be relaxed. There

[1] F. W. S. Craig, *British Parliamentary Election Results, 1885–1918* (London 1974), pp. 527, 533, 543, 553, 559, 562; *The Times*, 22 Dec. 1905.

was also a second identifiable influence on the development of Sinclair's ideas on the land question: the report of a commission of farmers and other agricultural experts who had visited Denmark in 1904. The proportionally large rural population of that country favourably impressed Sinclair, as did the efficiency of its agriculture and the social condition of smallholders. A well-structured system of agricultural education and the importance of the principle of co-operation clearly lay behind these successes.[2]

It is important, however, to note the points where Sinclair's scheme diverged from these recommendations. Brand's opinions were as much concerned with ensuring a continuing role for his Crofters' Commission, which by 1903 was running out of judicial work. Nevertheless, on no occasion did he argue that crofter tenure should be extended to the rest of Scotland; he confined himself to echoing the contents of the 1895 bill. The connection between the Danish report and the Small Landholders (Scotland) Bill is even more tenuous. The report made it clear that, apart from education and co-operation, what stimulated Denmark's rural prosperity was peasant proprietorship; statutes of 1899 and 1904 empowered the State to grant 90% loans for smallholders to purchase land.[3] Sinclair's espousal of dual ownership, however, rested not upon expert opinion but upon the dictates of Liberal ideology. Land purchase in Scotland had traditionally been rooted in Conservative thought, and Sinclair's rejection of it was based on that fact, as much as on his protestations about the expense to the State of such a policy. The argument that the demand for purchase did not exist was also used, with the experience of the CDB being given as evidence;[4] but this was a difficult argument to sustain. In fact, the failure of the CDB and of the unpopular policy of purchase was inevitable once the Liberals came to power, since they were pledged to abolish both the policy and the institution. The Small Landholders (Scotland) Bill was an intensely ideological measure, only tenuously based on informed analyses of the land problem in the Highlands and beyond.[5]

The Small Landholders (Scotland) Bill was introduced on 28 July 1906. The bill had been heralded in the King's Speech in February and, despite the complexity of the issues, by the middle of the year there was some impatience that it had not been forthcoming. It actually seems that the measure did not receive serious consideration by the Cabinet until May, when it was discussed and a committee to deal with it was

[2] SRO, AF43/6/1, Memo to Captain Sinclair, by Sheriff David Brand, Edinburgh, 25 Aug. 1903; SRO, SLFP, GD325/1/12, 'Farming in Denmark as seen by the Scottish Agricultural Commission of 1904'.

[3] Ibid., pp. 36–8; F. Skrubbeltrang, *Agricultural Development and Rural Reform in Denmark* (Rome, 1953), p. 213

[4] *PD*, 4th ser., vol. 162, cols. 260–2, 28 Jul 1906; ibid. 4th ser., vol. 171, col. 697, Sinclair, 19 Mar. 1908.

[5] *Oban Times*, 9 Jun 1906.

established.[6] The Scottish Secretary, Sinclair, then explained the bill's principal elements to the House of Commons. It was based on the Crofters Act of 1886, but with some important amendments, and was to apply to the whole of Scotland, not merely the crofting counties. Its most contentious parts were the compulsory provisions for creating new crofter holdings: new institutions were to be set up to oversee the creation of the new holdings, and if they failed to secure agreement with the proprietors, an element of compulsion could be introduced. The government was to provide the finance for equipping of the new holdings.[7]

The government was keen to emphasise the successes of the Crofters Act, in order to present it as the basis for a model of land tenure for the rest of Scotland. An independent report written by, among others, Ronald Munro-Ferguson and several members of the commission which had visited Denmark in 1904, cast doubt on this premise. Their principal conclusion about the operation of the Crofters Act was that, although it had undoubtedly improved housing conditions and removed the sense of grievance which crofters had felt prior to 1886, conditions in the crofting counties still continued to be primitive. In particular, despite the best efforts of the Crofters' Commission and the CDB, agricultural practice remained backward. They concluded that whatever improvement was evident was based on the capital provided by the offspring of crofters working in the South. Elsewhere, Munro-Ferguson argued that the establishment of dual ownership in the crofting counties had been no more than a recognition of the *de facto* situation. It was the case that the crofter provided his own improvements and equipment for his own holding – not for any deeply rooted historical or cultural reason, but because of the simple economic fact that they were worth so little that there would be no investment value for a proprietor in providing them.[8]

Not only the special circumstances of the crofter, but also the particular demands of the time, were used to invalidate the government's use of the 1886 Act as a basis for new legislation. The agitation of the 1880s had created a political imperative for crofter legislation, but there was no such demand from tenants in the Lowlands in 1906. Furthermore, the historical bases of the Crofters Act were held to be critical defining characteristics. Despite the Act's vague definition of these, they were not perceived as an encroachment on landowners' rights in the same way as the provisions of the new bill. These criticisms

6 BL, CBP, MS Add. 52512, fo. 47, Report by the Prime Minister to the king, on Cabinet meeting, 9 May 1906.

7 *PD*, 4th ser., vol. 162, cols. 258–64, 28 Jul. 1906; *Glasgow Herald*, 10 May 1906; *Oban Times*, 4 Aug. 1906.

8 'Government Land Bill: new light from the Crofters Act: a weighty report', *Glasgow Herald*, 21 Jan. 1908; R. C. Munro-Ferguson, 'The Scottish Small Landholders Bill', *National Review*, l (1907).

carry substantial weight. The government found it difficult to provide evidence that the landlord–tenant relationship outside the crofting counties was in need of such drastic reform as it proposed. Modern historiography has confirmed the validity of this contemporary impression in certain respects. It has been argued that the peasantry of the North-East, who shared at least some characteristics with Highland crofters, missed their opportunity to secure protection in 1886 by failing to articulate their case independently to the government; unfortunately, Trevelyan's 1895 bill, which would have given them crofter tenure, did not reach the statute-book. According to a recent historian, the eventual Small Landholders (Scotland) Act 'gave too little protection and was much too late'. In addition, the government's arguments concerning the national benefit to be gained from the creation of new smallholdings did not really succeed in moving the debate into a new context.[9]

It is important to put the 1906 bill into the context of the debate on Highland policy over the previous two decades. The 1886 Act had been based on 'dual ownership' or 'compulsory hiring', to use the contemporary terms by which it was described: that is to say, the crofter was still a rent-paying tenant of a proprietor, but, at the same time, he had security of tenure, the right of compensation for improvements, and the right to appeal to the Crofters' Commission to set a fair rent for the holding. The 1897 Act, on the other hand, had been based on the concept of land purchase: its aim – although this remained largely unfulfilled – was that the crofter would cease to be a tenant and would become an owner-occupier. The new bill was a direct repudiation of the 1897 concept, and an attempt to strengthen and extend the provisions of the 1886 Act. As Sinclair's wife and biographer wrote:

> As regards the formation of new holdings, like most Liberals at that time, he was not anxious to obtain the necessary land by purchase, because he did not want to turn the smallholders into peasant proprietors or tenants of a government department.[10]

The bill's introduction was greeted by heavy criticism of its drafting and substance. In particular, there was some surprise that the government had resorted to the concept of 'dual ownership', and ill-concealed horror that such a concept was to be extended beyond the crofting counties; it was argued that the system had not worked well in

[9] I. Carter, *Farmlife in North-east Scotland, 1840–1914* (Edinburgh, 1979), pp. 171–2; I. Carter, 'Unions and myths: farm servants' unions in Aberdeenshire, 1870–1900', in T M Devine (ed.), *Farm Servants and Labour in Lowland Scotland, 1770–1914* (Edinburgh, 1984), pp. 213–15; G. Malcolm, 'The Small Landholders (Scotland) Bill', *Factors Magazine*, vii (1906–7); SRO, GD176/1400, Memorandum on the Small Landholders Bill, 1907.

[10] M. A. Sinclair, Lady Pentland, *The Rt. Hon. John Sinclair, Lord Pentland. A Memoir* (London 1928), p. 87; R. Shannon, *The Crisis of Imperialism, 1865–1915* (London, 1984 edn), pp. 392–3

the Highlands, and not at all in Ireland. Also, it was attacked on the grounds that it did not stem from any thorough investigation of the Scottish land problem – and indeed, it does seem peculiar that Sinclair had not waited for the report of the departmental committee which was investigating the subject of smallholdings.[11] Nevertheless, despite these criticisms, Scottish ministers attempted to convince the Prime Minister that the bill was proving popular in Scotland; Lord Advocate Shaw wrote, indeed, that it was being received with 'positive enthusiasm'.

The departmental committee (whose members included Munro-Ferguson, a Liberal MP and Easter Ross landowner) reported in December 1906, some months after the introduction of the Small Landholders (Scotland) Bill. It was certainly in favour of government action to meet the perceived demand for the creation of more smallholdings; however, it was equally certainly not in favour of action in the direction advocated in Sinclair's bill. The committee was of the opinion that a system of dual ownership would be highly detrimental to the 'sense of responsibility which should accompany ownership'; in its view, such a system would be impossible to administer in the face of proprietorial opposition, and would lead to insecurity among farming tenants outside the crofting counties. With these points in mind, its report concluded:

> Experience has proved that a system of dual ownership of land is one which, under ordinary economic conditions, cannot be permanent, and while it lasts, is fatal to the proper maintenance of holdings, to harmony between landlord and tenant, and to the prosperity of agriculture.

This provided ammunition for Sinclair's critics, who felt that he was flying in the face of informed opinion.[12]

Owing to pressure on the parliamentary timetable, the bill was withdrawn from the 1906 session; but it was reintroduced the following year, and this marked the beginning of the real debate on its fate. It is important not only to examine the course of events throughout the lengthy period up to the bill's passage in 1911, but also the arguments which the government used to defend it. The debate has often been crudely characterised as a conflict between the Liberals on the one hand, and the Conservatives and the House of Lords on the other.[13] But it will be shown here that the politics were considerably more complex than that portrayal suggests: opinion on the bill cut through the Liberal Party and the Cabinet. Moreover, the country was divided geographically

[11] BL, CBP, MS Add. 41227, fo. 174, Shaw to C-B, 20 Sep. 1906, *Glasgow Herald*, 30 Jul., 13 Aug. 1906; *The Scotsman*, 1 Jun., 23 Jun., 30 Jul. 1906.

[12] *PP*, 1906, LV: *Report of the Departmental Committee on Small Holdings*, p. 33; *Glasgow Herald*, 25 Dec. 1906.

[13] Hunter, *Crofting Community*, pp. 190–3; Grigor, 'Crofters and the Land Question', ii, p. 85.

along the Highland line. This division went across both party and social lines, with an alliance of sorts arising between the Highland MPs, the representatives of the proprietorial interest in the House of Lords, and the newly formed Scottish Land and Property Federation

II

In the 1907 session the bill was introduced to the Commons in March, in an unchanged form. After a second reading in April, it was sent to the Lords in August, only to be rejected there by a majority of 162 to 39. This session saw most of the arguments which had been used in the 1906 debates develop further. The main argument which the government used to defend the bill demonstrated its attempt to emphasise the fundamental nature of the land problem in society. The bill's main objective was to halt rural depopulation, and hence temper overcrowding in urban areas; the secure tenure and capital incentives which it offered were designed to retain the existing rural population on the land, and to provide opportunities for new generations of smallholders through the increased facilities for creating new holdings. The theory was to create smallholdings of a sufficient size to deal with congestion and end the cottar problem.[14] There was a tendency to idealise the smallholder and the smallholding as progressive forces in society.

This idea that the land problem could be manipulated to achieve desired social ends was not particular to Scotland at the time. As far away as Russia, Tsar Nicholas II's chief minister, Peter Stolypin, held similar views. Stolypin's conception of the land problem was similar in some respects to that of the Scottish Conservatives. In the aftermath of the 1905 revolution in Russia, he sought to create an independent peasant class which he hoped would be 'defenders of order, a support for the social structure'; he argued that such people would have a sufficient stake in society to become opponents of revolutionary ideologies.[15]

The year 1907 also saw Small Holdings legislation passed for England. This left the administration of the new procedures for creating smallholdings in the hands of county councils, and did not interfere with the relations between the proprietor and his new tenants Lord Carrington, the President of the English Board of Agriculture, had acted astutely in waiting for the departmental committee on Small Holdings to report 'out of politeness', not because of the weight of its likely

[14] *Oban Times*, 20 Jul. 1907.

[15] A. Levin, 'Peter Arkad'evich Stolypin: a political appraisal', *Journal of Modern History*, xxxvii (1965), pp. 459–60; F E. Huggett, *The Land Question and European Society* (London, 1975), chap. 5

recommendations.[16] However, in so doing he could not be accused, as Sinclair was, of producing a baseless bill. Nevertheless, the importance of this report as a foundation for the English legislation should not be exaggerated, as it recommended purchase for smallholders. This Act has generally been well received, but it is interesting to note that members of the CDB who visited England in 1911 to report on its workings, were not favourably impressed: they reported that the price paid for the holdings was excessive and the improvements were proving to be similarly expensive.[17]

This English Act is important, owing to the contrast it provides in the ease of its passage through Parliament. Further, the Conservatives argued that since the agricultural conditions in Lowland Scotland were similar to England, the same procedures could be applied there. This was felt to be preferable to the Scottish bill, which would, in effect, extend crofting tenure to the Lowlands. Arthur Balfour put this point in Parliament, in reply to Sinclair:

> Anyone with even the most superficial acquaintance with the facts of the case knows that the difference between Berwickshire and Northumberland is incomparably less than the difference in farming between Berwickshire and the crofting counties of Scotland.[18]

In addition, Conservatives often expressed a worry that because of the similarity between the conditions in Lowland Scotland and England, the provisions of the Scottish bill could not logically be confined to Scotland. This threat of the 'crofterisation' of the entire UK was a scare tactic to stir up opposition to the Scottish bill; the statement was often made, but the mechanics of how the much-feared process was to take place were never fully explained.[19]

These were not arguments confined to the Conservative ranks in the Lords. Lord Rosebery, the former Liberal Prime Minister, and still nominally a member of that party, pursued them vigorously, to the embarrassment of his former colleagues. He described crofting as the most 'backward' agricultural system in the country, and pointed to the absurdity of extending it to an area where he believed the agricultural system was unrivalled.[20]

Opposition to the terms of the Small Landholders Bill did not only come from ageing and fractious politicians. Much expert agricultural

[16] Brown, 'Land legislation', p. 76.
[17] SRO, AF42/8399, 'Notes of the inspections of English small holdings visited by Mr Mackintosh and Mr Coles'.
[18] *PD*, 4th ser., vol. 171, col. 704, AJB, 19 Mar. 1907; BL, AJBP, MS Add. 49859, fo. 167, Balfour to Portland, 6 Aug. 1907.
[19] *Oban Times*, 10 Aug., 24 Aug. 1907.
[20] R. R. James, *Rosebery* (London, 1963), pp. 461–2; R. Crewe-Milnes, Marquess of Crewe, *Lord Rosebery* (London, 1931), ii, p. 609; *PD*, 4th ser., vol. 180, col. 988, 13 Aug. 1907; NLS, Rosebery Papers, MS 10019, fo. 244, R. C. Munro-Ferguson to Rosebery, 28 May 1907.

opinion objected, in particular, to the idea of extending crofter tenure to the Lowlands. The Scottish Chamber of Agriculture consistently opposed the bill's terms. This organisation – composed as it was of factors, landowners and tenant farmers – should be seen as a repository as much of Conservatism as of agricultural expertise. It complained that the terms of the bill would discourage investment in Lowland agriculture, and much was made of the supposed failure of dual ownership in Ireland. That was a difficult argument to counter, as both parties had introduced land purchase measures in Ireland. The government attempted to do so, however, by pointing out that the Scottish bill did not provide for free sale, a critical component of dual ownership.[21]

Certainly the Liberals were encountering massive problems with their Scottish land legislation in the Lords. This problem was also encountered with other pieces of government legislation. Yet the Lords did not attack Liberal legislation indiscriminately: major social legislation had been passed in 1906, most importantly the Workmen's Compensation Act. This suggests that the Lords were operating tactically rather than ideologically; they tended to pick on soft targets – bills which lacked support from important sections of the Liberal constituency, like Birrell's Education Bill of 1906, which was unsatisfactory to Nonconformist opinion. The Lords saw themselves as acting to revise bills which had not received proper treatment in the House of Commons, due to government control of that House. The problems encountered with the legislative programme were also the 'result of powerful restraining forces among the Liberals themselves'.[22]

In the case of the Scottish land bill, the 'restraining force' was the paucity of support for it within the Cabinet. Knowledge of this was far from being confined to the privacy of the Cabinet room; for instance, Lord Hamilton of Dalzell had resigned from his position in charge of Scottish business in the Lords, because he felt he could not involve himself with the Small Landholders Bill.[23] By the autumn of 1907, Sinclair found himself increasingly isolated in the Cabinet, despite the support of his long-time political ally Campbell-Bannerman. He felt that only Asquith and Lord Loreburn, the Lord Chancellor, were sincere supporters of his measure. R. B. Haldane, the Secretary for War, thought that half the Cabinet opposed the bill, and that only Sinclair and the Prime Minister were wholeheartedly for it.[24]

21 *The Scotsman*, 25 Apr. 1907; BL, CBP, MS Add 41230, fos. 183–5, Resolutions of 17 Jul., 10 Oct., 1907; J. Spier, 'The Small Landholders Bill', *Factors Magazine*, vii (1906–7).

22 G. L. Bernstein, *Liberalism and Liberal Politics in Edwardian England* (Boston, 1986), pp. 83, 90; J. Ridley, 'The Unionist Opposition and the House of Lords, 1906–1910', *Parliamentary History*, xi (1992) pp. 235–53; J. F. Harris and C. Hazlehurst, 'Campbell-Bannerman as Prime Minister', *History*, lv (1970), p. 375

23 *Glasgow Herald*, 1 May 1907; BL, Marquess of Ripon Papers, MS Add. 43640, fo. 109, Hamilton to Ripon, 6 Jan. 1907; fos. 111–12, Ripon to Hamilton, 7 Jan. 1907.

24 BL, CBP, MS Add. 41230, fos 203–4, Sinclair to C-B, 12 Dec 1907; NLS, Murray of

There had been an attempt to rally Liberal opinion behind the bill in the summer of 1907. The Scottish Liberal Association organised a special conference in Perth to draw attention to it, which was an undoubted success in terms of the turn-out, with every constituency in Scotland represented. The political advantage was somewhat muted, however, with the Master of Elibank being forced on to the defensive, in his speech, to counter rumours that the bill was about to be dropped by the government. He attempted to introduce a more positive note by arguing that 'it was the fixed and settled determination of the Government' to proceed with the bill.[25] Liberal divisions were completely exposed in November when Lord Tweedmouth, in a speech also in Perth, stated that while he was not 'lukewarm' about the Scottish Small Landholders Bill, as had been suggested, he did prefer the arrangement of the English Act, which left the creation of new smallholdings in the hands of the local authorities. This incensed the normally amiable Sinclair, who wrote to Tweedmouth in the strongest terms, pointing out that his speech had made the government 'appear ridiculous and contemptible'. In this he had the support of the faithful, but by now ailing, Campbell-Bannerman, who felt the situation to be 'nasty'. Not the least embarrassing aspect of Tweedmouth's position was its coincidence with that of Rosebery.[26]

The second defeat of the Small Landholders Bill in the Lords left the government in a difficult position. The Lords, like the Conservatives in the Commons, objected to the extension of crofter tenure to the Lowlands. Throughout 1908, therefore, pressure was exerted on the government to divide the bill and make special provisions for the Highlands. As early as 1907, Balfour had argued that the Highlands would suffer if the bill was rejected out of hand. The Liberal Unionists did not accept the radical conception of the land problem shared by the Liberals, but they did accept that the Crofters Act was in need of modification, and that some new holdings could safely be created. Thus in 1908, the government was accused of using the bill deliberately to escalate the confrontation with the House of Lords, and of ignoring opportunities to settle for legislation which would deal with grievances in the Highlands.[27] Meanwhile, the position of government institutions in the Highlands was becoming increasingly difficult. The Crofters' Commission and the Congested Districts Board knew that their abolition was being attempted, but were equally aware that this would not be

Elibank Papers, MS 8801, fo. 135, Asquith to Murray of Elibank, 10 Oct. 1907; J. Wilson, *C-B: A Life of Sir Henry Campbell-Bannerman* (London, 1973), p. 600.

25 EUL, SLA Papers, no. 8, Minute Book, 1904–9, fos. 422–3, 433.

26 *The Scotsman*, 11 Nov. 1907; *Oban Times*, 31 Aug., 30 Nov. 1907; BL, CBP, MS Add. 41230, fos. 206–7, Sinclair to Tweedmouth, 12 Dec. 1907; fo. 208, C-B to Sinclair, 1 Jan. 1908.

27 BL, AJBP, MS Add. 49859, fo. 167, Balfour to Portland, 6 Aug. 1907; *Glasgow Herald*, 12 Feb. 1908; *The Scotsman*, 7 Feb. 1908.

effected quickly. It was a particular problem for the CDB, which, as has been seen, was now required to support a different policy from that which it had been constituted to implement.

III

There was surprise among Conservative opinion when Sinclair produced his bill, largely unchanged, for a third time in February 1908. Many felt that the government was not so interested in attempting to pass land legislation, as in providing targets for the Conservative majority in the Lords, in order to fuel the confrontation between the two Houses, and so further the case for constitutional reform. In presenting the bill to the Commons, Sinclair reached new heights of rhetoric in describing the benefits to be gained from an increased smallholding population. He spoke of the nation's 'physical deterioration', stemming from rural depopulation and the consequent loss of industrial efficiency and military effectiveness. On a more practical level, he tackled the problem of the bill's consequences for the concept of land ownership, arguing: 'This Bill does not touch in any shape or form the question of ownership of land. It deals solely with conditions of occupation by the cultivating tenant.'[28] Whether this represented an attempt to make the debate more vociferous by deliberately annoying the Conservatives, or a genuine misunderstanding on Sinclair's part of the way his bill was perceived, is unclear. Certainly, the ongoing Vatersay dispute indicated that Sinclair was unable to appreciate that landowners believed the procedure of creating smallholdings, with security of tenure under an existing proprietor, to be an imposition which would have a deleterious effect on other parts of their estates. He found it difficult to understand why proprietors should prefer the government to purchase land, if new smallholdings were to be created. Lord Lovat wrote privately about Sinclair: 'he regards a farm like a block of buildings up a street, and cannot see why if one feu is let, why it may alter the value of other similar feus, in fact he fails absolutely to grasp the point'.[29]

Rightly or wrongly, landowners, particularly outside the crofting counties, believed that the creation of protected tenancies on their land, possibly against their will and with inadequate compensation, was an infringement of their rights of ownership; their power to set a rent for a holding, or evict an unsuitable tenant, was to be placed in the hands of the Land Commission which the bill proposed to set up. This perception was prevalent in the crofting counties. On the Mackintosh estates, at Moy and Brae Lochaber in Inverness-shire, the bill was strongly deprecated for going far beyond the terms of the 1886 Act and any amendments which that Act required; the principal criticism was the fact

28 *PD*, 4th ser., vol. 184, cols. 657–69, 18 Feb. 1908.
29 SRO, SLFP, GD325/1/12, Lord Lovat to George Malcolm, 20 Nov 1908

that it would enlarge the rights of the tenant and reduce those of the landowner.[30]

The essential difference between the Highlands and the Lowlands was that, in the former, the equipment on a croft was provided by the tenant, so it was right that he should be compensated if he left the holding. However, in the Lowlands, the improvements were made by the proprietor who owned the land, and to whom it reverted when a lease fell in; consequently, there was no call for compensation to the tenant. Indeed, settling protected tenants on holdings which had been equipped by the proprietor was a definite infringement of his rights. The Liberal conception of ownership, however, was more simple, tending to see land as absolute property, unaffected by the type of tenants to whom it was leased. Sinclair himself argued in the Commons:

> The land remains the property of the landlord, to sell, to bequeath, or to mortgage. He retains his mineral, his timber and his sporting rights. He is to get fair rent for it equipped as it is, and a fair rent for his capital. His capital and his improvements are protected by statutory conditions which he can enforce and which the land court are bound to help him enforce.[31]

It was often argued that the effect of introducing dual ownership to the Lowlands would be to provide a disincentive for proprietorial investment in agriculture. Those opposed to the bill argued that a landowner was unlikely to invest in improving land, if there was the possibility of its being used for the creation of smallholdings, possibly against his will. On the other hand, Liberals were keen to point out that the operation of security of tenure in the Highlands had had the effect of releasing capital. Freed from the threat of eviction, the crofter had the security to spend money on improving his holding and especially his housing conditions. This process would be duplicated in the Lowlands if the bill was passed. The Master of Elibank argued that 'security of tenure seems to me to call forth the best characteristics of the Scottish race; and if can make the people prosper surely the land will prosper likewise'.[32]

But, faced by the overwhelming Conservative dominance of the House of Lords, these arguments were academic. The bill was rejected for a third time in March 1908. Sinclair's problems increased in April, when Campbell-Bannerman resigned as Prime Minister and died three weeks later on 22 April. Regardless of the relationship with his successor, Sinclair would never be as close to the new premier, H. H. Asquith, as he

30 SRO, GD176/1400, Memorandum on the Small Landholders Bill, 1907.

31 *PD*, 4th ser., vol. 171, col. 708, 19 Mar. 1907; ibid., 4th ser., vol. 184, col. 665, 18 Feb. 1908.

32 Ibid., 4th ser., vol. 171, col. 704, 19 Mar. 1907; BL, CBP, MS Add. 41243B, fos. 257–66, Notes for a speech on the Small Landholders (Scotland) Bill; NLS, Elibank Papers, MS 8801, fo. 171, Murray to Rosebery, 16 Jun. 1908.

had been to Campbell-Bannerman; as his biographer put it, 'the frank and friendly days with C-B were over'.[33] Although publicly the new Prime Minister was committed to the bill, he did not accord it such a high priority as his predecessor; it was not immediately reintroduced, and, as late as October 1909, Asquith informed Scottish Liberals that while he saw the need for land reform, he did not propose to 'make a pronouncement as to time and place'. Asquith was well aware of the divided nature of the Party and the Cabinet on this issue, and did not want to exacerbate the situation by forcing the bill on reluctant colleagues.[34]

The situation in 1908 had changed, so far as the Highland MPs were concerned. They had seen Highland land reform linked to an unpopular general measure for Scotland which stood little chance of becoming law before a general election and constitutional reform. Fearful of facing a Highland electorate with nothing to show in the shape of land reform, they began to take steps to secure a measure specifically providing for the crofting counties. Conservative opinion in the North was amenable to such a move, believing that the Liberals had cynically neglected the interests of the Highlands for the purpose of engineering a dispute with the House of Lords. The *Northern Chronicle*, an Inverness newspaper with a distinctly Conservative editorial line, asked: 'When are the crofters to see that they are used as pawns in a political game in which they are not interested.'[35]

Lord Lovat, a Conservative peer, had introduced a land bill into the House of Lords in February 1908. It was limited to the crofting counties, and provided for the merging of the Crofters' Commission and the CDB – both of which, he argued, were moribund – to create a new Land Commission which would have increased powers to create new holdings. He justified the introduction of another land reform bill, while the government measure was before Parliament, by the existence of a cross-party Highland consensus on the issue. Furthermore, he felt an individual initiative was necessary because he had no confidence that the government would listen to the claims of the Highlands, as the effect of its actions so far had been 'to sacrifice Highland interests in order to conjure up and strengthen an abortive attack on the House of Lords'.[36] However, this was not purely an attempt to head off Liberal attacks on the House of Lords (although that objective did exist), as the involvement of most of the Crofter MPs in the effort to gain separate legislation for the Highlands demonstrates.

33 Sinclair, *Sinclair Memoir*, p. 92.

34 EUL, SLA Papers, no. 10, Minute Book, 1909–20, fos. 38–9, H. H. Asquith to the SLA, 26 Oct. 1909; NLS, Haldane Papers, MS 5908, fo. 65, R. B. Haldane to Asquith, 8 Oct. 1908.

35 *Northern Chronicle*, 18 Mar. 1908; *The Scotsman*, 8 Jun. 1908; *Oban Times*, 28 Mar. 1908.

36 F. Lindley, *Lord Lovat. A Biography* (London, undated), pp. 153–4; *PD*, 4th ser., vol. 185, cols. 4–6, 27 Feb. 1908, *The Scotsman*, 28 Feb. 1908

A memorial had been sent to the Prime Minister, signed by eighteen MPs, including five of the six members for the crofting counties (the exception was John Dewar of Inverness-shire). They pointed out that the Small Landholders (Scotland) Bill would not pass until 'grave constitutional issues have been decided', and they went on to echo Lord Lovat's contention that a cross-party consensus existed on the principles of land reform for the Highlands. They demanded a conference between the Commons and the Lords on the land issue, and intimated their support for a private member's bill prepared by the Orkney and Shetland MP, John Cathcart Wason. The government rejected the idea of a conference between the two Houses, despite the fact that such meetings were part of Asquith's preferred method of settling disputes.[37]

However, some Liberals did stick to the party line: John Dewar, MP for Inverness-shire was one, and the Rev. Malcolm MacCallum, a former Deer Forest Commissioner, was another. They felt they would be deserting the Lowlands if they argued for separate bills. In general, the Liberal government declared its support for the structures proposed in the Small Landholders Bill; no doubt it was concerned that, should it do otherwise, it would be regarded as defeatist. Nevertheless, such a line allowed them to feel that they had escaped from an 'awkward situation'.[38] Despite this, a private meeting took place under the auspices of the Scottish Land and Property Federation, with Lord Lovat and the Liberal MP for Argyllshire, J. S. Ainsworth, present. At this meeting, the MPs were said to have expressed general agreement with the contents of Lord Lovat's bill. Their action in sending the memorial to Asquith, and in generally agitating for separate bills, bears out this contention. Another Highland landowner and prominent Conservative, The Mackintosh of Mackintosh, was told:

> Weir, Morton & Co [MPs for Ross-shire and Argyllshire respectively] are furious with the government, and think that Sinclair has sacrificed them and their crofter constituents to his desire to make a big splash himself.[39]

The idea that the best way to secure progress for the Highlands was to argue for separate legislation found some support in the government institutions in the Highlands. This is not surprising, as these bodies had to deal with the practical consequences of the legislative delays. William MacKenzie, Secretary to both the Crofters' Commission and the CDB, wrote of the 'clamant need' of legislation for the Highlands, and admitted that the case for the Lowlands 'was not so pressing'. He

[37] *Northern Chronicle*, 29 May 1908; *Oban Times*, 6 Jun., 27 Jun., 10 Oct. 1908; C. C. Weston, 'The Liberal leadership and the House of Lords veto, 1907–1910', *Historical Journal*, xi (1968), pp. 508–37.

[38] EUL, SLA Papers, no. 8, Minute Book, 1904–9, fo. 444; *Forward!*, 19 Jul. 1909.

[39] SRO, GD325/1/12, 'Conference between certain members of the House of Lords and of the House of Commons, 4 Jun. 1908'; W. Long to The Mackintosh, 11 Sep. 1908.

concluded: 'There were good provisions in Lord Lovat's bill of last year. In view of that fact I cannot think that the Lords would reject a reasonable government measure.'[40]

These events are important, not because they produced any progress (none of the incipient private member's bills proceeded very far), but because of the light they shed on the state of opinion on the land issue. The opposition of the Conservatives and of most of the proprietors in the Lords was not total, but conditional. They were prepared to see reform of the 1886 Act in the Highlands, and extension of the provisions of the more moderate English Small Holdings Act to the Lowlands of Scotland. In addition, the Liberal Party was split at almost every level, from the Cabinet down, on the best way to tackle the land issue. This was recognised by the Master of Elibank, when he refused to let a deputation of Scottish Liberals see the Prime Minister on the grounds of the 'divided state of the party'; if one deputation was allowed access, others arguing for different policies would demand similar treatment.[41] Liberal division was countered by a Highland coalition crossing party and social lines, which pointed out to the government the importance of settling outstanding Highland grievances immediately.

The bill's rejection caused many problems on the ground in the Highlands. Lord Lovat and others had argued that institutions such as the Crofters' Commission were moribund. However, it is important to understand why. In the case of the Commission, its most important work – that of revising rents – had been completed. But this could not be said of the Congested Districts Board, which made it clear, in 1907, that it was the existence of a bill for its abolition that was the main thing restricting its activities. Of course, when the Board made this statement, it was not to know that the bill would not pass until the end of 1911. Thus it had to work for five years at a reduced level of intensity, while the problems which it had been constituted to tackle proliferated.[42]

The attitudes of the government and the crofters in the disputes in the Southern Hebrides and Kilmuir was heavily influenced by the controversy over the Small Landholders Bill. Lady Gordon Cathcart was able to fight a successful rearguard action against the government's attempts to involve her in a scheme based on the provisions of the Small Landholders Bill. She was strongly opposed to such a course of action and was in a good position to defend her point of view as long as the bill was not passed. Because the government had no legislative structure to back up its arguments, she was able to set the agenda for the debate and introduce her own conditions at any time.[43]

40 SRO, AF42/6330, Minute by William MacKenzie, 9 Jul. 1909.
41 EUL, SLA Papers, no. 8, Minute Book, 1904–9, fos. 534–5.
42 *CDB Annual Report, 1906–7*, p. v.
43 SRO, AF42/3858, CDB to Comptroller and Auditor General, 8 May 1907; AF42/5344, SEG to H. Cook, 16 Oct. 1908; *Oban Times*, 28 Mar., 10 Oct. 1908.

IV

The year 1909 saw John Sinclair elevated to the House of Lords, with the title Lord Pentland. Asquith assured him that the reason for the move was to redress the lack of effective government management in the Lords. Sinclair felt that there was more to it; he resented his removal from the Commons, which his wife later described as akin to 'vanishing from real political life'. Sinclair had made few political allies with his persistent advocacy of the Small Landholders (Scotland) Bill, but given his close association with this bill, it would have been inexpedient of Asquith to dismiss him before it reached the statute book. However, Sinclair was dismissed in February 1912, almost immediately after the bill was passed, which strengthens the impression that he was not an integral member of Asquith's Cabinet.[44]

The years 1909 and 1910 were dominated by the larger dispute with the House of Lords over the 1909 budget. The two general elections of 1910 saw the Liberal vote hold up well in the crofting counties, while it was being eroded elsewhere. Indeed, the Liberals performed better in Scotland than at any time since 1885, and once again swept the crofting counties. This performance was not matched in rural England, however, where there was a marked swing back to the Conservatives, leaving Liberal strength concentrated in industrial areas.[45] Many felt that it was support for the Scottish land legislation which kept the Liberal vote so healthy in Scotland. Certainly, land was one of the major issues at both elections. The Conservatives fought them on a dual policy of land purchase, by means of local government, for existing smallholders, and of granting amendments of the Crofters Act where necessary. This policy was distinctly unattractive, despite the Party's undoubted unity behind it. Nevertheless, both in Scotland and south of the Border, Conservatives and Unionists were in little doubt that it was the land issue and widespread distaste for landowners which had lost them the election in Scotland; Austen Chamberlain candidly admitted that as long as land was an election issue, his party would have little success in Scotland.[46] The Liberal Party had succeeded in polarising the land issue in its favour: the traditional Scottish antipathy to the landlord was skilfully exploited by invective against the 'House of Landlords', who were portrayed as the culprits in holding up the Small Landholders (Scotland) Bill. This argument was very successful, despite the best efforts of *The Scotsman*, which pointed out that 'it is the Secretary for Scotland not the

[44] Sinclair, *Sinclair Memoir*, p. 93; Brown, 'Land legislation', pp. 84–5.

[45] Blewett, *Peers, Parties and People*, pp. 380–3, 400–3.

[46] *Glasgow Herald*, 14 Jan. 1910; SRO, GD433/2/140/103, Letter from R. B. Finlay, 20 Dec. 1909; Blewett, *Peers, Parties and People*, p. 402; BL, AJBP, MS Add. 49860, fos. 213–15, H. Seton Karr to A. J. Balfour, 5 Feb. 1910.

House of Lords that is responsible for the lack of any new legislation on the Highlands'.[47]

Although Scottish land legislation was off the agenda from mid-1908 to mid-1911, the year 1910 provides an interesting footnote on the depth of the Liberal commitment to the cause of the smallholder. The death of Edward VII in May 1910 led the Liberals and the Conservatives to convene a conference on constitutional issues, in order to prevent the necessity of forcing a crisis on the new monarch. By the middle of the summer, this conference was deadlocked. David Lloyd George, the Liberal Chancellor of the Exchequer, then produced a plan for a coalition government which would circumvent constitutional issues and press on with the work of social reform; this was very much an individual initiative, without Asquith's explicit blessing. It is interesting, in this context, because Lloyd George wrote a lengthy paper laying out the basis for such a coalition, which included a section on land reform. He argued, 'the small holdings craze is of a very doubtful utility', and went on to point out the lack of agricultural expertise among smallholders, before concluding that a system of 'farming on a large scale with adequate capital' would be the system most worthy of state support.[48] The incipient coalition did not materialise, but this memorandum demonstrates that another member of the Liberal Cabinet was lukewarm in his commitment to the idea of extending smallholdings. Although the memorandum's objectives – to attract Conservatives to a coalition – should be kept in mind when considering the views of Lloyd George, it does show, in the words of one historian, that he 'regarded the small holding programme as politically divisive and economically dubious'.[49]

V

Given the controversy generated when it was first introduced in 1906 and continuing down to the second rejection by the House of Lords in 1908, it is curious to find that the Small Landholders (Scotland) Bill was passed without acrimony in 1911. But the circumstances and rhetoric which accompanied its reintroduction were somewhat different.[50] It was now introduced as a private member's bill by Sir Donald MacLean, the member for Peebles, and Arthur Murray of Elibank.[51] This fact set the tone of the subsequent deliberations at a less intense level than had been the case in 1906–8, as is evident from the Lord Advocate's speech in the House of Commons at the second reading stage in June 1911, which declared:

47 Leneman, *Fit For Heroes?*, p. 7; EUL, SLA Papers, no. 10, Minute Book, 1909–20, fo. 109.

48 K. O. Morgan (ed.), *The Age of Lloyd George* (London, 1971), p. 154.

49 A. Offer, *Property and Politics, 1870–1914* (Cambridge, 1981), p. 358.

50 Brown, 'Land legislation', p. 84; Leneman, *Fit For Heroes?*, p. 8.

51 A. C. Murray, *Master and Brother: Murrays of Elibank* (London, 1945), p. 90.

> We are in a judicial frame of mind. We have learned a good deal during the last few years. I think we are prepared to meet each other on fair and even friendly terms. I hope the promoters of this Bill will not dwell unduly upon the new heaven and new earth that we sometimes hear predicted of land measures.

Even the acerbic and individual Liberal MP R. C. Munro-Ferguson chose to remark on the beneficial effects of the more consensual style of debate which had emerged on this issue.[52]

Nevertheless, changes in tone, by themselves, would have been insufficient to bring about the rapid settlement which occurred. It was changes in the substance of the bill that proved to be instrumental. Two such changes stand out. First, in the case of compensation claims amounting to more than £300, the landlord was accorded the right to call in an independent arbiter. Secondly and more importantly, a new category of tenants, to be known as 'statutory small tenants', was created. As noted above, one of the principal problems with the Small Landholders (Scotland) Bills of 1906–8 had been a worry that the provisions of the Crofters' Holdings (Scotland) Act were to be extended uncritically beyond the crofting counties. Clause 32 of the 1911 bill went some way to dealing with this problem, by redefining crofter tenure and extending it beyond the crofting counties. Yearly tenants of holdings of less than fifty acres, or of holdings rented at less than £50, were to be known as 'small landholders'; they were to have security of tenure, the right to have their rents fixed by the Scottish Land Court, and the right to be compensated for their improvements when they left their holdings. As for the 'statutory small tenants', they were defined as those, mostly outside the crofting counties, whose improvements had been paid for by their landlords, and they were now admitted to the partial protection of the Act. This politically necessary compromise on the differing conditions between the crofting and non-crofting counties was unpopular among the more doctrinaire Liberals, such as J. A. Bryce, MP for Inverness Burghs, who regarded it as an unnecessary admission of error in earlier versions of the bill.[53]

The new limitations faced by the Lords played a part in the process. In the years from 1906 to 1910 they had selectively disrupted the Liberal programme by attacking vulnerable legislation. The Parliament Act invalidated such a tactic. Now, rather than opposing the bill outright without any hope of success, the Lords, and the opposition generally, took a more constructive attitude. By judicious argument at the committee stages in both Houses, they were able to extract some concessions. After the resulting small amendments, the opposition then accepted the inevitability, if not the complete desirability, of the bill's passage, and allowed it to pass without a division.

[52] *PD*, 5th ser., vol. 26, cols. 1424, 1402.
[53] Ibid., 5th ser., vol. 31, cols. 756–7; *Oban Times*, 22 Jul. 1911.

The Small Landholders (Scotland) Act of 1911 made important alterations to preceding land legislation, and codified a series of Acts which now became known as the Small Landholders (Scotland) Acts, 1886 to 1911. The Crofters' Commission and the CDB were abolished, after a profoundly unsatisfactory five-year hiatus in their work; their roles were taken on by the Scottish Land Court [hereafter the SLC] and the Board of Agriculture for Scotland [BoAS]. The most important changes which were made to the 1886 regime concerned the machinery for extending the area under smallholding tenure. The 1886 Act's limited provisions were replaced by an apparently radical process, by which no only could holdings be enlarged, but completely new tenancies could be established on privately owned land. The consent of the landowner would make the process simple, but, if this was not forthcoming, the BoAS could place the necessary details before the SLC, and an element of compulsion could be introduced. In the event of a mutually agreeable scheme, the landlord would be compensated by an amount decided by the SLC; if the claim exceeded £300, the claim could be settled by arbitration.[54]

Under the 1911 Act, a sum of £200,000 was to be made available for the purpose of Scottish land settlement. This was to be made up of £15,000 under the Agricultural Rating Act of 1896, and a further £185,000 to be voted annually by Parliament. It was to be known as the 'Agriculture (Scotland) Fund', and was to be used principally for equipping the new holdings created under the Act. However, all compensation claims and the Board's administrative expenses had to be paid out of it. It is important to note that this sum was for the whole of Scotland and not for the exclusive benefit of the crofting counties, as had been the case with the £35,000 available annually to the CDB.

VI

One of the less significant events of these controversial years was the creation of a new Highland Land League in 1909. Strongly critical of its predecessor's close ties to the Liberal Party, the new League was based on the assumption that 'official Liberalism has been the deadly enemy of the Highland proletariat'. It proposed an alliance of crofters and workers to campaign for the nationalisation of the land and the advancement of Labour in the Highlands. Thomas Johnston, editor of the newspaper *Forward!*, which supported the Independent Labour Party, came to the leadership of the League with a background as a trenchant critic of landlords. His propagandist critique of their social position, *Our Noble Families*, originally written for *Forward!*, became a best seller. Nevertheless, the League could never hope to match the

54 MacCuish, 'Crofting law'

intensity of the Crofters' movement of the 1880s, when the depth of the perception of grievance in the Highlands was much greater than during the Edwardian period. Furthermore, the movement in the 1880s had been strong at the grass roots, whereas the new League was largely the creation of a small number of urban-based activists. The new League was much more sectarian, politically, than its predecessor. Admittedly, the Crofters' movement had established close ties with the Liberals, but these were essentially a feature of the post-1886 period, when the original League was in decline; prior to that, the strength of the movement had been its political independence. But the new Highland Land League singularly failed to break the Liberal monopoly in the crofting counties, and its main policy of land nationalisation was not seriously considered by either of the two main parties. In the event, its pre-war activities were limited to minor publishing ventures and abortive attempts to run candidates in the 1910 elections in Caithness.[55]

VII

In terms of the ongoing debate on Highland policy, the years 1906 to 1911 are significant for the Liberal advocacy of the idea of dual ownership and the specific rejection of land purchase and land nationalisation. The Small Landholders (Scotland) Bill attracted criticism from all quarters. Conservative opinion, notably in the concerted campaign by *The Scotsman*, was firmly against the extension of dual ownership to the Lowlands. Many Liberals, some of them landowners like Munro-Ferguson and Rosebery, were equally opposed to these provisions. Another portion of Liberal opinion, while committed to the concept of the multiplication of smallholdings, was concerned that Sinclair's bill was badly thought out, and preferred the more moderate provisions of the English Small Holdings Act. Opinion in the growing Labour movement was not well-disposed to the bill either, condemning it for being insufficiently anti-landlord. Finally, the majority of Crofter MPs were opposed to the government's attitude to the Highlands. The feeling was that the bill was being used to provoke the Lords, and was not a sincere attempt to improve the lot of the crofter. As early as 1907, Thomas Shaw, the Lord Advocate, was discussing the Small Landholders (Scotland) Bill in the context of the 'coming conflict with the House of Lords'. This demonstrates that, if it was not deliberately employed to provoke the peers, leading Liberals were certainly aware of its disruptive potential.[56] Also, the campaign of informed agricultural opinion, carried

[55] *Forward!*, 4 Sep. 1909, 6 Nov. 1911; Grigor, 'Crofters and the Land Question', ii, p. 95; G. Walker, *Thomas Johnston* (Manchester, 1988), pp. 10–13; J. Hunter, 'The Gaelic connection: the Highlands, Ireland and nationalism, 1873–1922', *SHR*, liv (1975), p. 195.

[56] Hutchison, *Political History of Scotland*, p. 243; *Forward!*, 6 Apr. 1907, 16 May 1908.

out by the various landowners' and factors' organisations, should not be underestimated.

The scale and diversity of the opposition to the bill, therefore, makes it difficult to argue consistently that ideological obstruction by the Unionist peers was the primary obstacle to its passage. This argument can only be adopted if the Liberal propaganda of the time, which skilfully portrayed the debate in these terms, is accepted uncritically. Some Liberals argued in 1913, in debates on the Scottish Home Rule Bill, that it was the absence of a Scottish Parliament which had delayed the passage of the Small Landholders (Scotland) Act for so long.[57]

Although Sinclair often referred to the Crofters' Holdings (Scotland) Act as an authoritative precedent for his proposals, it is difficult to argue that the Small Landholders (Scotland) Bill represented a serious, objective attempt to settle outstanding issues in the Highlands. Indeed, the perception that the Liberals were ignoring the crofting counties in favour of provocation of the Upper House led to a tactical realignment of Highland opinion in 1908. Liberal MPs and proprietors from the Scottish Land and Property Federation came together to lobby the government for separate Highland legislation. This further detracts from the simple 'Liberal-versus-Unionist, tenant-versus-proprietor', interpretation of the debate. It also damages the reputation of the Campbell-Bannerman and Asquith governments, on this issue at least, as administrations prepared to sacrifice ideology for practical solutions. Above all, the arguments for land reform in this period, whether articulated by Liberals like Sinclair or by Labour movement figures like Thomas Johnston, took little account of the need for specific Highland policies. Rather, they were based on nebulous ideas of the national benefit which was to be gained from rural regeneration.

57 Leneman, *Fit For Heroes?*, pp. 5–9; H. J Hanham, *Scottish Nationalism* (London, 1969), p. 100

CHAPTER SEVEN

Land Settlement, 1911–1919

After the years of frustration during the protracted passage of the Small Landholders (Scotland) Act, 1911, expectations for the land settlement that it would achieve were extremely high. Liberal rhetoric presented the Act as a panacea for the problems of the Highlands, and as a curative for a plethora of social ills.[1]

The Act finally came into operation in April 1912, when the institutions created by its provisions began their work. The Board of Agriculture for Scotland [BoAS] and the Scottish Land Court [SLC] took over from the Congested Districts Board and the Crofters' Commission. The BoAS was composed of three executive officials. One, Sir Robert Wright, was Chairman. There was a division of labour between the other two members of the Board: R. B. Greig was given the task of supervising its duties in the areas of agricultural education and improvement of livestock husbandry; while John Sutherland, a former Oban solicitor and estate agent, was appointed specially to deal with the creation of smallholdings. As Small Holdings Commissioner, Sutherland was in charge of the entire work of the Board's Land Division; his final decisions were based on information gathered by a network of sub- and assistant sub-commissioners who were allocated geographic areas of responsibility. A former Scottish Office civil servant, H. M. Conacher, filled the post of Secretary to the Board.[2] As for the SLC, it continued the legal functions of the Crofters' Commission. The SLC's Chairman, N. J. D. Kennedy, had been David Brand's successor as Crofters' Commission Chairman; he was now a peer, with the same status as a Judge of the Court of Session. Lord Kennedy was of Highland descent, his father having been a Free Church Minister in Sutherland.[3]

I

The initial tasks of the BoAS were to establish how great a demand there was for land, and to identify what land was available for the creation of smallholdings. The availability of land was governed by section 7(16) of the Act, which stated that farms of less than 150 acres, home farms, or

1 *Glasgow Herald*, 5 Jan., 7 Mar., 1912.

2 SRO, E824/869, KLTR to Cabinet Land Settlement Committee, 3 Sep. 1920; PRO, CAB27/105/256, 294–6, BoAS, Land division, duties and procedure.

3 *Northern Chronicle*, 13 Feb. 1918.

lands under leases in force at Whit Sunday 1906 (or 1911 in the case of the non-crofting counties), could not be taken for smallholdings. One obstacle to the initial search for land was the highly particular nature of the demand. Many applicants wanted to be settled on specific lands, either in their immediate localities or in the areas of their origins; a 'disinclination' to consider alternatives was a serious problem for the Board.[4] The scale of demand was considerable: new facilities for land settlement encouraged a huge number of applicants of varying qualifications to try their luck. In total, 5,352 applications were submitted to the BoAS: 3,370 for new holdings and 1,982 for enlargements of existing holdings. Of the applications for new holdings, 2,760 came from the crofting counties – of which, more importantly, 1,300 came from the Outer Hebrides, in particular Lewis. The Board anticipated that this bias towards the crofting counties would even out over time, as tenants in the south of Scotland became aware of the benefits to be gained from the Act's operation.[5]

When a body of applications was received and some potentially available land had been identified, a smallholdings scheme could be contemplated. The sub-commissioners for the particular areas had a duty to keep themselves informed regarding farms which were, or were about to fall, out of lease;[6] these were inspected by the sub-commissioners and their reports submitted to the Small Holdings Commissioner. Then, if the scheme was to proceed, negotiations were opened with the management of the estate in question. By 1915, however, the BoAS had realised that estates could, if they so desired, slow the process down at this stage; so BoAS officials were instructed to act promptly and be vigilant over potential delaying tactics. At this point there were three alternatives. First, the settlement could proceed by agreement, in which case the estate had no right to subsequent compensation if the scheme failed. Secondly, if the proprietor had no real objections to the scheme, but wished to ensure the right to subsequent compensation (under section 17(2) of the 1911 Act) should it prove a failure, then an unopposed compulsory order could be sought from the SLC; this was the cause of many problems, because the SLC was flooded with cases which would have been dealt with better by a more simple procedure. Thirdly, if the negotiations did not produce agreement, then application could be made to the SLC for a compulsory order, for which the approval of the Secretary for Scotland was required. The SLC's procedure involved the hearing of witnesses and counsel's opinion for both parties, the BoAS and the estate; in addition, the SLC had a duty to inspect the ground in question. If the SLC approved the scheme, the next stage was the selection of holders for the smallholdings.

4 *BoAS Annual Report, 1912*, p. viii.

5 Ibid., p. xi.

6 PRO, CAB27/105/298, Duties and procedure; *BoAS Annual Report, 1914*, p. ix

Genuine proprietorial observations were taken into account at this stage.[7]

The finances of the BoAS were governed by section 5 of the 1911 Act. The Agriculture (Scotland) Fund was composed of £15,000 under the Agricultural Rating Act of 1896, supplemented by a maximum of £185,000, to be voted annually by Parliament. That meant that up to £200,000 a year was available to the BoAS, but the 1911 Act was an expensive method of constituting smallholdings, and the Board hinted that the limits of the Agriculture (Scotland) Fund would be the most important constraint on its work.[8]

There were many calls on this money during the settlement of a smallholdings scheme. The tenant of land which was being used for land settlement could claim compensation for the disruption of his tenancy; while the landlord could demand compensation for damage to the letting value of his land caused by the creation of smallholdings. BoAS officials were warned by the Small Holdings Commissioner to distinguish carefully between 'direct' loss, such as increased management overheads, and 'indirect' loss, 'such as the possible depreciation of value of the estate in consequence of the establishment thereon by small holders'. This question of whether landlords had the right to claim compensation for the loss of 'selling value' plagued the Board. Landlords argued that the establishment of smallholdings on an estate took away 'many of the advantages of ownership', making the property less marketable; the Board felt that such a claim was not covered by the Act; and, further, disputed whether such depreciation actually took place. There was little evidence one way or the other, and the debate quickly became sterile.[9] If the compensation claimed by a proprietor or a tenant exceeded £300, the final award would be settled by an arbiter appointed by the Court of Session, but otherwise the SLC was to settle the amount. The demand for compensation beyond £300 could be genuine, or it could be a tactic to delay the scheme. This was a badly drafted clause. The proprietor did not have to establish a claim of more than £300; he merely had to intimate that he would be claiming compensation in excess of that sum. Once some experience was gained of the working of the Act, there was widespread dissatisfaction with the inconsistent awards of the arbiters; but inconsistency is hardly surprising, since the arbiters were a group of randomly chosen individuals who could not look to the Act for any guidance.

The compensation had to be met out of the Agriculture (Scotland) Fund. Clearly a large number of compensation awards would prejudice

7 CAB27/105/277, Duties and procedure; *BoAS Annual Reports, 1913*, pp. viii–ix; *1914*, p. viii; SRO, AF83/177, A. N. Wilson to BoAS, 20 Oct. 1913; AF83/153, A. Lowis to BoAS, 13 Dec. 1912.

8 *BoAS Annual Report, 1912*, p. xiv.

9 PRO, CAB27/105/302, Duties and procedure.

the ability of the BoAS to set up smallholdings schemes. It could only abandon schemes in which the compensation was deemed to be excessive – hardly an ideal course of action.[10] Apart from compensation, the Board had to bear the inevitable losses consequent on the establishment of smallholdings on privately owned land. These occurred on several fronts. There was a difference in what farm buildings were worth to the landlord or tenant farmer, and to smallholders; indeed, they could have been useless to the latter. Also, the rent of the land under smallholdings could well have been less than when the property was rented as a whole farm. Thirdly, the stock on the farm might not have been relevant to the needs of smallholders and would have to have been sold at a loss, compared to the acclimatised value.[11] Thus the Act was not a straightforward piece of legislation, but it had many potential loopholes. The exploitation of these loopholes by adroit landowners seeking to exploit areas of ambiguity would be the main feature of its short and troubled history.

II

Most of the demand for new holdings came from the Outer Hebrides, and in course of time the bulk of BoAS activity would be concentrated in that area. Lewis was the site of the most long-standing and deep-seated difficulties, and various institutions had already failed to come to terms with the land issue there. Nevertheless, expectations for speedy progress were high in the years prior to 1914. But the Board, at the outset of its work in this area, was well aware of the difficulties involved: Lewis was particularly characterised by scarcity of land and poverty-stricken applicants.[12]

These expectations overran in the western parish of Uig at the end of 1913. Fourteen crofters in the townships of Valtos and Reef cleared the neighbouring farm of Reef of its stock of 200 sheep and five head of cattle.[13] This 600-acre farm had been the subject of attention by the Deer Forest Commission in the 1890s. In the first decade of the new century, the Congested Districts Board [CDB] had examined the farm and discovered it to be unsuitable for the formation of smallholdings. But expectations had been increased by the 1911 Act, and the raid was a symptom of the fact that, as early as 1913, frustration had grown to a serious level.[14] Reef farm was isolated and largely composed of machair land, with little ground being suitable for cultivation. That aside, in

[10] *BoAS Annual Reports, 1912*, p. ix; *1914*, pp. xi, xvii.

[11] PRO, CAB27/105/302–5, Duties and procedure.

[12] *BoAS Annual Reports, 1913*, p. vi; *1914*, p. vi.

[13] SRO, AF67/61, Police report, Miavaig, Lewis, 28 Nov 1913; Memo by the Chief Constable of Ross and Cromarty Police, 29 Nov. 1913.

[14] Mather, *State Aided Land Settlement*, p. 12; C. A. Logan, 'Attitudes to the Land on Lewis, 1886–1914' (St Andrews University M.A. dissertation, 1993).

terms of the 1911 Act it was 'statute barred', as its rent was less than £80 a year. There was a school of thought in the island that section 27 of the Act, which referred specifically to Lewis, superseded this provision. This section denied landholder status to tenants of holdings rented at more than £30 or extending to more than thirty acres, and it was widely held that such farms were available for the creation of smallholdings. Indeed, it was in this particular area of Lewis that the demand for the clause had originated. However, the combination of a refusal by the BoAS to implement section 27, and the fact that it shared the earlier view of the CDB that the farm was unsuitable for smallholdings, ensured that the raiders' demands were denied. There was a clear gap between the popular expectations, which had been conditioned by the rhetoric surrounding the land issue in the period 1906–11, and the reality of the Board's power, which was limited by the provisions of the 1911 Act. Colin MacDonald, an assistant sub-commissioner in Lewis, wrote to the Small Holdings Commissioner, telling him that 'it was next to impossible to get the men to realise that the Board has no power to deal with their case'.[15]

Nevertheless, the problems over Reef farm caused a certain amount of consternation, both at the BoAS and in the Scottish Office; the trouble had come so soon after the passing of the 1911 Act, and before the BoAS had had the opportunity to achieve any significant progress in Lewis. Indeed, the fact that the BoAS had achieved so little in Lewis had helped to cause the raid. As the superintendent of police in Stornoway noted, 'the whole proceeding is a game to hurry up somebody'. Some elements on the Board, led by Robert Greig, were inclined to start negotiations with the estate over Reef.[16] However, the consensus of opinion was that, although the raid was primarily a publicity stunt, it could have worrying consequences if it were not handled correctly. Experienced officials were well aware that once agitation began in Lewis, it was difficult to eradicate it. Secondly, there was a worry that, if raids were seen to influence the new regime favourably, it was likely to encourage their repetition.[17] However, despite the potential political consequences of the raid, the Lord Advocate did not consider it serious enough to initiate a criminal prosecution, and advised that the estate should proceed with a civil action. The raiders were sentenced to six weeks for breach of interdict in March, but were released the following month, after giving an undertaking not to encroach on the farm.[18]

15 Day, *Public Administration*, pp. 230–1; SRO, AF67/61, BoAS Secretary to Under Secretary for Scotland, 1 Dec. 1913; C. MacDonald to J. Sutherland, 20 Dec. 1913.

16 SRO, AF67/62, Supt. of Police, Stornoway to Chief Constable of Ross and Cromarty, 30 Jan. 1914; AF67/61, Memo for Secretary for Scotland, 4 Dec. 1913.

17 AF67/61, N. MacLean to J. Sutherland, 8 Dec. 1913.

18 AF67/61, Note by the Lord Advocate, 29 Dec. 1913; *The Scotsman*, 20 Mar., 2 Apr. 1914.

A major factor in the Reef difficulties was the simultaneous attempt by the BoAS to implement smallholdings schemes in Lewis. The Board prepared schemes for four farms: Galson in Ness in the north-west, Orinsay and Stimervay in Lochs in the south-east, Carnish and Ardroil in Uig, and Gress, to the north of Stornoway. These farms covered a total of nearly 23,000 acres, and it was proposed to create around 130 smallholdings.[19]

The proprietor of Lewis, Major Duncan Matheson, was represented by Skene, Edwards and Garson, the famous firm of Edinburgh solicitors. They acted for a number of Highland proprietors, and had experience of crofting law going back to 1886. In each of the four cases considered here, Matheson's solicitors reacted negatively, on his behalf, to the Board's proposals. They argued that the formation of smallholdings on the estate had been unsuccessful in the past; and they ascribed to smallholders a tendency to let rent arrears accumulate, and to be deficient in the stewardship of land. They also noted that the proprietor, together with the rest of the non-smallholding population, would face an increased burden of rates.[20] There were two reasons for this: first, the creation of smallholdings decreased the overall rateable value of a parish; secondly, small landholders received a number of rating dispensations which meant that they only had to pay three-eighths of their half of the rates for their holdings. It was also pointed out that the sporting value of the estate would be reduced – an unlikely eventuality as none of the farms had any real sporting value, but this was a very vague area, because sporting values were so subjective.[21] At each stage of the procedure Skene, Edwards and Garson were obstructive and uncommunicative.[22] This pattern of events continued until 1916, by which time it was clear that the estate would oppose every move of the BoAS. At this stage the Board considered its options, whether or not to proceed, and if not, whether to postpone or abandon the schemes. In the event, with most of the applicants for land away on active service, a postponement was sought: the SLC was informed that the Lewis applications were to be withdrawn until the end of the war. There had been divisions in the BoAS over this policy, with the Chairman holding out against it, and the postponement was only carried out on the sanction of the Secretary for Scotland.[23] In effect, this was an indefinite suspension. The BoAS had to weigh the costs of continuing the schemes against the likelihood of renewed lawlessness if they were withdrawn.

19 SRO, AF83/71–3, 352–8, 360–2

20 AF83/71, SEG to BoAS, 7 Jun. 1913.

21 AF83/352, Report on Orinsay and Stimervay, 27 Jan. 1913; AF83/355, Report on Carnish and Ardroil, 30 Jul. 1913; PRO, CAB27/105/302, Duties and procedure.

22 SRO, AF83/72, SEG to BoAS, 4 Dec. 1913; BoAS to SEG, 22 Jan. 1914.

23 AF83/73, BoAS to Secretary for Scotland, 16 Mar. 1916; Memo on land settlement in Lewis, 15 Mar. 1916; BoAS to Under Secretary for Scotland, 30 Jul. 1917; AF67/390, Memo by R. P. Wright, 15 May 1917; *BoAS Annual Reports*, *1916*, p. vii; *1919*, p. xv.

This obstruction had exacerbated the intense demand for land in Lewis, as one of the assistant sub-commissioners noted in 1916: 'the Lewis people, having had these farms dangled before them for some years will break the peace if the thing is postponed more or less indefinitely'. The Board was aware that, owing to the level of recruitment on the island, it would be compelled to take action at the end of the war, whenever that might be.[24]

The proprietor's obstructive tactics were a major obstacle to land settlement. During the Board's deliberations on the fate of the Lewis schemes, Skene, Edwards and Garson's 'various means of obstruction' were given high priority in the Board's explanation of its own failure.[25] Nevertheless, other reasons can be given for why these schemes were unsuccessful. A large part of the problem was the quality of land in Lewis. Neither the CDB nor the BoAS considered the farm of Reef suitable for smallholdings. The other farms were also far from ideal. Orinsay and Stimervay were isolated, as the road system in that part of Lewis was almost non-existent; the arable land was not plentiful, and the old arable, now used for sheep, was of doubtful quality. And, while Carnish and Ardroil were supposed to make a potentially prosperous scheme because of the prospects for fishing in their area, the sub-commissioner noted that although this may have been true at one time, it was no longer so, for, in view of the modern methods of fishing, smallholders could not hope to compete; and there were also difficulties over working the arable land due to drifting sand. Indeed, a BoAS official regarded Galson as the only farm he had seen on Lewis which was suitable for smallholdings.[26]

There was also an ongoing debate, between Skene, Edwards and Garson and the Board, as to whether the Lewis applicants were fit to take on any smallholdings. The former were decidedly of the opinion that they were not. The BoAS seemed to be divided on this question, although it was not overly critical of the applicants' abilities. Neil MacLean, an assistant sub-commissioner with the Board, directly contradicted the estate's position: his belief was that they had 'considerably extended' the amount of arable land in Lewis.[27] There was unlikely to be a meeting of minds on this issue. Skene, Edwards and Garson had built a reputation on preventing land settlement in various ways since 1886. In this case, the proprietor they were representing was equally opposed to the formation of smallholdings on his estate. On the other hand, the BoAS network of local officials was often quite close in its opinions to the applicants for land. After all, these officials were

24 SRO, AF83/73, N. MacLean to BoAS, 10 Mar. 1916.
25 AF83/73, Memo on land settlement in Lewis, 15 Mar. 1916.
26 AF83/355, Report on Carnish and Ardroil, 30 Jul. 1913; AF83/71, Memo with regard to Lewis, Jun. 1912; AF83/352, Report on Orinsay and Stimervay, 27 Jan. 1913.
27 AF83/73, Memo with regard to Lewis, Jun. 1912; Memo on Lewis applications for small holdings, Dec. 1914.

usually natives of the area in question, and the close contact they had with the applicants may have reduced their objectivity.

Nevertheless, despite these points, there can be little doubt that the fundamental difficulty was the structure of the Small Landholders (Scotland) Act. Its labyrinthine complexities were exploited to good effect by Skene, Edwards and Garson. The lengthy procedures, and the number of different institutions involved (the BoAS, the SLC and the Scottish Office), were ideal for the development of obstructive tactics. By 1914 the Board admitted this itself.[28]

There were many areas in the Act which could lead to confusion. Thus differing interpretations of section 27 – the so called 'Lewis Clause' – had led to problems in Reef in 1913–14. Essentially, what the estate was doing was exploiting the lack of definition in the Act over what constituted a 'scheme'. Section 7(3) established that it was the Small Holdings Commissioner's duty, once he had established the existence of demand and available land, 'to negotiate with the landlords of such land with a view to the adjustment of a scheme for the registration by agreement of any one or more new holders in respect of such land'. There was no indication as to how much detail the landlords had to be given, in the course of such negotiations. Nor, indeed, was there any indication as to what should constitute 'negotiation'. Skene, Edwards and Garson exploited both these areas to the full.

They constantly attempted to put the blame on the BoAS for the delay in coming to an agreement, and even went so far as to 'take exception to the sub-commissioner's statement that any attempt to negotiate can only result in a "useless waste of time"'. Indeed, in the case of Galson, by November 1913 the two parties were even unable to agree if any negotiations had actually taken place![29] The hard-pressed officials of the Board were under no illusions that it was the structure of the 1911 Act which was really at the root of their problems in Lewis; in the crucial year of 1916, indeed, they were discussing the schemes in the context of the need for the Act's amendment.[30]

III

The second major arena of BoAS activity was the southern Hebridean estate of Lady Gordon Cathcart, which covered Benbecula, South Uist, and Barra (except for the northern part). She was also represented by Skene, Edwards and Garson, and had been for over thirty years. As is discussed in earlier chapters, the CDB had implemented a number of

[28] *BoAS Annual Report, 1914*, p. viii

[29] SRO, AF83/71, SEG to BoAS, 7 Jun 1913, AF83/72, SEG to BoAS, 24 Nov. 1913, AF83/356, SEG to BoAS, 2 Oct. 1913, 18 May 1914; AF83/352, SEG to BoAS, 7 Jun., 7 Nov 1913; AF83/353, SEG to BoAS, 20 May 1914, AF83/354, SEG to BoAS, 23 Jul. 1914.

[30] AF83/73, N. MacLean to BoAS, 10 Mar. 1916.

schemes on her estates, in Barra, Vatersay, and South Uist. Now, in this period, four schemes were developed in the southern Hebrides. Three were on her ladyship's estate on the island of South Uist; at Ormiclate, Bornish and Milton, at Glendale, and at Askernish. The fourth, at Eoligarry in Barra, was on land which had been bought by its tenants in 1900, at the time of the formation of smallholdings in the area by the CDB.[31] The Board proposed the formation of 133 new holdings and forty-seven enlargements, and the land involved covered around 25,000 acres.[32]

There were a number of differences between these cases and the situation in Lewis, where, even if all the farms had been taken for smallholdings, there would still have been a considerable cottar problem. In the case of South Uist, the population was much smaller and the congestion, although serious, was not chronic. The sub-commissioner for the West Highlands argued, in his submission to the SLC in the case of Ormiclate, Bornish and Milton, that the three schemes which had been prepared would, if implemented, represent a complete solution to the land and housing problems in South Uist.[33]

Skene, Edwards. and Garson were unimpressed with the Board's statements in these cases. They used broadly the same arguments, but they did not pursue the obstructive tactics to the same extreme. They argued that South Uist was saturated with smallholders (something which could not be said for Lewis): schemes implemented by the CDB had seen the establishment of eighty holdings. They did not accept the argument that the new holdings created would represent a complete solution to the problem on the island, because they had heard it before; the CDB had already said that the formation of fifty holdings would have the desired effect. They claimed now that none of the South Uist farms was available, or suitable, for smallholdings. Further, they attempted to establish that the demand for land in South Uist was not genuine, maintaining that 'there were no really necessitous cases to be dealt with'. The Board disagreed, on the grounds that, due to the smallness of the holdings, the demand for land was 'very strong and urgent'.[34]

The estate also pursued the line of argument that crofters were agricultural vandals. This had been a constant refrain of Lady Gordon Cathcart since 1886. She was fundamentally opposed to the crofting system for a variety of reasons, both agricultural and social. As has been

[31] AF83/74–6, 144–6, 190; AF67/143.

[32] SRO, AF83/75, Report on Ormiclate, Bornish and Milton, 9 Apr. 1913; AF83/76, Precognition for the SLC, 25 Feb. 1913; AF83/144, Preliminary report on Glendale, 12 Oct. 1912; AF83/190, Minute to BoAS Land Committee (undated).

[33] AF83/76, Precognition for the SLC, 25 Feb. 1913.

[34] AF83/74, SEG to BoAS, 4 Jun., 4 Oct. 1912; AF83/75, SEG to BoAS, 3 Feb. 1913; AF83/76, Precognition for the SLC, 25 Feb. 1913; AF83/144, SEG to BoAS, 29 Jan. 1914; AF83/190, SEG to BoAS, 2 Sep. 1919.

noted throughout this book, she took pains to articulate her views to the government at every possible juncture, and this period was no exception. The BoAS was informed that it was undesirable to extend the crofting system, because it 'keeps the energetic man down to the level of the least enterprising'. Furthermore, the fact that the applicants for land were imbued with the culture of crofting made them 'unsuitable for small holdings', according to the estate, which went to considerable lengths to impress the Board with evidence of this unsuitability. It was pointed out that the crofter was as negligent in looking after grazing as he was incapable of working arable; and to back this up, particulars of the fate of an enlargement given to eighty-one crofters in 1897 were produced.[35]

The Board used a large number of assistant sub-commissioners to report on the farms in which they were interested. They were unlikely to be employed by the Board if they were opposed to the idea of land settlement, but, beyond that, there could hardly be any consistency of view among them. It has been noted above how one assistant sub-commissioner on Lewis was very impressed with the ability and endeavour of the crofters in relation to the arable land on the island. The sub-commissioner who reported on the South Uist farms took a more sophisticated attitude. He suggested to the BoAS that 'more of the success depends upon the tenant than on the holding'; and went on to enumerate the qualities required for the successful running of a smallholding: as well as industry, considerable knowledge of stock husbandry and marketing had to be allied to knowledge of agriculture and sound business sense. His conclusion was that 'the value of land in the Hebrides would be improved if crofters practised better agricultural habits'.[36] In an ideal world, agricultural ability and knowledge would have been the main criteria for choosing smallholders, and only the most suitable farms would have been broken up for smallholdings. However, land settlement was as much a political, as an administrative and technical, task, and many other influences had to be taken into account.

Three additional factors influenced the Board in these schemes. First, there was the revival of incidents of land raiding Secondly, as in Lewis, the structure of the Act was extremely significant Thirdly, the less than ideal nature of the farms involved in the schemes caused problems.

The scheme for Ormiclate, Bornish and Milton had progressed to maturity with the setting up of ninety-nine new holdings and forty-four enlargements. Perhaps because of this, frustration boiled over at Glendale in the south of the island. The BoAS decided to postpone the scheme there, due to wartime conditions and to the fact that 'a good deal had already been done in South Uist, at considerable cost, under the scheme for Ormiclate, Bornish and Milton'. December 1916 saw a threat

[35] AF83/75, SEG to BoAS, 3 Feb. 1913; AF83/74, SEG to BoAS, 16 Nov 1912
[36] AF83/75, Report on Ormiclate, Bornish and Milton, 9 Apr 1913

to raid the farm and this, allied to the fact that the lease was to expire at Whit Sunday 1918, led the BoAS to consider reviving the scheme. However, the likely cost of compulsory proceedings and subsidising applicants deficient in capital was enough to dissuade it from doing so.[37] The Board was also not assured of straightforward progress once the farm was out of lease: there was nothing to stop a proprietor re-letting a farm, even when it was under consideration by the BoAS for a smallholdings scheme. There were strong suspicions that some estates were doing this deliberately, in an attempt to hamper the Board's work, and to collect the maximum amount of compensation possible.[38] In the case of Glendale, the scheme's postponement in 1918 was followed by a raid. Lady Gordon Cathcart had been opposed to the taking of the whole farm for smallholdings. The Board offered an alternative scheme in which only half of the farm would be affected, but proprietorial opposition remained implacable. Eventually she relented in the spring of 1919. Part of the reason for this change of heart may have been the intervention of Sir Reginald MacLeod, a Skye landowner and former Under Secretary for Scotland. He took care to explain to Lady Gordon Cathcart that she need not lose out financially by agreeing to a scheme: the BoAS would take over the stock and equipment on the farm, and would make good any difference between the farm rent and the fair rent, set by the SLC, for the new smallholdings. Demand was so high that the Board had to amend its original scheme for twelve new holdings to accommodate twenty-two.[39]

There was also a raid at Askernish in late 1919. This was a clear example of the BoAS being forced into a scheme which it would otherwise not have contemplated, through the pressure of raids and the absence of suitable alternatives. The sub-commissioner stated bluntly, 'Askernish Farm is not the sort of place I would wish to select for small holdings if I had a choice'. The estate management claimed not to take the raid seriously, blamed government weakness for the renewed raiding, and advocated that the raiders should be dealt with firmly. However, in 1920 Lady Gordon Cathcart relented, as she tended to do, and allowed a scheme to proceed.[40]

The scheme at Eoligarry in the north of Barra was similarly troubled by land raids. Despite having been offered potato ground, cottars raided part of the farm in April 1917. The Board declined the offer of purchase

[37] AF83/144, BoAS memo concerning Glendale, 29 Jan. 1919.

[38] *BoAS Annual Report, 1914*, p. ix.

[39] SRO, AF83/144, BoAS memo concerning Glendale, 29 Jan. 1919; AF83/145, Report on Glendale, 14 Feb. 1919; AF83/146, BoAS to Under Secretary for Scotland, 3 Oct. 1921; AF67/146, Sir Reginald MacLeod to Lady Gordon Cathcart, 5 Mar. 1919; E824/574, BoAS to the Treasury, 7 Oct. 1921.

[40] SRO, AF83/190, Report on Askernish, 17 Jul. 1919; BoAS to Under Secretary for Scotland, 11 Dec. 1919; SEG to BoAS, 28 Apr. 1920.

and stated its determination to proceed, according to the 1911 Act. The inevitable delay led to further raids in September 1917.[41] The difficulty was increased by the fact that Eoligarry was the only land left on Barra which was remotely suitable for the creation of smallholdings. The demand was such that the BoAS realised that it would have to take over the whole of the farm – something that was also necessary because, since it was an owner-occupied estate, any part of it left untouched, would be claimed as a home farm and hence would be excluded under section 26, sub-section 3(g). There were of course the usual objections to using the 1911 Act. The sub-commissioner advocated purchase, under the Congested Districts (Scotland) Act, 1897, which was supposed to have been superseded by the 1911 Act; his reasoning was that the compensation and arbitration expenses would exceed the cost of an immediate purchase. The owners, through the inevitable Skene, Edwards and Garson, offered to sell at £12,000. The members of the Land Court favoured this option. Their advice was eventually taken in the spring of 1919, and Eoligarry was finally purchased.[42]

The case of Eoligarry represents an extreme example of the growing view within the Board that the 1911 Act was more trouble and expense than it was worth. Admittedly, it was a special case, a small owner-occupied estate in an area of congestion, where there were no suitable alternatives for land settlement. Nevertheless, in general there was a strong strain of dissatisfaction, based on experience, with the 1911 Act, and also, a realisation that it was the Act itself, as much as proprietorial opposition or the difficulties caused by raids, which had held up progress in the southern Hebrides. The Board's influential Sub-Commissioner for Small Holdings in the Highlands was clear in his view as to the worth of the 1911 Act, referring to it variously as 'absurd and mischievous' and 'imperfect and unsatisfactory'. His view was passed on to the Scottish Office by the Board. It argued, with reference to Askernish farm, that the cost of using the 1911 Act 'would be heavy relatively to the results secured'.[43]

It is thus clear that in the southern Hebrides, as well as in Lewis, monocausal explanations of the failure of the Small Landholders (Scotland) Act, focusing on proprietorial opposition to the BoAS's land settlement schemes, are simplified misrepresentations of a complex picture. As we shall see, in North Uist and Harris the element of

41 SRO, AF67/143, BoAS to Barra Cottars, 20 Mar. 1917, Police report, Castlebay, Barra, 5 Apr. 1917, Under Secretary for Scotland to SEG, 15 Sep. 1917, Police report, Castlebay, Barra, 2 Sep. 1917.

42 AF67/143, T. Wilson to R. Wright, 7 Nov. 1917; Supplementary report on Eoligarry, Barra, 7 Nov. 1917; SLC Note, 7 Dec. 1917; SEG to Under Secretary for Scotland, 14 Jan. 1918; BoAS to SEG, 10 Jan. 1918; *BoAS Annual Report, 1918*, p. x, Leneman, *Fit For Heroes?*, p. 108.

43 SRO, AF83/145, Report on Glendale, 14 Feb. 1919; AF83/190, BoAS to Under Secretary for Scotland, 11 Dec. 1919.

proprietorial opposition was much less prominent, but the BoAS's record in these islands in this period was equally unsuccessful.

IV

The land issue in North Uist should be examined alongside that of Harris. The BoAS proposed the setting up of forty new holdings on the 4,100 acre farm of Cheesebay in North Uist, for the benefit of cottars from the congested island of Taransay off Harris. It was not an ideal location for smallholdings, as it was heavily interspersed with small lochs typical of the North Uist landscape. In an echo of the debate between the duke of Argyll and the BoAS in Tiree (see below), the estate stated its preference for fewer and smaller holdings. It also objected to the influx of Harris cottars as it felt that this 'would create strife with the locals'.[44] The BoAS was of the opinion that in selecting applicants for a scheme, it did not have to be limited to those who reside 'in the immediate vicinity of the farm or even in the same parish or county', and it had obtained legal opinion which confirmed this view.[45] The difficulties with this scheme led to some thought on the question of migration. Indeed, it was questioned whether this scheme could really be called migration at all: movement over the same distance in the Lowlands would certainly not be called migration, and no such objection would be taken to it. It was also pointed out that, if proprietors and applicants for land persisted in their negative attitude to movement, no progress could be made 'unless the view is taken that congestion in the Highlands is never to be relieved except from the estate on which it exists (surely an impossible attitude)'.

The Cheesebay scheme was another which the Board considered postponing for the duration of the war. The possibility of expensive arbitration was a major consideration in favour of postponement. However, the Taransay element of the equation complicated matters. It was widely recognised that Taransay was 'one of the most miserable spots in the Hebrides', and that the Board would be ignoring its duty if nothing was done to relieve congestion there. There was also the possibility of renewed raids if the cottars had the prospect of settlement on North Uist removed. The Board was aware that it would be open to justified vilification if it were not ready, at the conclusion of the war, to put the scheme into effect 'as part of the general policy of relieving congestion in the Outer Hebrides'.[46]

In this case the proprietor, Arthur Campbell-Orde, was at least willing to put forward suggestions as to how the scheme might be altered. At his

[44] SRO, AF67/144, Police report, Lochmaddy, North Uist, 23 Jul. 1914; AF83/385, Memo by T. Wilson, 24 May 1913.

[45] AF83/385, Report on Cheesebay, North Uist, 20 Sep. 1913; AF83/386, Notes for a meeting concerning North Uist, 18 Mar. 1914.

[46] PRO, CAB27/105/299, 312, Duties and procedure.

suggestion, the number of holdings to be formed was reduced from fifty-two to thirty-two – but this had the side-effect of not accommodating all the applicants from Taransay. The BoAS did, however, have a duty to take reasonable landlord suggestions into account during the negotiation. Land settlement could not work if the proprietor whose land was being used for smallholdings had no input into the process. Similarly, genuine proprietorial suggestions should not be confused with landlord opposition – though that, of course, is not to argue that the latter did not exist.[47]

V

Tiree, part of the estate of the duke of Argyll, was a major arena of BoAS activity. Here a number of distinctive features merit examination. One is the attitude of the proprietor: the estate became fully involved in the discussions surrounding the attempted creation of smallholdings on the island, without ever being obstructive. Another is that, whereas in the other parts of the Highlands the limitations on the Board had been chiefly political or financial, in the case of Tiree the obstacle was physical – although the potential for successful settlement on this island was high, due to its fertility and to its history of large holdings which had been encouraged by the estate management.[48]

The Board prepared schemes for five farms on Tiree: Hynish, Greenhill, Baugh, Balephetrish, and Heylipol. It was proposed to form seventy-one new holdings and eight enlargements, and the schemes encompassed 3,557 acres.[49] Numerous indications of a high demand for land – there were, for example, 126 applications for four new holdings and four enlargements at Baugh – led the Small Holdings Commissioner to conclude that the demand was 'pronounced' and that action should be taken with 'urgency'. However, the Board did note that its own concentrated activity in a particular area tended to swell the demand abnormally.[50]

Such a large demand, mainly from the sizeable cottar population, together with the limited amount of farmland available for land settlement – 3,500 acres – set the context for the debate about the size of holdings which would characterise the land issue on Tiree. For political reasons, the Board wished to satisfy as much of the demand as possible. The debate surfaced particularly over the farm of Balephetrish which

47 SRO, AF83/390, BoAS to Under Secretary for Scotland, 26 Jun 1917, *BoAS Annual Report, 1914*, p. xi.

48 J. R. Coull, 'The island of Tiree', *SGM*, lxxviii (1962), pp. 17–24.

49 SRO, AF83/111–12, 152–3, 157–8, 249–50, 433–5.

50 AF83/158, Statement of facts to SLC concerning Baugh, Tiree, 1913, AF83/111, Memo for the Small Holdings Commissioner, 16 Oct 1912, AF83/250, BoAS to Under Secretary for Scotland, 18 Mar 1914, *BoAS Annual Reports, 1913*, p. vi, *1914*, p. vii.

extended to 1,400 acres, and where it was proposed to establish eight new holdings and four enlargements. The scheme had been withdrawn during the war following a land raid, and after it was realised that the compensation awarded to the tenant by an arbiter was greater than the capital value of the farm.[51] But it was revived in the early part of 1919. By that time, sixty-three new holdings and twenty-seven enlargements of holdings had already been formed on Tiree. Nonetheless, there were still 218 outstanding applications for new holdings, and forty-eight for enlargements. Ninety-four of these applicants specified Balephetrish as their preferred site of settlement.[52]

The duke was prepared to assist the BoAS in this scheme, on the condition that the holdings formed were larger than those in the previous schemes; he advocated the formation of holdings with a rent of £30–£40. As an incentive for the Board, he offered to allow the application to the SLC to go forward unopposed, and to let them set the level of compensation.[53] The duke's analysis had unlikely allies in the shape of former cottars, who had been given land in the scheme for Greenhill farm before the war. They complained to the Secretary for Scotland about 'the scraps given off in Greenhill instead of moderately sized holdings from which we could make a decent living'; they found they were still burdened with cottars; and they even went so far as to claim that their holdings were so small that it was not worth while building houses.[54] The Board was well aware of the political imperative for creating large numbers of smallholdings. By this method, more of the demand would be satisfied and the potential for lawlessness reduced. This was noted in 1913, while the Hynish scheme for the Land Court was being prepared:

> while the Board realise that it is desirable to make the holdings of substantial size they found it was impossible in an Island like Tiree to approximately meet the needs of all the applicants without diminishing the size of the holding.[55]

In 1922, the Board eventually settled twenty-seven applicants on large new holdings and fourteen on smaller units. This was carried out under post-war legislation. The BoAS, under pressure of threats of renewed lawlessness, contemplated buying the land, but eventually proceeded with a scheme which left it in the hands of the duke.[56] Despite this

[51] SRO, AF83/249, Minute by the Small Holdings Commissioner, 28 Jan. 1913; BoAS to Lindsay, Howe and Co., 27 Jun. 1914.

[52] AF83/250, Memo concerning Tiree, 31 Jul. 1920; AF67/165, Memo regarding Tiree, Feb. 1918.

[53] SRO, AF83/250, Lindsay, Howe and Co. to BoAS, 7 Jan. 1919.

[54] AF83/153, Tiree crofters to T. MacKinnon Wood, 14 Apr. 1913.

[55] AF83/111, Notes for SLC evidence concerning Hynish, Tiree, 11 Jun. 1913.

[56] SRO, E824/515, BoAS to the Treasury, May 1921; KLTR to Treasury, 15 Jul. 1921; AF83/251, BoAS to Lindsay, Howe and Co., 29 Mar. 1922.

political influence, by the time of the post-war Balephetrish scheme the Board had come to realise that the formation of a large number of smallholdings would not eradicate congestion in the long term. The duke's offer of an unopposed scheme proved too tempting to turn down.

Thus, in the case of Tiree, the Board found that, as well as the usual political pressures and financial limitations allied to the customary problems of the procedures of the 1911 Act, it had physical and intellectual problems to deal with as well.[57]

VI

The attitude of the duke of Sutherland was at the opposite extreme to that of Major Matheson and Lady Gordon Cathcart. Indeed, his habit of offering large pieces of his estate to the Board for land settlement, sometimes as gifts, was disconcerting. The first instance was in 1912. In response to a speech by the Chancellor of the Exchequer, he offered 200,000 acres of deer forest to the government, at £2 per acre; subsequently, he reduced the price to £1 2s 6d per acre. He followed this up with a further offer of 200,000 acres – mostly of sheep-grazing – in the parish of Tongue. Of course, the duke could well afford such 'generosity'; at this time he was the largest landowner in the country. His estates totalled 1.3 million acres; most of them were in Sutherland, but he also owned valuable land in Shropshire and Staffordshire. The timing of such an offer was also propitious. Sheep-farming was no longer profitable and mature mutton, such as was commonly produced in Sutherland, no longer appealed to the public taste. So, in the words of the *Glasgow Herald*, it represented 'excellent business' to try and off-load it on to the government, for a considerable sum of money. The theme of Lloyd George's argument was that there was a vast amount of land in the Highlands, otherwise suitable for smallholdings, under deer. This was a widely held radical belief which, despite the reality of its findings, the 1892 'Royal Commission (Highlands and Islands)' had not dispelled. The reactions of Lloyd George and other Liberals to the duke's offer were disingenuous. In the acerbic words of Lord Lovat, after having 'harped continually' on the agricultural value of such land they now 'turn round and say that it would not keep a mouse'.[58]

A third offer by the duke of Sutherland involved the 16,000-acre sheep farm of Shinness, near Lairg.[59] This was rented at £527, with a valuable sheep-stock of 3,500. It was under lease until Whit Sunday 1918, when the duke proposed to allow the BoAS to carry out a scheme

57 Leneman, *Fit For Heroes?*, p. 17

58 *Glasgow Herald*, 29 Oct., 31 Oct. 1913, 1 Jan 1914, SRO, GD325/1/223, Lord Lovat to the SLPF, 3 Nov. 1913.

59 L. Leneman, 'Borgie: a debatable gift to the nation', *NS*, ix (1989), p. 81

of land settlement – an offer which the BoAS described as 'patriotic'. The scheme contemplated the formation of twenty-one 'self supporting' smallholdings, each to be supplemented by a share in the hill grazing and a stake in a sheep club stock. The Board predicted that these arrangements 'assured ... exceptional success'.[60]

Despite expenditure of nearly £15,000 in loans and grants to the holders, a number of problems with the settlement soon emerged. They did so on two fronts: the fate of the sheep-stock, and the expense and quality of housing on the settlement. The former was to become a particular problem in land settlement in Sutherland after the war, and the events in Shinness presaged such difficulties. The capital that most holders had was insufficient for them to afford the valuable flocks which were commonly found in a classic sheep-farming county such as Sutherland. In the case of Shinness, the successful applicants were given entry to their holdings at Martinmas in 1919. However, they refused to sign bonds for the ownership of the sheep-stocks, and so it remained in the management of the BoAS, at considerable expense.[61] The holders could not be persuaded to take it over until 1923; and by 1928, the club stock had fallen into severe financial difficulties.[62] There was little the Board could do to prevent such a state of affairs. The stock could be sold, but if sold at auction it would not realise its valuation price, and the Board would have to bear the loss. There was a general problem with handing over the management of large sheep-stocks to smallholders, for the majority of them had no experience in the complex business of managing such flocks. This had been noted with reference to a farm on Tiree: a sub-commissioner there pointed out that the management of a sheep-stock involved constant buying and selling to maintain the stock's value, which 'can only be undertaken with success when capital, ripe experience, considerable skill and judgement is at the command of the tenant'.[63] Through no fault of their own, few applicants for smallholdings could be expected to have these qualifications.

The second problem with the Shinness settlement concerned the settlers' housing. Vast sums of money had been spent on the houses. However, unlike what normally happened in the Outer Hebrides, where the holders largely built their own houses, at Shinness contractors did the work at great expense; so great, that suspicions of profiteering were voiced. In 1915, BoAS officials had been warned of the dangers of burdening smallholders with large housing costs. Even with the low level of interest on BoAS housing loans, expensive buildings could cripple a

60 SRO, AF83/614, Scottish Office/BoAS memo, 24 Sep. 1917; *BoAS Annual Report, 1917*, p. x.

61 SRO, AF83/614, Scottish Office/BoAS memo, 24 Sep. 1917.

62 AF83/615, Sir A. Sinclair to the Secretary for Scotland, 8 Apr. 1924; Leneman, *Fit For Heroes?*, p. 67.

63 SRO, AF83/111, Report on Hynish, Tiree, 30 Nov. 1913; *BoAS Annual Report, 1914*, p. xiv.

holder's chance of success, especially when he was a man of limited capital, as many were; and, in the case of outgoing tenants, extravagant buildings could make the holding difficult to let. The SLC would not compensate holders on the true value of the buildings, but on their value 'to the holding'.[64] However, in the case of Shinness, despite the considerable outlay, the quality of the buildings was not high, and complaints continued throughout the 1920s and 1930s. The necessary improvements were not made until after the Second World War.[65]

Thus, although in contrast to other areas discussed, the prospects for dealing with the land issue in Sutherland would seem to have been good, since proprietorial opposition was not a factor, there were few physical constraints, and large, potentially self-supporting, holdings could be contemplated, in the event the expected progress did not take place. Part of the problem may have been that the BoAS was carrying out land settlement on somebody else's terms. Given the slow progress over the years since 1911, the Board could not afford to turn down the duke's offers. However, if it had been left to its own judgement, the Board is highly unlikely to have chosen a property such as Shinness, with only 1,300 arable acres out of a total of 16,000, as being suitable for land settlement. The Borgie scheme, like Glendale in Skye, was viable because it had scope for subsidiary income, through the forestry work available for the settlers. Yet again, the complex political dictates generated by the structure of the 1911 Act, which reduced the pace of land settlement to a crawl, forced the Board to grasp at any opportunity to satisfy demand.

VII

As well as proprietorial opposition to individual schemes of land settlement, there was also a more general campaign against the provisions of the 1911 Act. This was conducted by the Scottish Land and Property Federation [hereafter SLPF], an organisation which had been set up for the very purpose of preventing the Act from becoming law. There was a feeling among landowners, following the establishment of the BoAS and the SLC, that the Act was an attempt to 'despoil their property'. This belief was particularly prevalent in the non-crofting areas, where there had been no previous experience of the operation of such institutions[66] – and the bulk of the SLPF's membership came from the non-crofting areas. Nevertheless, its views on the course of land settlement are worthy of discussion.

The SLC and its Chairman, Lord Kennedy, were particularly targeted

64 PRO, CAB27/105/300–1, Duties and procedure.
65 Churchill College, Cambridge, Thurso Collection, THRS, V1/1/200, Lord Novar to Sir A. Sinclair, 19 Jun. 1924; Leneman, *Fit For Heroes?*, pp. 68–70.
66 SRO, E824/869, KLTR to Cabinet Land Settlement Committee, 3 Sep. 1920

for criticism. The SLPF asked its members to detail experiences of the proceedings of the SLC. From this evidence, it argued that the SLC was an unsatisfactory tribunal. Faults included Lord Kennedy's unjudicial manner, his acceptance of hearsay evidence, his distrust of expert evidence submitted by proprietors, and his clear bias towards smallholders throughout his work.[67] The SLC was compared unfavourably to the old Crofters' Commission, which was held in high regard by landowners and crofters alike.[68] However, the root of the opposition lay deeper than this. The SLPF, although not representative of all landowners, was fundamentally opposed to the whole concept of land settlement. It stated that clearly in 1914, when it argued that the creation of smallholdings by compulsion was an 'intrusion of the rights of ownership'; whereas, in contrast, the BoAS regarded the setting-up of new smallholdings as the 'primary purpose of the Act'.[69] The SLPF was the voice of active landlordism and it would have been surprising, given its history, if it had not campaigned against the operation of a nationwide system of land settlement. But a much greater influence on the implementation of public policy in the Highlands was the individual proprietor, who slowed down the process of land settlement on his or her own estate.

Despite vociferous espousal of the measure during the years 1906–11, period, some Liberal opinion soon turned against the terms of the 1911 Act. Lloyd George set up a number of small committees to investigate the land issue – rural and urban – throughout the whole of the British Isles; the chairman of the Scottish committee was J. Ian MacPherson, MP for Ross-shire and an acolyte of the Chancellor of the Exchequer. Lloyd George's motivations for such a comprehensive examination of the land issue were manifold. He believed that it was impossible to tackle social inequalities without first taking on the power of the landed classes; the corollary was that land reform would make all social reform possible. Also, faced with mounting fiscal demands, Lloyd George believed that a national land tax would be the best way of raising revenue. The land enquiry committees were to provide a basis for a subsequent Land Campaign which was to put the land issue at the top of the political agenda. The period 1912–14 was one of great difficulty for the Liberal Party; it was losing by-elections and was embattled, as ever, over the Irish question. By June 1914 Liberal backbenchers were becoming restive, and complaints on the budget reached the ear of Asquith.

[67] SRO, GD325/1/14, Returns to schedule on Small Landholders (Scotland) Act; GD325/1/25, Notes on the administration of the Small Landholders (Scotland) Act; SEGP, deed box A6, Lady Gordon Cathcart, no. 6, bundle 2, Memo on Small Landholders (Scotland) Act.

[68] SRO, GD325/1/210, Account of meeting at SLPF, 8 Aug. 1913; Leneman, *Fit For Heroes?*, p. 11; Day, *Public Administration*, p. 229.

[69] SRO, GD325/1/148, Memo on administration of Small Landholders (Scotland) Acts, 1 Mar. 1914; PRO, CAB27/105/263, Duties and procedure.

Moderate Liberals were unhappy with the land proposals, and many were concerned at the range of objectives being pursued under the guise of the Finance Bill. For their part, Conservatives were quite happy to sit back and observe the implosions in the Liberal Party. Problems were compounded when the land proposals in the Budget were dropped in June 1914; this enraged the radicals in the Party.[70]

Notwithstanding the failure of the longer-term objectives of the land enquiry committees, the Scottish Report provides an interesting commentary on the 1911 Act. Many sensible criticisms were made. The right of the proprietor to go the Court of Session to have an arbiter appointed to adjudicate compensation of more than £300 was lamented; the potential expense to the Board, as has been noted, caused a number of schemes to be cancelled. It was felt that the headings under which compensation could be claimed should be reduced. The problem of proprietors letting farms while the Board was contemplating a smallholdings scheme was also recommended for reform. And, finally, the Board's limited financial resources, especially given the lack of capital among many applicants, was held to be a major obstruction to land settlement.[71]

Thus, by 1914, the Small Landholders Act had few friends. Frustrated applicants, unhappy landowners, and now the disaffected element in the Liberal Party which had created it, all added to the difficulties of the Board, which was trying hard to implement this most imperfect piece of legislation. A further difficulty was the task of trying to continue its operations in wartime. The most obvious problem here was the fact that many of the Board's officials were on active service, and operations had to be conducted using a skeleton staff. In addition, many of the estate officials, and potential applicants, were also absent for the same reason. A second problem was the rise in prices of the materials required for land settlement, such as timber, iron, wire, lime, and cement. The price of livestock and farm implements also increased several-fold. This stretched the finances of the Board, which were reduced during the war years, and burdened the new holders with high annual charges.[72] For these reasons, land settlement was largely in abeyance during the war. In particular, the rise in the price of livestock caused considerable problems: the Board could not afford to take over farms which had large sheep-stocks because of the likelihood of a large difference between the

70 B. B. Gilbert, 'David Lloyd George: land, the budget and social reform', *American Historical Review*, lxxxi (1976); B. B. Gilbert, 'David Lloyd George: the reform of British landholding and the budget of 1914', *Historical Journal*, xxi (1978); H V. Emy, *Liberals, Radicals and Social Politics, 1892–1914* (Cambridge, 1973).

71 Scottish Land Enquiry Committee, *Scottish Land, Rural and Urban* (London, 1914), pp. 115–22.

72 SRO, E824/869, KLTR to Cabinet Land Settlement Committee, 3 Sep. 1920; *BoAS Annual Report, 1915*, pp. x–xi; D. T. Jones *et al.*, *Rural Scotland During the War* (London, 1926), pp. 242–4

acclimatisation and the market values.[73] Nevertheless, despite these difficulties, some effort was made to implement schemes which had been conceived before the war.

It is clear that weaknesses in the Act were the fundamental difficulty faced by the BoAS. Its imperfections allowed some proprietors to prevent the Board from carrying out its duty, and to hold it to ransom over the issue of compensation. Also, the general provisions of the Act lacked clarity and definition. It is important to relate this to the Act's origins. The legislation was designed with short-term political objectives in mind, and the Act's operation clearly demonstrates that these objectives militated against technical efficiency. The BoAS and the SLC were criticised for the speed at which they worked and were accused of political bias. There may have been some substance in such allegations. However, it should be understood that they were working with an imperfect implement. Furthermore, the political environment in which they were created, and the political objectives of the 1911 Act, made it difficult for them to appear a-political.

Difficulties also originated in the problems which the Board faced. Available land did not, and never could, match the precise demands of the applicants. The problem was potentially exacerbated when a Court of Session decision in 1917 created the class of absentee crofters. Previously, it had been the case that to qualify as a small landholder, a person had to live and continue to live within two miles of the croft. However, the ruling established that it was sufficient if this condition was satisfied on the 1 April 1912, when the 1911 Act came into force. This did not affect new BoAS settlements, as in most cases they chose their landholders from a large field of applicants. But it was a problem, in that established croft land could fall into the hands of people who were not particularly motivated to utilise it effectively; this could be incongruous in areas where the demand for land was high.[74] Another problem arose when the BoAS discovered, as had the Crofters' Commission and the CDB before it, that crofters were reluctant to migrate. This elevated the physical constraints on land settlement in the Hebrides to a matter of high importance. It forced the Board to create holdings of a smaller size than it, and the more helpful proprietors, were comfortable with. Therefore, settlements created by the Board tended to struggle in economically testing conditions – a difficulty that was beginning to emerge, even within the short period examined here. The fact that land settlement proved problematic, even in areas where proprietorial co-operation was forthcoming, substantiates the conclusion that other factors merit attention.

[73] *BoAS Annual Report, 1917*, pp. ix–x.

[74] *Court of Session Cases, 1917*, pp. 453–63, Rogerson v. Chilston; J. Scott, *The Law of Smallholdings in Scotland* (Edinburgh, 1933), p. 71.

VIII

Despite the difficulties, some progress was achieved, and it is important to examine its extent. The following table relates the number of new holdings (NHs) and enlargements (Es) created under the Act to the real demand (RD) for land in each county (real demand has been calculated by subtracting withdrawn or invalid applications from the total number of applications that were submitted). In the final column (% RD settled), the number of land settlements (NHs + Es) in each county is expressed as a percentage of the real demand: that is one way of demonstrating how much of the demand was actually satisfied. As the table shows, over the Highlands as a whole, the settlement of real demand works out at no more than 10.3%: a figure that can only be regarded as unsatisfactory.

Table 4: *Land Settlement under Small Landholders (Scotland) Act, 1911, April 1912–December 1919*[75]

County	NHs	Es	RD	% RD Settled
Caithness	73	1000	691	25.0
Sutherland	45	61	1308	8.1
Ross	14	14	1865	1.5
Inverness	195	128	3234	10.0
Argyll	155	94	1409	17.7
TOTAL	482	397	8507	10.3

A number of the figures reflect the conclusions drawn from the specific studies of individual geographical areas made in this chapter. The high number of holdings on Tiree inflate the settlement percentage in Argyll. The high demand for, and complete failure of, land settlement in Lewis,[76]is evident in the disastrously low percentage of settlement in Ross. Even in areas where the demand was comparatively low, the success rate under the Act was poor; in Caithness, for example, only 25% of applicants could be settled.

However, a statistical exercise such as this can only present part of the overall picture. Questions can certainly be raise about the viability of the policy of creating large numbers of small units. Thus even the high figure of settlement for Argyll, for example, cannot be used as an infallible index of successful land settlement. And, in general, what the figures demonstrate clearly is that the 1911 Act, for all the reasons explored here, was an imperfect vehicle for land settlement in the Highlands. Further legislation was required: it came in 1919.

[75] From *BoAS Annual Report, 1919*, appendices 1, 2

CHAPTER EIGHT

Land Settlement from 1919

The Land Settlement (Scotland) Act, 1919, was passed in very different circumstances to those of its predecessor of 1911. All the parties now attempted to avoid the controversies which had hitherto characterised debate over land legislation. The Lord Advocate, T. B. Morrison, winding up the first reading of the new bill in August 1919, spoke of the 'very strong disposition on all sides' to bury the former arguments on land policy. However, when the Secretary for Scotland, Robert Munro, opened the same debate, he presented the bill in much the same rhetorical manner as the 1911 Act had been presented: the 'freshness, freedom and peace' of rural life was contrasted to the 'drive, artificiality and fever' of an urban existence. The political power of the Coalition government had much to do with the ease with which the 1919 Act was passed. It was presented as an attempt to fulfil the pledge given to recruits that they would receive land on their return from the war.[1] This, however, was only a part of the Coalition's motivation. By 1919 the deficiencies of the 1911 Act had become all too clear. Minor pieces of wartime legislation could not, and were not intended to, provide a comprehensive solution to the Scottish land problem. The Land Settlement (Scotland) Act was the Coalition's attempt to provide this.[2]

I

The debate between two competing mechanisms for creating new smallholdings was a constant theme of the history of government policy in the Highlands since 1886. The 1886 Crofters Act and the 1911 Small Landholders Act provided for the creation of new holdings on privately owned land, while the 1897 Congested Districts Act provided facilities for crofters to become the owners of their holdings. The 1919 Act contained elements of both ideas. Part I empowered the BoAS to acquire land, compulsorily if necessary. It could then either act as a landowner, or sell the land on to applicants for smallholdings; the powers of the 1897 Act for the assistance of owner-occupiers and the adaptation of holdings remained in force. More importantly perhaps, given the events

[1] *PD*, 5th ser., cols. 1806–7, 1857; *The Scotsman*, 12 Nov. 1919.

[2] Leneman, *Fit For Heroes?*, p. 20; *PP*, 1928, XI: *Report of the Committee on Land Settlement in Scotland*, pp. 10–11; 'Land settlement for soldiers and sailors', *SJA*, i (1918).

of recent years, Part II of the Act was an amendment of the 1911 Act. Three areas of amendment are of particular note. First, the SLC's role was reduced: the BoAS now had the power to issue an order for the establishment of new holdings without reference to the SLC, though the sanction of the Secretary for Scotland was required, and if he had reservations concerning the scheme he could ask the SLC to investigate. Secondly, the procedures for compensation were altered: the landlord's right to appeal to an arbiter for claims of more than £300 was removed, and all claims were now to be settled by the SLC Thirdly, the landlord's right to claim compensation for loss of selling value was abolished. In 1920 it was noted that, while the high compensation awards had been a major obstacle to the operation of the 1911 Act, the new procedures limited compensation awards effectively.[3]

A completely new area in the Act was the provision for the preferential treatment of ex-servicemen, for a period of two years after the Act became law. Later, a public announcement was made that no applicant would be preferred if his application was not received by 1 March 1921. The Board did not enforce this rigorously, and the ex-service preference only lapsed in 1926. The ex-service applications accounted for a major proportion of the demand for new holdings in the immediate post-war era, as is demonstrated in Table 5:

Table 5: *Ex-Service Demand for Land Settlement, 1920–1924*[4]

Year	Total Applications	Ex-Service Applications	%
1920	2273	1720	76
1921	1416	617	44
1922	814	453	56
1923	606	384	63
1924	705	342	49

This pattern of demand is consistent with that following earlier pieces of legislation: demand tended to peak when legislation was new and to fall away later. After 1919, however, the ex-service dimension complicated matters, and may have dissuaded civilians from applying during the early post-war years; as can be seen from the table, the civilian demand rose proportionately as time went on. On the other hand, much of the ex-service demand in the immediate post-war years was nominal: the mere existence of the opportunity for ex-servicemen encouraged some to apply for land who would not otherwise have done so. The BoAS

[3] PRO, CAB27/104/96, 142, Land Settlement Committee; 'Small Holdings in Scotland', *International Labour Office Geneva, Studies and Reports*, series K, no. 3 (Nov. 1920).

[4] From *BoAS Annual Reports, 1920*, p. xiii; *1921*, p. xv; *1923*, p. xiii; *1924*, p. xii; *1925*, p. x.

attempted to deal with this problem in 1922 by issuing a circular to all ex-servicemen whose applications had been received before January of that year. As a result, 1,584 applications were removed from the Board's lists – either because the men intimated that they no longer wished to be considered for land settlement, or because they did not reply to the circular or to the reminders that followed it.[5]

The financial provisions of the Act are also of interest. The Board was empowered to borrow a sum of up to £2.75 million from the Public Works Loans Commissioners. In July 1920, only seven months after the passing of the Land Settlement Act, the Cabinet considered that demand for land was much higher than what the available funds could meet. But the possibility of discontinuing land settlement was rejected, in view of the likely social, as well as law-and-order, consequences. Due consideration was given to the fact that pledges had been made at the time of military recruitment and during the 1918 election campaign. It was agreed that a Cabinet committee, including the Secretary for Scotland, Robert Munro, should be set up to consider the 'policy and machinery of land settlement'.[6] The main issue before the committee was whether the problem was administrative, and so capable of being solved by devolving responsibility for Highland land settlement to a separate body, and by bringing Lowland land settlement into line with the English county council arrangements.[7] The Secretary for Scotland held a different view, arguing that the financial provisions of the 1919 Act were inadequate; he conceded that economies could be made to release more money for land settlement, but believed that it would be necessary to settle 1,000 holders a year in order to keep pace with demand.[8]

The main objection to the idea of decentralising the process of land settlement was that it could not be funded by local contributions. There were also grave doubts over the value of seeking the co-operation of Highland county councils, since they had no experience in the field of land settlement. Munro repeatedly asserted that the problem 'was entirely one of money'. But the view emerged from the committee's deliberations that the problem of land settlement in the Highlands was entirely different from that in the rest of the country, and that there was a good case for preferential treatment.[9]

The committee's report was submitted to the Cabinet in late November 1920. It confirmed that Highland land settlement was

5 PRO, CAB27/105/250–1, Notes on the memo by the Secretary for Scotland, 8 Oct. 1920; *BoAS Annual Report, 1922*, p. ix; 'Land settlement in Scotland', *SJA*, xv (1932), p. 245.

6 PRO, CAB23/22/5–9, Cabinet conclusions, 15 Jul., 13 Aug. 1920.

7 PRO, CAB27/105/368–94, Memos by members of the Land Settlement Committee, Oct.–Nov. 1920.

8 CAB27/105/400–3, Memo by the Secretary for Scotland, 10 Nov. 1920.

9 CAB27/104/156–63, Land Settlement Committee, 2 Nov. 1920; SRO, E824/869, K. MacKenzie (KLTR) to Land Settlement Committee, 3 Sep. 1920.

unique, and recommended that it should be put under the sole authority of the Director of Land Settlement, Sir Arthur Rose, who would have direct access to the Secretary for Scotland. Economies should be effected by acquiring land which was already equipped, and by reducing the size of new holdings. Expenditure was to be tightly controlled. Robert Munro dissented from elements of the report, particularly the administrative provisions which amounted to a side-lining of the BoAS in favour of the Director of Land Settlement. He also differed over one of the suggested methods of economising: it had been recommended that loans to new holders to purchase stock should be limited to 50% of the value of the stock, but Munro pointed out that this would be 'an insuperable obstacle' to the settlement of ex-servicemen.[10]

The committee also recommended that an extra £1 million should be made available to the BoAS for land settlement – the bulk to be allocated to the crofting counties. This represented a victory for Munro. When the report was at the draft stage, it was only proposed to allocate an extra £333,000 to Scottish land settlement, but Munro argued that this 'would be of little value in solving the problem'. In the event, it was agreed to find an extra £750,000.

In many ways this committee exemplified problems which could be traced back to the 1906–11 period, when Highland and Lowland land settlement were conjoined. It was the contention of many in the Highlands that this was a mistake. The war added to the immediacy of the problem, and the land raids, which were common in the immediate post-war period, added to the case for special facilities for the Highlands. Clearly, however, it would be politically impossible to alter the 1919 administrative regime radically, so early in its life. The alternative was to instruct the Director of Land Settlement to favour the Highlands, without actually making a policy statement to that effect. The Cabinet agreed this shift in policy in January 1921.[11]

The second point to emerge is that Highland land settlement should not be regarded simply as part of the general post-war reconstruction policy. Furthermore, it was not simply an ex-service problem. The impression that it was arose because the new legislation followed so quickly after the end of the war. Also, in this period, land settlement was taking place right across Europe. The problems faced on the Continent, however, were considerably greater and were qualitatively different, as in some areas much farm land had been destroyed by the fighting, and there was a general history of peasant proprietorship.[12] Land settlement

10 SRO, AF66/27, Land Settlement Committee, final report.

11 PRO, CAB23/24/19–21, Conclusion of a conference of Ministers, 4 Jan 1921

12 'Smallholdings in France: acquisition by military pensioners and victims of war', *SJA*, i (1918), pp. 489–90; 'Agricultural reconstruction in France', *SJA*, ii (1919), pp. 549–51; 'Soldier settlement in Italy', *SJA*, iii (1920), pp. 84–6; C. Bathurst, 'The land settlement of ex-servicemen', *Nineteenth Century and After*, lxxviii (1915); H Bernhard, 'Land settlement in Switzerland', *SJA*, ii (1919), pp. 546–8.

in the Highlands, on the other hand, was an ongoing process, with roots as far back as 1886, although it was given new impetus by the debate on reconstruction.[13] The 1919 Act was not a new policy departure, but the latest in a series of Acts dealing with Highland land. This made it possible to regard the Highlands as a special case. Thus the problem being discussed by the committee was a manifestation of the continuing crofting problem, and not a new ex-service problem.[14] The 1919 Act had been passed to accelerate land settlement and to amend existing legislation, and, although the government rhetoric in 1918 and 1919 concentrated on the idea of fulfilling a pledge to war veterans, the internal government discussions made it clear that the Act was primarily intended as an improvement to existing procedures. The problems with the 1911 Act were so serious, and were evident so quickly, that the war probably delayed, rather than encouraged, its amendment.[15]

The Board's right to borrow from the Public Works Loans Commissioners was reduced to £3 million following publication of the *Report of the Committee on National Expenditure* in 1922. This committee (the 'Geddes Committee') has often been seen as a reaction to the heavy expenditure incurred in the immediate post-war era. It followed on the heels of the vocal anti-waste movement, which had campaigned vigorously for reduced public expenditure, and the political impact of the anti-waste movement was among the forces which made the government act. The Treasury may have been suspicious of the Geddes Committee, because of institutional jealousy of outsiders' involvement in the policy-making process, but there can be no doubt that, as far as Scottish land settlement was concerned, they shared the same parsimonious view. Nevertheless, the Geddes Committee echoed the 1921 Cabinet committee in stating that the Highlands were a special case, which should be exempt from the wider economies recommended in the Board's operations. Instead the main areas affected by the 'Geddes Axe' were Lowland land settlement, which was to return to the pre-war basis, and the BoAS's administrative and personnel costs.[16]

A recent author has argued that 'the initial impetus for land settlement during the war years did not emanate from the Highlands of

[13] H. F. Campbell, *Highland Reconstruction* (Glasgow, 1920).

[14] PRO, CAB27/104/134, Land Settlement Committee, 14 Oct. 1920; SRO, AF83/54/1, Land Settlement, Departmental Committee, 6 Mar. 1922; E824/469, Treasury memo, 15 Jul. 1920.

[15] SRO, AF66/41, Memo on land settlement by Under Secretary for Scotland, 13 Mar. 1922; AF66/54, Memo on land settlement in Scotland, 12 Feb. 1924; E824/869, KLTR to Treasury, 3 Sep. 1920.

[16] *PP*, 1922, IX: *Second Interim Report of the Committee on National Expenditure*, pp. 43–4; SRO, GD325/1/369, Memo on Geddes Committee's report; A. MacDonald, 'The Geddes Committee and the formulation of public expenditure policy, 1921–22', *Historical Journal*, xxxii (1989), pp. 643–74; K. O. Morgan, *Consensus and Disunity: The Lloyd George Coalition Government, 1918–1922* (Oxford, 1979), pp. 287–96.

Scotland but from England'.[17] This is a striking thesis. It is based on the existence of committees in the Department of Agriculture and Fisheries, which considered the settlement of ex-servicemen on the land. Certainly, such committees did advocate land settlement; and, moreover, they recommended settlement in colonies, by tenancy, not by purchase.[18] Yet there is no evidence to link these recommendations with Scotland; the ideas are consistent with the details of English land settlement. So far as Scotland, and in particular the Highlands, is concerned, the impetus for post-war land settlement came from the experience of the crofting counties since 1886.

The 1919 Act represented a considerable improvement on its 1911 predecessor, with the removal of the SLC stage leading to much quicker settlement of schemes. Nevertheless, procedure was still complicated, and fresh complaints soon arose about the ponderous nature of the BoAS.

II

The island of Lewis took up a considerable proportion of the BoAS's time and energy. A new consideration was the personality and wealth of its post-war proprietor, the plutocratic Lord Leverhulme, who had acquired the island in 1917. In May 1917, the Board considered that it was time for land settlement proceedings on Lewis to be revived. It was not proposed to carry out the schemes there and then, but rather to prepare them so that they could be implemented swiftly following the end of the war.[19]

When the Board contacted the new proprietor to establish his views on land settlement, it found that he was opposed not only to land settlement, but also to the crofting system. Leverhulme had grandiose plans for the island's development. He argued that he had bought the estate without being aware of the existence of the land settlement schemes.[20] This seems unlikely; but, if it is true, it represents a major failure on the part of his legal agents. It is possible that Skene, Edwards and Garson chose not to advertise the fact specifically that these schemes were pending, in an effort to make the property seem more attractive; by 1917, Major Matheson was in a near bankrupt condition and was desperate to sell Lewis. Despite this possibility, Leverhulme must have been aware of the existence of the general, ongoing, process of land settlement.

Leverhulme regarded crofting as an unhealthy and uneconomic mode

17 Leneman, *Fit For Heroes?*, p. 20.
18 *PP*, 1916, XII. *Report of the Departmental Committee on Land Settlement for Soldiers and Sailors*.
19 SRO, AF67/390, Memo by R. P Wright, 15 May 1917
20 SRO, AF83/73, R. P Wright to T Wilson, 21 Aug. 1918

of life, and its extension by the government a 'gross waste of public money'. He pointed out that a croft occupied only a small proportion of a man's time for a very small return, and regarded it as a millstone round a potential wage labourer's neck. At this stage he was only in favour of granting very small allotments which could be worked in the employee's spare time. He pointed out that the Lewis farms were not big enough to meet the demand for smallholdings even if they were all utilised, and a partial settlement could only lead to more agrarian trouble. Therefore, he suggested that the Board should not proceed with the schemes until it had had an opportunity of evaluating his own contribution to the island.[21]

The Board and the government were reluctant to give such an undertaking at this stage, while the new legislation was going through Parliament and just after it was passed. At the same time, they were aware of the scale of Leverhulme's commitment to the island, and did not want to be identified as the cause of his withdrawing his own plans, with all their potential benefits. It was estimated, in March 1919, that the demand for smallholdings and enlargements in Lewis extended to 1,273 applications. Against this, the schemes which the Board had prepared for the farms of Galson, Gress, Carnish and Ardroil, and Orinsay and Stimervay could only cater for 150 applicants. However, if Leverhulme's opposition to land settlement were dropped, another 254 holdings could be created on farms with rentals in the £30–80 category. The Board was keen that land settlement should proceed alongside Leverhulme's plans; it was hoped that the latter would absorb a considerable amount of the latent demand for land. Leverhulme's absolute position stemmed from the fact that he believed that the breaking up of farms, particularly those near Stornoway, would prejudice the milk supply for the enlarged urban population which he hoped to establish there.[22] But the Board warned Leverhulme that, while it appreciated his good intentions and the scale of his investment, the level of commitment to crofting tenure amongst the population should not be underestimated; and further that, should he persist in his absolute opposition to land settlement, his popularity would be eroded.[23]

The issue was complicated by the renewal of raiding in Lewis when the veterans of the Great War returned. News of raids at Tong, Coll and Gress reached the BoAS at the end of April 1919. The raiders stated that they would have nothing to do with the proprietor's schemes, and declared their absolute and unconditional demand for land; they were willing to deal only with the BoAS, which they regarded as having a duty

21 SRO, AF67/248, Hume, MacGregor and Co. to BoAS, 8 Oct., 9 Oct. 1919; Leverhulme to R. Munro, 21 Sep., 7 Nov. 1918; AF67/251, Leverhulme to R. Munro, 24 Jul. 1919.

22 SRO, AF83/363, Memo on land settlement in Lewis, 5 Mar. 1919.

23 AF83/363, T. Wilson to BoAS, 1 May 1919; AF83/73, R. P. Wright to T. Wilson, 21 Aug. 1918.

to provide them with new holdings. Thomas Wilson, the Board's senior sub-commissioner in the Hebrides, reported that raids could be expected at Galson, Carnish and Ardroil, and Reef.[24] The farms of Coll and Gress became the focus of the three-cornered struggle between the raiders, Leverhulme and the BoAS. For the raiders and the proprietor the issue was straightforward. The former wanted land, while the latter wanted to undertake projects which required the land coveted by the raiders. The situation was more complex for the BoAS. It had a statutory duty to attempt to carry out schemes of land settlement, and Coll and Gress were 'available' as defined by the Act. However, it realised that it would be open to justified vilification, if it were perceived as the cause of Leverhulme's carrying out his threat to cancel his projects if land settlement on these farms was carried out. Fortunately, by the autumn of 1919, the raiders had been persuaded to leave the farms.

The year 1920 saw the situation become much more serious, as the three-dimensional nature of the argument on Lewis was made clearer. Indeed, 1920 was a difficult year for the Board. In the autumn, it decided that its funds were fully committed, and it announced that it could not consider any new schemes. Compulsory procedure could be used to carry out land settlement on Gress, but in the case of Coll, which was rented at less than £80, Leverhulme's co-operation was required.[25] Renewed raids in January 1920 produced a crisis situation.[26] Leverhulme adopted a twin-track approach, abandoning all his projects in the rural districts of Lewis and deciding to concentrate solely on Stornoway and on Harris. He also took out interdicts against the raiders, in an attempt to prevent them from occupying Coll and Gress. One of Leverhulme's constant refrains was that the problems caused by an isolated minority, who insisted on raiding farms, did not blight his relationship with the people of Harris – who had appealed to his vanity by renaming the township of Obbe in his honour.[27]

Misinterpretation followed the government's attempt to deal with the raiders in the autumn of 1920. The Lord Advocate, T. B. Morrison, was sent to Lewis to meet the raiders and ascertain their views. He obtained an undertaking from them that they would withdraw from Coll and Gress and not renew their occupation until the following spring, but made no mention of any promise that land would be found for them. For their part, however, the raiders believed that such a promise had been made, and agreed to withdraw 'in the confident belief', as they put

24 AF83/363, C. MacDonald to BoAS, 16 Mar. 1919; AF67/251, R. Graham to BoAS, 27 Apr. 1919; T. Wilson to BoAS, 1 May 1919; AF67/324, Police reports, Stornoway and Back, 8 Apr. 1919.

25 AF67/325, BoAS to the Scottish Office, 15 Mar. 1920; *BoAS Annual Report, 1920*, p. xv.

26 SRO, AF67/252, R. Graham to BoAS, 19 Jan. 1920.

27 N. Nicolson, *Lord of the Isles: Lord Leverhulme in the Hebrides* (London, 1960); Leneman, *Fit For Heroes?*, p. 120; SRO, AF67/251, Leverhulme to J. Morrison, 18 Aug. 1919; Leverhulme to R. Munro, 18 Aug. 1918.

it, 'that there will now be no further delay on the part of the Board'.[28] Whatever the truth of the opposing claims surrounding the Lord Advocate's mission to Lewis, the raiders certainly thought that they had elicited a promise from the BoAS. Meanwhile, the Board was putting pressure on the government in October 1920. It described the immediate aftermath of Morrison's report as an 'opportune moment' to proceed with land settlement, and stressed that this window of opportunity would close if no progress was made by the spring.[29]

Leverhulme spent the winter of 1920 organising meetings throughout Lewis, in which his proposals were put to the vote. The majority of these meetings endorsed his projects, but, significantly, those in the district of Back, where Coll and Gress were situated, were more equivocal. As a scientific test of opinion, these meetings did not satisfy the Board. Nevertheless, Munro, the Secretary for Scotland, agreed to Leverhulme's demand that he should be allowed to pursue his development plans for ten years, and be given a pledge that no farms would be broken up for land settlement. Before making this agreement, Munro had informed the Cabinet of the situation in Lewis, pointing out that the conditions demanded by Leverhulme – a cessation of raiding and a promise that the BoAS would not use its compulsory powers for ten years – could not be met in full. It is also clear, from Munro's memo to the Cabinet, that he would have preferred land settlement and the development projects to proceed simultaneously. He felt that Leverhulme's plans, if successful, could provide a more comprehensive solution to the problems of the island than any government policy; therefore he recommended that Leverhulme should be given 'his chance'. In return for this, Lord Leverhulme offered five farms on the west coast: Maelistra, Carnish and Ardroil, Timisgarry, Reef, and Dalbeg.[30] They were quickly settled, using Part II of the Land Settlement Act, and the holders were given entry to the fifty-seven new holdings and 170 enlargements on Whit Sunday 1921. Unfortunately for the future peace of the island, the Coll and Gress raiders would not accept land on the west coast.[31] They still regarded themselves as the parties to an agreement with the BoAS whereby they would receive holdings on the farms of Coll and Gress – although the Secretary for Scotland was at pains to assure them that no such promise existed.[32]

June 1921 saw the third of an annual series of raids on Coll and

28 SRO, AF67/254, Report by the Lord Advocate, 12 Oct. 1920; M. Campbell and M. Graham to T. B. Morrison, 20 Oct., 23 Oct. 1920.

29 AF67/254, BoAS to R. Munro, 22 Oct. 1922.

30 AF67/254, Leverhulme to R. Munro, 1 Nov. 1920; PRO, CAB24/117/265–8, Land settlement in Lewis: memo by the Secretary for Scotland, 27 Dec. 1920.

31 SRO, AF83/718, Memo *re* agreement between BoAS and Lord Leverhulme, 1 Feb. 1921; A. Rose to J. Lamb 17 Feb. 1921; D. Shaw to BoAS, 2 Mar. 1921.

32 SRO, AF67/333, M. Graham and A. Graham to R. Munro, 14 Apr. 1921; R. Munro to M. Graham and A. Graham, 25 Apr. 1921; *BoAS Annual Report, 1920*, p. xix.

Gress. These were to have profound results. Leverhulme had no hesitation in stopping all his development works. In September, therefore, Munro informed Leverhulme that, from his point of view, the agreement of December 1920 had been breached, and that he intended to proceed with land settlement on Coll and Gress. He justified his action in terms of the duty conferred on him, as Secretary for Scotland, by the 1919 Land Settlement Act. Munro has been criticised for the 'alacrity' with which he withdrew from the agreement of December 1920. However, at the time the agreement was reached, Munro was far from convinced of the value of Leverhulme's plans; and, moreover, he was aware of the agreement's likely effect. He informed the Cabinet:

> I fear that if and when a public announcement is made that only a very small and local scheme of land settlement is to proceed, raiding will be renewed, and Lord Leverhulme will cease his operations. This risk, I think, must be faced.[33]

Munro was not only uneasy about concluding the agreement, but less than sanguine about its value. It is not surprising that he should have taken the first opportunity to withdraw from it.

Coll and Gress contained only a small proportion of arable land. A scheme was also proposed for Orinsay and Stimervay in Lochs, which were described as being of 'little agricultural value'. An appeal was made to the Treasury to grant the necessary money for this without having the usual detailed estimates supplied; the 'special urgency' of land settlement on Lewis was used as a justification for such an unusual procedure. The Treasury agreed reluctantly, on the condition that the expenditure was limited to £200 per holding.[34]

As there were more applicants than holdings, a ballot had to be conducted. Leverhulme tried unsuccessfully to persuade the Board that the raiders should be excluded from it. The Board, however, was well aware that their exclusion would lead to renewed and intensified trouble. It was therefore decided that involvement in a raid would not be regarded as a disqualification for being given a holding.[35]

The year 1922 saw repeated threats of raids on the farm of Galson on the west coast. Leverhulme was opposed to a land settlement scheme for this farm. But the government argued that its promise, of December 1920, not to use compulsory powers need no longer stand, as Leverhulme had breached his part of the bargain by stopping his

[33] SRO, AF67/331, Leverhulme to R. Munro, 8 Jul. 1921, R. Munro to Leverhulme, 3 Sep., 17 Oct. 1921; PRO, CAB24/117/268, Land settlement in Lewis. memo by the Secretary for Scotland, 27 Dec. 1920; Nicolson, *Lord of the Isles*, p. 181.

[34] SRO, AF83/760, Report on Gress, 17 Nov. 1921, Report on Coll, 17 Nov 1921; Report on Orinsay, 17 Nov. 1921, BoAS to Treasury, 19 Nov 1921, Treasury to BoAS, 25 Nov. 1921

[35] SRO, AF67/331, BoAS to the Scottish Office, 12 May 1922; AF83/760, N MacLean to BoAS, 13 May 1922

development works. Galson, 6,115 acres in extent, was the last remaining substantial farm which had not been broken up. The BoAS had prepared a land settlement scheme for it in 1912, but this had never been implemented, due to the combined difficulties of the war and the unsatisfactory provisions of the Small Landholders Act. The new scheme involved the creation of fifty-seven new holdings. The government still retained a slight hope that Leverhulme would restart his works, and was worried lest the use of compulsory powers would occasion a 'complete break' with him. By January 1923, however, it was clear that all the works were at a standstill and were likely to remain so.[36] In the following month, the Board approached the Treasury to sanction expenditure of £10,069 for the fifty-seven new holdings on Galson. The Treasury was advised to grant this request as the 'district is dangerous',[37] and, despite Leverhulme's opposition, the scheme went ahead.

By 1924, all the large farms and some of the smaller ones had been utilised for land settlement. Leverhulme was now taking steps to dispose of Lewis and concentrate his activities on the less troublesome island of Harris. His proprietorship of Lewis has led to considerable historical debate.[38] Among other things, it has been argued that his departure was a lost opportunity for the island. It has been further conjectured that some judicious compromise by the raiders and the government, as well as by Leverhulme, could have seen land settlement proceed alongside the development works. It is impossible to be certain on these points. But it should be borne in mind that Leverhulme held the crofting system in utter contempt, and had done so from his earliest connection with the island. He was an 'individualist', and felt that action taken in common could never be successful: land settlement, in his view, 'made the permanent solution of the problems of Lewis impossible'.[39] There does not seem to be any basis for compromise in such an attitude. On the other hand, Leverhulme was capable of agreeing to land settlement in certain circumstances. His consent to the schemes on the Uig farms, in the winter of 1920–1, was in his view a realistic price to pay for the security of an agreement with Munro that the compulsory powers of the BoAS would henceforth be suspended.

There were a number of considerations which added to the difficulty of the situation. Coll and Gress had become the focus of the Lewis land problem. Prior to the concession over the west-coast farms in 1921,

36 AF83/767, BoAS to Under Secretary for Scotland, 1 Dec. 1922; Scottish Office memo, 2 Dec. 1922; BoAS to Scottish Office, 20 Jan. 1923; Scottish Office memo, 7 Feb. 1923; Report on Galson, 14 Mar. 1923.

37 SRO, E824/572, BoAS to Treasury, 10 Feb. 1923; KLTR to Treasury, 14 Feb. 1923; Treasury to BoAS, 20 Feb. 1923.

38 Nicolson, *Lord of the Isles*, p. 277; Leneman, *Fit For Heroes?*, pp. 118–25; Hunter, *Crofting Community*, p. 277.

39 Nicolson, *Lord of the Isles*, pp. 178–9; SRO, AF67/248, Leverhulme to Munro, 7 Nov. 1918; AF67/331, Leverhulme to Munro, 9 May 1921.

Leverhulme used every argument at his disposal in an attempt to dissuade the Board from breaking up these farms. Their proximity to Stornoway, in particular, had allowed him to argue that land settlement would prejudice the milk supply to that town. This argument was attacked at the time by BoAS officials, and historians have also pointed out its weakness. It may have given a point for discussion, but Leverhulme elevated it to the position of a fundamental obstacle to the break-up of the farms. The Board's view, however, was that if Stornoway developed as Leverhulme anticipated, Coll and Gress would never be able to supply it with milk. Although compromise should have been possible on this point, in reality it was extremely unlikely, given Leverhulme's general aims.[40]

The land raids at Coll, Gress and Orinsay, and the threats at Galson, undoubtedly intensified Leverhulme's opposition to land settlement. It was his belief that the raiders were an isolated minority, and that their point of view was abhorred by the rest of the population. He informed the Board that 'out of the 32,000 people in Lewis, only thirty are raiders' – who he described as a 'small number of misguided men'[41] The establishment figures in Stornoway – business men and senior local government officials – supported Leverhulme.[42] As for the rural areas, Leverhulme made much of the fact that, in 1921, he was able to garner 9,000 signatures for a petition supporting his schemes. The series of public meetings organised later that year also seemed to indicate majority support for him. However, there were problems with both these tests of opinion. The petition was a simple statement of support for the development plans, but Leverhulme used it in an attempt to isolate the raiders. Clearly, most people were likely to support the plans with their promise of prosperity; yet this did not preclude them from having sympathy, at least, with the raiders. The Lord Advocate reported that his impression was that the majority of the population actually wanted the land settlement and Leverhulme's development plans to proceed together. The same point applies to Leverhulme's meetings. In addition, the BoAS did not regard them as valid, because there was no way of ascertaining whether the attendance was representative or not; it would have preferred an individual, rather than a mass, test of opinion.[43]

Much attention has been given to a meeting held at Gress in March 1919, supposedly attended by 1,000 people. Leverhulme addressed this

[40] AF67/252, Memo by R. Wright for the Secretary for Scotland, 15 Mar 1920; Nicolson, *Lord of the Isles*, pp. 130–2

[41] AF67/256, Leverhulme to R. Munro, 9 Mar 1920, AF67/331, Leverhulme to Munro, 18 May 1921.

[42] PRO, CAB24/117/273, A. Munro to R. Munro, 27 Nov 1920.

[43] SRO, AF83/363, C. MacDonald to BoAS, 16 Mar 1919; AF67/251, Memo by T. Wilson, 23 Sep. 1919; AF67/252, Memo, Mar. 1920; AF67/254, Lord Advocate's Report, 12 Oct. 1920; *The Scotsman*, 20 Oct. 1919, 24 May 1920

meeting, outlined his projects, and predicted the prosperity which they would bring about. The intervention of one of the anti-Leverhulme faction drew a rapturous response. However, so did Leverhulme's contribution. The date of the Gress meeting is significant: March 1919 was before the first of the raids on Coll and Gress, and before the main government attempt to persuade Leverhulme to give up the farms for land settlement. Nicolson's comment, 'it was not easy then to assess where the majority feeling lay', therefore seems the most sensible conclusion.[44]

The raiders argued that the rest of the population 'understood' what they were doing. Significantly, they also pointed out that the raids did not necessarily indicate opposition to Leverhulme; merely that they considered their claim to the land to be of more importance.[45] What is very clear is that Leverhulme quickly developed an intense dislike for the raiders and their actions – so much so that he wished to exclude them from the ballot for holdings on the farms. Leverhulme was not used to dealing with obstacles that could not be cleared immediately with a judiciously applied sum of money. The commercial world to which he was accustomed could not prepare him for the complexities of dealing with land raids in Lewis. Even government officials with long years of experience found this a task of considerable difficulty!

In his attempt to prevent Coll and Gress being taken for land settlement, Leverhulme pointed out that these farms would not be sufficient to satisfy the demand for land on the island, and that if they were taken it would only increase the potential for trouble. He also argued that it was impossible to create 'economic' or self-sufficient holdings on the farms; it was obvious that Coll and Gress – indeed all the farm land in Lewis – was insufficient for this purpose. However, it seems contradictory for Leverhulme to have made this assertion, if he truly believed that the raiders were in such a small minority. Settlement of Coll and Gress might have taken the heat out of the situation; as it was, the fact that other farms were settled before Coll and Gress only added to the feeling of grievance among the raiders.[46]

In general, it seems that most of the population of Lewis were prepared to give Leverhulme's projects the benefit of the doubt while they were likely to go ahead. Once that likelihood passed, however, they returned to their demands for land. In 1919, the total demand for new holdings and enlargements in Lewis amounted to 1,273 applications. The corresponding

[44] Hunter, *Crofting Community*, pp. 197–8; Leneman, *Fit For Heroes?*, p. 119; D. MacDonald, *Lewis: A History of the Island* (Edinburgh, 1978), pp. 179–80; Nicolson, *Lord of the Isles*, p. 139.

[45] Ibid., pp. 140–2.

[46] SRO, AF67/256, Leverhulme to R. Munro, 9 Mar. 1920; AF67/331, Leverhulme to Munro, 18 May 1921; AF67/238, Report on Coll and Gress, 4 May 1921; Nicolson, *Lord of the Isles*, p. 178.

figure for 1923, after the settlement of the four west-coast farms and the suspension of Leverhulme's development projects, was 1,098.[47]

Insufficient attention has been paid to the years prior to Leverhulme's proprietorship. The land raids were not isolated, discontinuous events. There had actually been a long-standing attempt by government institutions to create new holdings in Lewis. But the CDB, and the BoAS up to 1921, had been singularly unsuccessful in this regard. Indeed, it could be argued that Leverhulme was an easier proprietor to deal with than Major Matheson had been. He was far from reticent in stating his position, whereas Matheson had tended to hide behind a screen of legal technicalities.

Finally, despite all the attention given to the Leverhulme period, the most noticeable point about it has been ignored by past historians. This is the fact that, despite the strong opposition of the proprietor, practically all the available farmland in Lewis was, in fact, eventually utilised for land settlement. In the period from 1919 to 1925, 237 new holdings were created on eleven farms, at a total cost of £71,809.[48] This clearly demonstrates the superiority of the Land Settlement (Scotland) Act over all the other previous legislation.

III

In contrast to the difficulties which the BoAS encountered on Lewis, the operation of the 1919 Act on Skye was much more straightforward. Skye had been the scene of major land settlement in the first decade of the century, and the events at Kilmuir and Glendale have been discussed in detail above. Nevertheless, there was still considerable outstanding demand for land. The principal area of activity for the Board in the post-war period was in the west and south of the island. Employing the provisions of Part I of the 1919 Act, the Board acquired 60,000 acres from MacLeod of MacLeod. The family was in dire financial straits, and the £56,809 which it received in 1920 was much needed. The Board, in attempting to convince the Treasury that such expenditure was useful, referred to the intensity of demand in Skye and the likelihood of trouble if nothing was done. The estate contained eighty small-sized holdings in need of enlargement. The entire 60,000 acres allowed the Board to create 142 new holdings and enlarge a further seventy-five, for a total expenditure of £140,136.[49] The reference to potential raiding can partly

47 SRO, AF83/363, Memo on land settlement in Lewis, 5 Mar 1919; AF67/391, BoAS to the Under Secretary for Scotland, 21 Apr 1923

48 SRO, AF83/760, BoAS to the Treasury, 19 Nov. 1921, AF83/718, Minute to BoAS concerning Lewis farms, 13 Jul. 1921, E824/572, BoAS to the Treasury, 10 Feb., 1923, E824/606, BoAS to the Treasury, 6 May 1925.

49 E824/615, BoAS to the Under Secretary for Scotland, 23 Mar 1920; Treasury to BoAS, 27 Mar. 1920.

be explained as the BoAS's tactic to persuade the Treasury of the immediate need for expenditure. Nevertheless, there was some substance to the claim. Over the period from 1919 to 1922, there had been seven raids in Skye, including three on the land which the Board purchased from MacLeod of MacLeod.[50] In addition, the Board received nine statements of intent to raid, three of which emanated from the former MacLeod estate.[51] In this period, the Board was inundated with threats of raids, from all over the crofting counties. A large number of these could be, and were, safely ignored; but in Skye and the Outer Hebrides, a long-standing tradition of raiding meant that threats from those areas merited cautious treatment. One of the reasons for the persistence of the disturbed atmosphere in Skye, after the purchase of this land, was that the Board could not proceed immediately to break it up. The farms on the estate only became available to the Board as the leases expired.[52]

The farms of Drynoch and North Talisker came into the Board's hands in 1923. North Talisker was used to settle migrants from Lewis and Harris, in the first large scale migration scheme since the idea became part of government policy in 1897.[53] A migration scheme had wider significance than the mere movement of people from one place to another. It represented an honest attempt to see land settlement as a total policy, rather than as an *ad hoc* method of settling various local difficulties. At the same time, the BoAS had a specific desire to deal with the congestion in Lewis and Harris. The land available for settlement in those islands was insufficient to deal with the local demand, and that, together with the complications raised by Leverhulme, led to unrest. The likely contribution of a migration scheme to quelling such unrest was emphasised by the Board in their various submissions to the Treasury on the matter. The argument was successful, as the Treasury granted £30,000 for the scheme.[54]

The North Talisker settlement was eventually composed of sixty-eight holdings, sixty-three of which were tenanted by migrants from Lewis and Harris. The total population approached 400. The settlers were able to pursue a number of different methods of earning money. Some went to the East Coast to fish, while others were involved in the tweed industry. There was a club stock, with 1,600 sheep, on the grazing land of the farm, and there was also arable cultivation, though that took some

50 SRO, AF67/148, 151, 157, 171.
51 AF67/148, 150, 154, 156.
52 Leneman, *Fit For Heroes?*, p. 137.
53 *BoAS Annual Reports, 1920*, p. xiv; *1921*, p. xvi.
54 SRO, E824/659, BoAS to the Treasury, 7 Mar. 1923; Treasury to BoAS, 29 Mar. 1923; E824/538, BoAS to the Treasury, 6 Nov. 1923; Treasury memo, 27 Nov. 1923; BoAS to the Treasury, 29 Feb. 1924; 'Land settlement in Skye – Migration schemes', *SJA*, vii (1924).

time to gather momentum. On the whole, the variety of activity gives the impression of a thriving settlement.[55]

The settlers were better off as tenants of the BoAS than of a private landlord. With a government institution as landlord, there was an element of stability which was lacking even with the best of private landlords. Further, the support offered by the BoAS was second to none. As well as the various forms of monetary and practical assistance which were available, Board tenants had access to agricultural education facilities and expert advice on matters of cultivation and husbandry. Private landlords may have provided equipment on occasion, though very rarely in the crofting counties; the crucial difference was that they would charge a market rent based on the value of their contribution. The BoAS allowed the SLC to set a fair rent for all new holdings created under their auspices. Like Glendale, the most successful of the CDB settlements, North Talisker with its club stock had scope for producing income other than from the bare holdings of the settlers. Moreover, the involvement of the settlers in the tweed industry added another economic dimension.[56]

There were a number of other schemes in Skye in this period. The 1911 Act was employed to create twenty-one new holdings at Drinan and Glasnakille, near Elgol, on the Strathaird estate. Using the provisions of Part II of the 1919 Act, twenty-two new holdings and sixty-six enlargements were formed on the Waternish estate. The 16,000-acre grazing farm of Scorrybreck, north of Portree, part of the MacDonald estates, was acquired under Part I of the 1919 Act. The farm of Claigan, adjacent to Dunvegan, was also broken up under Part II (in the face of proprietorial opposition from MacLeod of MacLeod), to create fifteen new holdings. Two points are worthy of note here. In terms of policy, it proved easier to carry out schemes under Part I of the 1919 Act, that is purchasing the land outright prior to settlement, than under Part II, which, after all, was simply a more efficient version of the unpopular 1911 Act. Secondly, it is interesting to note that the BoAS deliberately used the fact that some farms had been raided and others were under threat as a tactic to persuade the Treasury to sanction expenditure. In general, in the period 1919–25, the Board's efforts in Skye resulted in the creation of 218 new holdings and 143 enlargements of existing holdings.[57]

Skye was thus one of the most fruitful areas of operation for the Board in this period – so much so that the BoAS Director of Land Settlement admitted to a Skye farmer, 'we have so much land being subdivided in Skye at the moment that the immediate pressure is

[55] SRO, AF83/30, Report on North Talisker, Dec 1924

[56] *BoAS Annual Report*, p. xvi, Leneman, *Fit For Heroes?*, pp 143–4

[57] SRO, E824/647, BoAS to the Treasury, 17 Jan. 1921; AF67/158, Memo on Strathaird; AF83/667, BoAS to the Under Secretary for Scotland, 7 Mar 1925.

relieved to a great extent'.[58] This success was based on a fortuitous state of decay among the proprietors of Skye. MacLeod of MacLeod was practically insolvent, and was only too happy to divest himself of 60,000 acres and receive over £56,000 for them. The MacDonald estates were under Trusteeship, due to the mental incapacity of Lord MacDonald, and the Trustees were keen to realise as many assets as possible; hence they responded favourably to the Board's enquiries concerning the farm of Scorrybreck, described by a government official 'as one of the best sheep farms in Scotland'.[59] The conditions for taking over farms under Part I of the Act were propitious. Part II schemes, however, remained a source of contention. This is entirely consistent with the proprietorial reaction to land settlement since the 1880s. Landlords, when faced with a proposal to break up a farm, would rather have it taken off their hands altogether than become involved in the business of creating and administering smallholdings.

IV

It has been noted that in some cases the BoAS used the existence and threat of raids in Skye to its own advantage in some cases. This, however, was not always possible; it could not, for instance, be done at Strathaird on Skye, or on Raasay. The land raids which took place there are significant because of the impact they had on the government's response to raids. The perennial government dilemma was that to grant the requests of raiders would only encourage other raids; while not to do so would only intensify the original grievances.

The case of Raasay is particularly interesting. It had come to the Board's attention before the war; but little could be done then because of the inadequacies of the 1911 Act. Raasay was owned by the Coatbridge firm of William Baird and Co., Ironfounders, which was interested in Raasay only for the exploitation of its iron ore deposits. It was not keen to have smallholdings established. By 1920, however, Baird's industrial operations in Raasay were at a standstill, and with the improved facilities of the 1919 legislation, the idea of a scheme for the island was revived. The BoAS began negotiations for a scheme of migration for men from Raasay and the neighbouring island of Rona, and the consequent enlargement of the remaining Raasay crofts; but these negotiations were interrupted when cottars from Rona took possession of lands at the south-eastern end of Raasay. The usual process of serving and breaching of interdicts led to the raiders' incarceration in late 1921. The Secretary

[58] AF83/663, H. A. Rose to J. T. Cameron, 23 Mar. 1921.

[59] SRO, E824/647, KLTR to the Treasury, 27 Jan. 1921; Clan Donald Centre, Lord MacDonald Papers, bundle 3666, fos. 7–9, Dundas and Wilson to Sir A. Abdy [Lord MacDonald's Curator], 28 Mar. 1919; bundle 3675, Memo by W. Murray, *re* Scorrybreck, 28 Jan. 1920.

for Scotland, Robert Munro, responded to this situation with uncharacteristic firmness, declaring that henceforth, raiding would operate as a bar to land settlement.[60] The BoAS, however, took a different view to that of the Scottish Office. It was much more sympathetic to the plight of the raiders; Thomas Wilson, who had visited them in prison, was especially sympathetic. There was no doubt that the conditions on Rona were dreadful. The problem was that only one of the raiders possessed the ex-service qualification, so they could not be given priority treatment, if the letter of the law was to be followed.

While the Scottish Office was declaring against land raids, the Board was approaching the Treasury with a proposition to purchase Raasay: the only possible method of preventing the raiders from reoccupying the land was to 'project a scheme at once'. The Treasury was horrified at the potential expense of purchasing Raasay and settling penniless cottars on new holdings, but it was eventually persuaded to allow the Board to go to £20,000 in an effort to purchase. The island was secured in March 1922 for £18,000. Tentative BoAS predictions indicated that a further £14–15,000 would be required to take over the sheep-stock and to equip the new holdings. The initial settlement of the island was hampered by an outbreak of typhus, which meant that only seven applicants were settled in 1922; but more progress was made the following year, when over thirty applicants were settled.[61]

There are a number of issues here which are worthy of exploration. Clearly, there was a good deal of sympathy for the conditions which the raiders had to tolerate on Rona: the Lord Advocate described them as 'dreadful'. However, at the executive level in the BoAS, and in the Scottish Office, this sympathy was tempered by awareness of the wider context. Dreadful congestion existed in other parts of the Highlands, and raids had occurred elsewhere. No politically defensible argument could be found for priority treatment for Raasay; indeed in 1920, when prioritising various land settlement schemes, the Board did not highlight Raasay. There was also a shortage of money for land settlement in 1920, which gave another reason for not taking action.[62] The BoAS subcommissioners, who were in contact with the raiders, persuaded the Board that the only way of dealing with the difficulty was to purchase the island, but they, of course, did not have any high political considerations; their brief was simply to ascertain the most effective way of dealing with given situations as they found them. There was also the usual worry about whether giving in to raiders would encourage raids in

[60] SRO, E824/369, BoAS to the Treasury, 30 Dec. 1921, AF67/149, Memo on Raasay, 19 Mar. 1921; Police reports, Portree, 2 Apr., 9 Apr. 1921; *BoAS Annual Report, 1922*, p. xvii.

[61] SRO, E824/369, BoAS to the Treasury, 30 Dec. 1921; Treasury memo, 3 Jan. 1922; BoAS to Treasury, 30 Mar. 1922; *BoAS Annual Report, 1922*, p. xv.

[62] SRO, AF67/149, Lord Advocate to Secretary for Scotland, 14 Oct. 1921, Memo on Raasay, 19 Mar. 1921

other places, which had been evident since the 1880s. Many felt that the continuation of raiding throughout the decades after the 1886 Act was caused by an initial failure to deal with it firmly. However, the issue was not as simple as that. There was a general expectation of land settlement in the Hebrides, and it was the Board's failure to satisfy this demand – an almost impossible task – which perpetuated raiding. Raiders, moreover, had never shown any signs of being discouraged by a firm hand; indeed, that tended to inflame already heated situations. Thus the Board had little choice, as the CDB had discovered earlier, but to deal sensibly with the raiders' demands.

A similar situation had arisen at Balranald in North Uist. Here, two separate raids had occurred by 1921, and extreme difficulty was encountered in removing the raiders. The BoAS proposed the establishment of sixteen new holdings and thirty-two enlargements. But once the raiders were removed, the Board faced the problem of going ahead with the scheme and including those who had broken the law. It did so, because it tended to view raids as a symptom of frustrated land hunger, rather than as a challenge to its authority, and realised that the only prospect of peace was to proceed with the land settlement scheme. Thus Balranald was acquired at Whit Sunday 1922, and a revised scheme for twenty-two new holdings and thirty enlargements was implemented.[63]

In the case of Raasay, the ex-service priority was an obstacle to land settlement. This was a general problem faced by the Board. In some areas it was impossible to find sufficient ex-servicemen to proceed with a scheme; but the virtual exclusion of civilians prejudiced the possibility of schemes for both categories. Clearly the men from Rona were needy applicants, regardless of their wartime activities. However, the government had realised that there was political mileage in generous treatment for war veterans. The problem was that, in the Highlands, land settlement was not a post-war innovation – as the Treasury, under pressure from the BoAS, recognised in 1922, commenting:

> Men have been waiting for holdings for some time, and their demands have been actively renewed since the war. In the peculiar circumstances of the crofting districts, the preference given by the 1919 Act cannot be absolute.[64]

[63] SRO, E824/524, BoAS to Under Secretary for Scotland, 11 Mar. 1921; BoAS to Treasury, 19 Apr., 21 Apr. 1921, 13 Oct. 1922; GD325/1/249, Correspondence relating to Balranald, May–Aug. 1921.

[64] *BoAS Annual Report, 1921*, pp. xvi–xvii; SRO E824/369, Treasury memo, 3 Jan. 1922.

V

Despite the considerable amount of land settlement activity which had occurred on the Gordon Cathcart estates on the Uists and Barra prior to 1919, there were a number of farms still available for settlement. Askernish, which was made available for smallholdings in 1919, proved a source of continuing difficulty, as has been discussed in Chapter 7, above. Activity in the post-1919 period also concentrated on the farms of Drimore and Drimsdale (on South Uist), and Nunton (on Benbecula).

The BoAS had made enquiries about Drimore before the war, but decided to drop the scheme in 1915.[65] However, 1919 saw renewed applications for this farm. The estate was still opposed to land settlement, arguing that the farm was an intrinsic part of a cluster of three farms which were worked as a group, and that it constituted the estate's home farm. The farm was then raided, in November 1919,[66] and the tenacity of these raiders in holding on to the land, coupled with a second raid in December 1920, induced the estate to enter into negotiations with the Board. The raiders were still in possession in March of the following year, making the proper working of the farm impossible, and actually producing entreaties from Skene, Edwards and Garson to the Board to constitute smallholdings! The fact that the tenant of the farm was prepared to offer concessions to the Board, on his departure from the farm, encouraged consideration of a scheme. A proposal for the constitution of eleven new holdings and forty-six enlargements was prepared and sanctioned by the Treasury.[67]

The pattern of events in South Uist and Benbecula mirrored very closely those of earlier periods. The estate initially stated its opposition to land settlement very strongly, but it seemed to cave in when raids occurred. This pattern was repeated in the case of Nunton farm, on Benbecula.[68]

This pattern of vacillation in the face of pressure had its origins in the growing disillusionment of the elderly Lady Gordon Cathcart with her Hebridean estate. By August 1921, her solicitors informed the Board that it was their view that 'the day for private ownership in these parts is passed'; and they advised the proprietor that due to the 'never ending' trouble of the estate, it would be in her interests to dispose of it. Contact was made with the Board in an attempt to arrange a sale, but nothing came of it.[69] There is no clear evidence as to why that was so. However,

65 SRO, AF83/206, SEG to BoAS, 27 Mar 1914; AF83/207, BoAS to SEG, 19 Mar. 1915.
66 AF83/207, BoAS to SEG 24 May 1919; SEG to BoAS, 26 May, 9 Aug., 6 Nov. 1919.
67 AF83/212, SEG to BoAS, 6 Dec. 1919, 7 Dec 1920, 16 Mar 1921, E824/560, BoAS to Treasury, 7 Sep., 1921.
68 SRO, AF83/230, Memo on Nunton Benbecula; SEG to BoAS, 15 Dec 1922, BoAS to SEG, 18 Jul 1923.
69 AF83/213, SEG to BoAS, 31 Aug. 1921, SEGP, deed box A6, Lady Gordon Cathcart, no. 6, bundle 5, Correspondence between Lady Gordon Cathcart and James Garson, Mar 1921

given the prevailing political conditions, it would seem likely that the Board would have found it difficult to gain Treasury sanction for the heavy expenditure such a purchase would involve. Furthermore, the Board would not have much to gain from such a transaction. By the early 1920s, most of the farms on the estate had already been broken up, and so, by acquiring the land, the Board would only have been increasing its management expenses at a time when it was under pressure to economise.

By the mid-1920s, the Board found that all the land available for smallholdings had been exhausted – though that is not to argue that all the demand for land had actually been satisfied. This was the area with the longest history of government-sponsored land settlement: the proprietor of North Uist had been the first to approach the CDB with land, considerable activity had taken place on the islands of Benbecula and South Uist, and the small islands of Barra and Vatersay were almost entirely in the hands of crofters by this time. The Board therefore warned that, in future, applicants from that region would have to consider migration or emigration if their demand for land was to be fulfilled.[70]

Developments in Sutherland and Caithness are also worth examining. In the case of the former, there was considerable continuity with the years before 1919. In that period there had been no shortage of land, but it was found that the agricultural conditions of the county, with its heavy reliance on sheep-farming, militated against successful land settlement. The most notable example of this continuing trend concerned the farm of Eriboll, in the north-west of the county. It had been purchased in 1919, for £12,000; but, by the time the BoAS obtained entry in 1921, it found that the price of the stock had risen by 45% compared to the 1919 estimates. Applicants were not forthcoming for the sixteen smallholdings which it was proposed to form on the land: the reason being lack of capital. This scheme was therefore abandoned on the grounds of expense. The loss on the sheep-stock, and the cost of managing the estate, led the Treasury to describe Eriboll as 'an expensive incubus'. Eventually, in September 1926, the BoAS sold Eriboll for £10,000 – £2,000 less than it had paid for it seven years earlier.[71]

The problem behind this failure was the fluctuation in stock prices in the immediate post-war era. Sheep, in particular, had risen in value. New holders were burdened with high annuity-payments for their stock, a difficulty which was accentuated when prices began to decline in the mid-1920s. There was also the problem of compensating the outgoing sheep farmers at high values, which was exacerbated when sheep prices

[70] *BoAS Annual Report, 1924*, pp. xxii–xxiv.

[71] SRO, E824/576, BoAS to the Treasury, 4 Dec. 1925; Treasury memo, 11 Dec. 1925; KLTR to the Treasury, 16 Dec. 1925; BoAS to the Treasury, 9 Sep. 1926.

plummeted in late 1921. Holders were now faced with a drastic reduction in their income. This also created a difficulty for the BoAS in cases where it had taken over sheep at the height of the market, and was forced to pass them on to holders after the fall in prices; the Treasury was disturbed at the prospect of being asked to bear the loss. The Board made much of the fact that the fall in prices was unexpected, but the Treasury had been aware of the likelihood of this as far back as 1919, and had warned the Board in 1920.[72]

In Caithness, the major issue to emerge was the size and economic viability of the holdings. The properties acquired for land settlement in Caithness tended to have a larger proportion of arable land than elsewhere in the Highlands. For example, the proposed holdings on the farm of Upper Dounreay were almost half arable and half pastoral. The farm of Watten consisted of 640 acres of arable land and 2,800 acres of pastoral. At Ormlie, 306 of the 410 acres on the farm were arable.[73] The distance of Caithness from central markets, transport difficulties, and the lack of employment opportunities meant that a larger size of holdings was defensible. In the case of Watten, the Treasury asked for the size of holdings to be reduced and for more men to be settled. The Treasury view of efficiency was to settle the maximum number of men; the KLTR, Sir Kenneth MacKenzie, had stated that ex-service land settlement was unlikely to be 'economic', and that 'the object is to try and get the ex-soldier settled at as small a cost as possible'.[74] The size of the holdings caused problems in attracting applicants. Equipment costs were high, particularly for buildings. Many applicants were short of capital and reluctant to take on heavy burdens; for those who did, difficulties were exacerbated by the sharp fall in the prices of agricultural produce in 1922. The Board's continuing concern over this was reflected, in 1923, by a decision to allow holders settled before 1922, in Lowland and Highland arable areas, to apply to the SLC to have their buildings revalued in the light of current prices.[75]

This debate was echoed in a scheme for Borlum farm, on the Lovat estates in Inverness-shire. It was 56% arable, and the BoAS proposed to form four large holdings of between sixty-five and ninety-eight acres. The Treasury once again complained of the expense of creating small numbers of large holdings, but the BoAS argued that special consideration should be given to the Highlands because of the poor

72 E824/298, BoAS to the Treasury, 1 Dec. 1919; Treasury memo, 19 Jan. 1920; KLTR to the Treasury, 9 Sep. 1920; E824/480, BoAS memo on sheep-stocks, Dec. 1921; Treasury to BoAS, 4 Jan. 1922; KLTR to Treasury, 2 May 1922.

73 E824/559, Treasury memo, 8 Jul. 1921; E824/671, BoAS to Treasury, 28 Nov. 1920; AF83/652, BoAS to the Under Secretary for Scotland, 23 Apr. 1920.

74 SRO, E824/671, Treasury to BoAS, 11 Dec. 1920; E824/559, KLTR to Treasury, 14 Jul. 1921.

75 E824/469, Treasury to BoAS, 21 Dec. 1922; *BoAS Annual Reports, 1921*, p. xvi; *1922*, p. xvi; *1923*, p. xvi.

quality of much of the arable land. Although the holdings were large, the rents were relatively low, at between £18 and £27.[76] Perhaps the key to the attempts at land settlement in Caithness, and at Borlum, was that there was not the same political imperative for maximum settlement in order to prevent raids. Large holdings, likely to be sufficient to sustain a family without recourse to ancillary employment, could therefore be contemplated.

VI

The qualitative contribution of the 1919 Act to the ongoing policy of land settlement is presented in the following tables. Table 6 shows the number of new holdings (NHs) and enlargements (Es) which were created throughout the crofting counties (excluding Orkney and Shetland). As in Table 5 (above, p. 167), the level of land settlement (NHs + Es) is presented as a percentage of the real demand (RD) for land. The figures for each county are divided into holdings created on privately owned land (P), and estates acquired by the BoAS (B).

Table 6: *Land Settlement in the Crofting Counties, 1912–1925*[77]

County		NHs	Es	RD	% RD Settled
Caithness	P	26	5	826	15.5
	B	84	13		
Sutherland	P	62	109	1351	22.6
	B	27	108		
Ross	P	312	369	2111	34.2
	B	40	—		
Inverness	P	275	288	3942	30.5
	B	467	172		
Argyll	P	226	103	1370	29.8
	B	52	27		
TOTAL	P	901	874		
TOTAL	B	670	320		
GRAND TOTAL		1571	1194	9600	28.8

The contribution of the 1919 Act to land settlement can be clearly seen. The percentage of the demand for land settled was obviously a vast improvement on the pre-1919 situation, which is illustrated in Table 5.

[76] SRO, E824/536, BoAS to Treasury, 26 Sep. 1921; Treasury memo, 3 Oct. 1921; KLTR to Treasury, 18 Oct. 1921; BoAS to Treasury, 13 Dec. 1921; Treasury to BoAS, 20 Apr. 1922.

[77] From *BoAS Annual Reports, 1912–1925*.

Table 7 illustrates land settlement in the Hebrides alone. These are the heartland of the crofting community, and both the demand and the rate of settlement were higher than in the crofting counties as a whole. In Skye, Lewis and the Southern Hebrides, however, land settlement was taken to its maximum level by 1925. This was only sufficient to settle around 40% of the demand.

Table 7: *Hebridean Land Settlement, 1912–1925*[78]

Island		NHs	Es	RD	% RD Settled
Skye	P	59	51	1304	38.5
	B	278	114		
Lewis	P	262	278	1344	40.2
	B	—	—		
Harris	P	32	27	337	17.5
	B	—	—		
North Uist	P	4	31	447	39.6
	B	87	55		
South Uist	P	140	87	546	41.6
	B	—	—		
Barra	P	3	33	392	26.3
	B	67	—		
TOTAL	P	500	507		
TOTAL	B	432	169		
GRAND TOTAL		932	676	4370	36.8

There were two outstanding difficulties for the BoAS in conducting land settlement in this period. First, the demand for land was vociferous. It was articulated most prominently by means of the land raid, especially in the Hebrides. The BoAS had noted in 1914 that the demands of the raiders were limited, which is consistent with the pattern of agitation since the 1880s.[79] But the political imperative for the maximum settlement of demand distorted the pattern of land settlement throughout the period. And what was achieved did nothing to prevent or blunt the impact of economic depression in the 1930s.

The second problem faced by the Board was the attitude of the Treasury to land settlement. It often voiced disquiet over expenditure on land settlement. The Board, however, was politically adept, and emphasised the volatile situation in the Highlands; it also stressed the importance of land settlement as a social policy which could not be judged by economic results alone. By the judicious use of such

[78] From ibid.

[79] *BoAS Annual Report, 1914*, p. xi.

arguments, the Board actually did fairly well in extracting money from the Treasury.[80]

The land settlement policy after 1919 was the culmination of various attempts to deal with the Highland land issue since 1886. For this reason, the ex-service preference merely added to the complications of land settlement.[81] Although those demanding land adapted their rhetoric to suit prevailing political conditions, the real basis of their demands went much deeper.

80 PRO, CAB27/105/5–7, Land Settlement Committee: Treasury memo; SRO, AF67/387, Memo by H. M. Conacher on economic conditions in the crofting counties, Mar. 1924; AF83/760, BoAS to the Treasury, 19 Nov. 1921; Treasury to BoAS 25 Nov. 1921; Memo by BoAS for the Under Secretary for Scotland, Dec. 1921.

81 AF67/387, Memo by H. M. Conacher; Churchill College, Cambridge, Thurso Collection, THRS, V1/1/12, Lord Novar to A. Sinclair, 18 Jul. 1923.

CHAPTER NINE

Conclusion

In 1883, the government rejected calls for a Royal Commission for the Highlands by arguing that it could not be seen to be taking special action in any particular area of the country. Indeed, it denied that there was such a concept as a peculiarly Highland issue to be dealt with. The Napier Commission and the Crofters' Holdings (Scotland) Act of 1886 were the first, and most important, breaches in this mode of thought. The former established that there actually was a particular Highland issue, and in the latter – after some considerable debate within the Cabinet – the Highland area was defined. The definition, which covered the majority of parishes in the counties of Argyll, Inverness, Ross and Cromarty, Sutherland, Caithness, Orkney and Shetland, remains in force to this day.

However, it was challenged. The abortive bill of 1895 included provisions to extend the crofting area to include parts of upland Aberdeen and Banffshire and Highland Perthshire, where conditions akin to crofting certainly did exist. The failure to extend the crofting area to such districts has led some to make the rather pedantic point that the Highlands are a wider notion than the crofting counties.[1] The Congested Districts (Scotland) Act of 1897 also employed a specialised version of the criteria laid down in 1886. But the statutes of 1911 and 1919 laid this definition aside; they applied to the whole of rural Scotland. This has persuaded various commentators to argue that crofting suffered from a 'loss of identity' in the years between 1911 to 1955, when crofter legislation was restricted again to the crofting counties.[2] However, if the analysis extends beyond the terms of the Acts to the substance of policy, such a view must be qualified. The stormy passage of the 1911 Act was partly caused by the problem of the Lowland proprietors' fear of crofting legislation; consequently, the bill was modified at a late stage to accommodate their worries. These modifications did not affect the provisions for the crofting counties. It is one of the ironies of this period that after much worry about the consequences for the Lowlands of crofting-type legislation, one of the most important and lasting effects of the extension concerned the

[1] H. A. Moisley, 'The Highlands and Islands: a crofting region?', *Transactions of the Institute of British Geographers*, xxxi (1962), pp. 83–4.

[2] MacCuish, 'Crofting legislation'

crofting counties. This was the creation of the concept of 'absentee crofter', in 1917, when the Court of Session adjudged – in a case which had originated in the Lowlands – that a landholder need not continue to reside on, or within two miles of, his holding, as long as those conditions had been satisfied at the time of the passing of the 1911 Act.[3]

So, in effect, there were two separate policies stemming from the one piece of legislation. The situation after 1919 was even more complex. The government was facing heavy fiscal pressure on its expenditure, and the BoAS did not escape the effects. Faced with the prospects of a reduced budget after 1922, it chose to focus most of its attention and the bulk of its money on the Highlands; the potential instability in the Highlands generated by the land raids which occurred in this period was a potent factor in this decision. So, despite the changes in the geographical range of Scottish land legislation in this period, the crofting counties constantly remained a special area needing a particular and unique policy. Meanwhile, however, government attitudes had been turned upside-down. In 1883, the government argued that tenurial problems in the Highlands could be dealt with within the general legal framework governing relations between landlord and tenant. Forty years later, after legislation which had its intellectual origins in the crofting counties was extended to the rest of Scotland, the government was forced to concede that such a framework could not cope with the special demands of the Highlands, which still merited exceptional treatment.

As is to be expected, the geographical range was not the only feature of legislation and policy to change. The forty years from the mid-1880s to the mid-1920s saw governments of many different hues, Liberal, Conservative, and Coalition. The Highland land issue was on the political agenda, at various levels, for most of this time, and in periods like the mid-1880s, 1906–11, and 1919–25 it was quite a high priority for the government of the day. But the aims and content of government policy varied over the period. The impression has often been given that the four major pieces of legislation examined in this book – the statutes of 1886, 1897, 1911 and 1919 – represented a continuous line of cumulative development, so that flaws and failure in one policy were rigorously identified and eliminated in the next Act, which faithfully built on the previous ones.[4] Connected to this is the idea that the increasing level of government intervention which each Act represented was logical: the 1886 Act was intended to regulate tenurial relations which developed by 1919 into provisions for the State itself to act as landowner. There are, however, two major problems with these ideas. First, the 1886 Act was not intended as the basis for a new code of

[3] *Court of Session Cases, 1917*, pp. 453–63, Rogerson v. Chilston.

[4] Day, *Public Administration*, pp. 231–2; W. C. MacKenzie, *The Highlands and Islands of Scotland: A Historical Survey* (Edinburgh, 1937), pp. 296–8; D. Turnock, *Patterns of Highland Development* (London, 1970), p. 70.

legislation; rather it was to be the final solution to a problem which, in Gladstone's view, had plagued British governments for over a century. It was definitely *not* meant to herald a new and permanent phase of interventionist policy in the Highlands. Furthermore, it was intended to right the wrongs which had been perpetrated by the various forms and phases of agricultural and social reorganisation which had taken place in the Highlands over the preceding century. In short, it was retrospective rather than prospective. (Of course, Gladstone's intellectual desire to salve the Victorian liberal conscience on this question is a motive not to be underestimated.) Secondly, and most importantly, to see policy from the 1880s to 1920s as cumulative ignores the political and intellectual tensions between the different Acts and the policies which they promoted.

The principal theme running through this book has been the identification and examination of this debate. Essentially, there were two contending concepts behind the policies advanced in this period. One, normally associated with Liberal administrations, was concerned with giving existing tenants protection and security in their relations with the landowners. This has sometimes been called 'dual ownership'.[5] Although the landlord still retained ultimate ownership of the land, the improvements and buildings were owned by the crofter. The Liberals had developed this policy in Ireland in 1881, and they took it much further in a Scottish context in 1911. As well as extending it beyond the crofting counties, they included provisions whereby new holdings could be created on privately owned land, even against the wishes of the proprietor. On the other hand, there was also the policy involving the concepts of land purchase and peasant proprietorship, which was associated with Conservative governments. Much of the impetus for that policy came from landowners. At first sight this may seem incongruous; but, from their perspective, it was logical and consistent. Most of the proprietorial interest in croft land had been removed by the 1886 Act, for the work of the Crofters' Commission had reduced rents to a nominal level. In that case, proprietors felt that it would be helpful to complete the process and transfer the entire ownership of the croft to the crofter. There was an element of Conservative ideology in such thinking; to endow crofters with the responsibilities of ownership would, it was hoped, move them in a conservative (if not a Conservative) direction. This policy was tentatively applied from 1897 to 1906, but the success rate was not high, for a combination of reasons: the undercapitalised nature of the crofting economy, which meant that crofters were unlikely to be able to afford the necessary annuities; the lack of funds available to the Congested Districts Board to acquire land for selling on to crofters; and, especially, the conservatism of the crofters. The policy's failure can be

[5] SRO, AF43/6/13, Memo on dual ownership.

seen in the fact that the land which was purchased for peasant proprietorship had eventually to be converted into state ownership – which led some mischievous polemicists to herald the advent of land nationalisation in the Highlands under a Conservative government.[6] Essentially, crofter loyalty to the 1886 regime was too strong. This was not an esoteric or ideological judgement on the part of the crofters. They were unwilling to enter into a purchase agreement at the cost of the low rents and rating concessions which they had acquired in 1886; and the security which they had under the 1886 regime was tantamount to ownership. The policy of peasant proprietorship was never resurrected after its initial failure. In the 1919 Act, Part I did empower the government to buy land, but there was never any intention to sell it on to crofters. The government, in the shape of the BoAS, was now satisfied to act as landowner. After all, that was the eventuality which had had to be resorted to in 1908, when the Kilmuir crofters had refused to buy their holdings from the CDB.

The contentious policy-division between the two parties has not been fully appreciated by past historians, who have examined this period in a cursory fashion. Many have simply been concerned to note the progress made in the period which culminated in the 1919 Act. This has been presented as the statute which finally returned the land that Highlanders had been deprived of during the previous century and a half. However, in reality the 1919 Act was an honest attempt by the Coalition government to construct a non-ideological approach to land settlement, following reflection on the failure of the ideologically motivated statute of 1911. It was characterised by its flexibility, encompassing arrangements for new holdings to be created either on privately owned land, or on estates purchased by the BoAS. Undoubtedly, this was the statute under which the greatest progress was made in the Highlands. A remarkably large number of new holdings were created, by comparison to what happened after previous Acts. Significantly, the quantitative success was most evident in the Hebrides, and particularly in Lewis[7] – where, until the early 1920s, it had proved impossible for the CDB or the BoAS to create new holdings in that most congested of islands, because of the weaknesses of existing legislation combined with proprietorial obstinance and eccentricity.

It is vital, then, for understanding the development of government policy in this period, to note the conflicting ideological origins of the different policies that were implemented. The ideological motivation reached its peak in the period from 1906 to 1911. In those years, the Liberal government made no real effort to hide the fact that it had wider objectives than the mere creation of new holdings in the Highlands and beyond. It actually had an open agenda of trying to create a new model

[6] C. Stewart, *The Highland Experiment in Land Nationalisation* (London, 1904), pp. 3–4.
[7] See Tables 5, 6, 7.

of life in the countryside, which would appeal to those in the overcrowded cities, and contribute to a general movement of population from urban areas – to the general good of the nation. However, it is contended here that there was also a hidden agenda. The various Small Landholders (Scotland) Bills were employed cynically in the campaign against the House of Lords. The conjunction of Highland and Lowland provisions in them was highly controversial and caused most of the problems in the Upper House. In response, a cross-party campaign, which included landowners and the representatives of crofters, argued that it would be sensible to introduce a separate measure for the Highlands, where there was a real demand for a measure to deal with identifiable grievances. No such amendment to the government's programme was made until after the reform of the House of Lords; and thereafter, only limited accommodation to the cross-party arguments was allowed, in the shape of amendments to the 1911 version of the bill. When this became law, its crudely ideological origins were betrayed in its short working life. Very little progress was achieved, because the 1911 Act proved to be riddled with loopholes which were exploited by landowners, notably Major Matheson of Lewis and Lady Gordon Cathcart, who were horrified at the extension of the concept of dual ownership which it represented. The Conservatives, too, were motivated to a certain extent by ideological considerations – but to a lesser degree, and in a more constructive fashion. The problem with the Conservatives' policy of land purchase, however, was that it had minimal support within the crofting community. They had not based its introduction on any solid base or test of opinion.

Although, viewed objectively, it can be seen that the ideological treatment of the Highland land issue militated against great progress towards its settlement, such a treatment was inevitable. Government policy is usually created in a political environment whose defining characteristics are polemical debate and differences of approach to any given problem. The Highland land issue had originated in an atmosphere of polemicism in the 1880s, which continued until 1919, when the political power of the Lloyd George Coalition was able to carry a flexible and comprehensive measure that cut through the debates and conflicts of the previous generation.

The role of landowners has always been a controversial issue in Highland history. In this period they have been condemned and relegated to the sidelines.[8] But the level of proprietorial involvement in policy, during the period under consideration here, makes that opinion appear to be a considerable historical misjudgement. To argue that landowners were more important than has hitherto been assumed is not, however, to place a value judgement on the morality or culpability of

8 Hunter, *Crofting Community*, p. 196; Cannadine, *British Aristocracy*, p. 386.

their activities. One major flaw in most of the assertions concerning proprietors is that these have tended to treat them as if they were a monolithic force. Examination of a wide range of proprietorial correspondence helps to lead to a different conclusion.[9] The first point to emerge is the multifaceted nature of political attitudes among proprietors. In the debates surrounding the 1886 Act, the range was considerable – from the constructive and thoughtful interjections of Cameron of Lochiel, to the crude and reactionary contributions of Fraser of Kilmuir. That is not to argue that landowners did not at times act in concert. In 1884–5 they came together to formulate proposals to deal with the grievances of the crofters. Later in the decade, the importance of the 'Memorial of Highland proprietors' to the marquess of Lothian, and its impact on policy has been noted. In the 1890s, Lochiel and MacLeod of MacLeod, as befitted their Conservative allegiances, were both influential advocates of land purchase. Proprietors responded to the Royal Commission of 1892 by setting up an organisation – the Highland Property Association – at a meeting in Inverness convened by Lochiel. This was not mere reaction: it involved the systematic gathering of information on the structure of estates, in an attempt to protect the landowning interest. However, it is in the period 1906–11 that the landlord position is most interesting. In contrast to their Lowland counterparts, Highland landowners like Lord Lovat, another Conservative, were keen to see legislation be passed. Although it was in this period that the Scottish Land and Property Federation was set up specifically to combat the threat of legislation, that was dominated by proprietors from Lowland Scotland, not by Highlanders.

Others were influential on the ground. Lady Gordon Cathcart persuaded a reluctant government to lay aside its preferred option for the settlement of the island of Vatersay on her estate. The government wished to create new holdings but to leave the ownership of the land in the hands of the proprietor. Yet her ladyship prevailed at almost every point in the lengthy debate over this small, but politically important, piece of land, and the government was eventually persuaded against its wishes to buy the island. The fact that this was perhaps the last time a proprietor was able to compel a government to do something illustrates the reality of the proprietors' changing role over this period. After 1911, certain proprietors could still be obstructive if they so wished, but now only a negative influence could be exerted – as the history of the island of Lewis clearly demonstrates. And, when they were faced with the complexity of the 1919 Act – which included not only provisions for the government to buy land, but also a more efficient method of the

[9] Hunter, *Crofting Community*, and Grigor, *Crofters and the Land Question*, are the two historians most inclined to make generalisations of this kind. Neither, it should be noted, have examined the records of Highland estates to gain a more detailed view of proprietorial concerns.

despised concept of 'dual ownership' – there was little the proprietors could do. Further, Highland estates were in a state of decay and their main produce, hill sheep, was unremunerative. So, the assertion that the 1886 Act saw the end of meaningful proprietorial influence in the Highlands greatly oversimplifies a much more complex process. Proprietors were able, for a time in the late 1880s and 1890s, to have their preferred options adopted by receptive Conservative administrations; but in the first decade of the new century, they had to struggle harder to make their voice heard; and from 1911 to 1919 they were reduced to blocking tactics, exemplified by those of Matheson of Lewis.

As well as the considerable diversity among landowners, the government had to contend with a considerable diversity of physical and social conditions in the crofting counties. Often this corresponded to the differing proprietorial attitudes. The island of Lewis presented special problems for the government throughout this period. In the years immediately after the 1886 Act, it was the area with the highest level of rent arrears for the Crofters' Commission to deal with. The social condition of the island was a concern of government in the 1880s, and remained so throughout the period. Many government investigations revealed it to be the area with the most chronic congestion, the poorest land, and the highest incidence of cottars and squatters. In addition, the Congested Districts Board reported that the level of agricultural practice and stock husbandry on the island was lamentable. Prospects for dealing with these problems locally were hampered by the minimal revenue which the local authorities were able to raise from the island. This was a result of the congestion, exacerbated by the fact that many agricultural 'subjects' were not entered on the valuation roll, and hence were not assessed but nevertheless received full services. All the problems of the Highlands seemed to be concentrated on the one island: congestion, lack of capital, and paucity of opportunity. These problems were compounded by the unco-operative nature of the estate management: no new holdings were formed in Lewis on any scale until 1923–4, which demonstrates the continuing power of proprietorial negativism. However, even when the government had broken up every farm on the island for smallholdings, it still did not satisfy the demand for land.

In other Hebridean areas, similar problems existed, but not to the same extent. Progress was possible in Skye, due to good fortune as much as to good planning. The landholding structure on the island was in a state of flux in this period: the traditional proprietors, Lord MacDonald and MacLeod of MacLeod, were in terminal decline, while Fraser of Kilmuir was heartily sick of administering a crofting estate by the early 1890s and was only too happy to sell out. This state of affairs allowed the government to intervene and purchase much of the island in the post-1904 period, through both the CDB and the BoAS. The estates of Lady Gordon Cathcart, from Benbecula southwards, also saw considerable government activity. In negotiations with the government she tended to begin from an absolute position of non-cooperation, and then undertake a controlled retreat. But even this tactic could be nullified by the 1919 Act, and in the 1920s the aged lady was demoralised and wished to sell her estates. Thus, on these estates, by the early 1920s most of the land suitable for land settlement had been utilised. Unlike on Lewis, this was sufficient to deal with the vast bulk of the demand for land.

The county of Sutherland provides a contrast to the Hebrides. Here there were congested crofting townships on the margins of vast acreages of sheep farms. The CDB and the BoAS were able to carry out substantial schemes of land settlement. The duke of Sutherland was generally co-operative, indeed, at times too much so. His habit of offering large swathes of his estate to the government created a new set of problems; the political atmosphere of the wartime and post-war period made it very difficult for the government to refuse such offers, even if they were not wholly suitable for its purposes. After all, there was certainly no shortage of land in Sutherland, and the demand for it was as vociferous as anywhere else in the Highlands.

There were other areas of the Highlands where there was very little government activity throughout the period: most notably, the districts of Lochaber, Badenoch and Easter Ross. In such areas there was an easier co-existence between large scale farming and crofting; indeed crofting townships were relatively isolated among farms of considerable size. In Lochaber and Badenoch, there was also a strong history of club farming among the crofting class. Thus, although classic crofting conditions did exist in these areas, the diversity of landholding marked them out from the heartland of the crofting community in the Hebrides and West Highlands.

Crofter agitation in this period was almost continuous. It is important, nevertheless, to distinguish between its different phases. Before 1886, there was a movement which has been dubbed 'The Crofters' War', which was concentrated in the Hebrides and particularly in Skye. The initial spontaneity of this movement cannot be denied. Its political impact was to alert the government to the existence of the Highland land issue, but beyond that its impact was minimal. It was never able to influence government positively; the arrival of the Crofter MPs at Westminster came too late to be important in the making of the 1886 Act. After 1886, the focus of the agitation shifted to Lewis and to the task of amending the Crofters Act. It was singularly unsuccessful in this regard: after a few large-scale and stage-managed incidents, the agitation declined to small-scale incidents, and then petered out. Thereafter, there were a number of land raids and other incidents. However, they were related not to any general political campaign, but to a series of specific and localised issues: the dispute over Vatersay, the argument over the farm of Scuddaburgh in Skye or the conflict over the farms of Coll and Gress in Lewis. These incidents seem to have been brought about largely by a small number of committed activists who held considerable sway over the rest of the communities in question.

What is striking about the whole course of crofter agitation is its extremely limited objectives. The land raids were not expressions of radicalism, but demonstrations of loyalty to the orthodoxy established in 1886. The institution of landlordism itself was not under threat; as has been noted, it continued to be influential until quite late in this period. Crofters achieved limited gains in 1886 and, with the exception of trying to bring more land into this regime, were content with them. The relationship with their proprietors had been modified to such an extent that the latter's involvement in the crofter's day-to-day life was minimal.

The occurrence of land agitation both in the Highlands and in Ireland in the same period has led to simple comparisons between the two.[10] In Ireland, however, the agitation and the government policy displayed a number of crucial differences from what happened in the Highlands. The Irish agitation was much more intense and widespread than anything found in the Highlands. It was also much more sophisticated: complex structures of protest, such as the 'Plan of Campaign' from 1886, were developed. The important feature which separated Irish agitation from Highland was the link between land and nationalism in Ireland, which gave the land movement there considerable impetus and direction. By comparison, the Highland land movement was parochial; indeed, attempts to link it to wider political concerns were a significant cause of the decline of the Crofters' movement. Irish small tenants, with the greater objective of Home Rule in view, were much more eager to embrace the concept of ownership of their holdings. Consequently, governments of both parties pursued this policy vigorously. Scottish crofters, with their limited objectives, were satisfied with the substance of the 1886 regime which left them as tenants. Attempts to interest Scottish crofters in ownership were abandoned effectively in 1908, and were not revived for a further sixty years.[11]

Another aspect of crofters' behaviour which has largely escaped the attention of historians is their standard of agriculture and stock husbandry. This was a concern of every government institution in the Highlands in the period covered here. As the Congested Districts Board discovered, improvement in these respects was not simply a matter of re-education, but was part of the whole process of social improvement. The grafting of new structures on to traditional undercapitalised crofting, as

[10] Grigor, *Crofters and the Land Question*, i, pp. 44–5.

[11] G. D. Goodlad, 'The Liberal Party and Gladstone's Land Purchase Bill of 1886', *Historical Journal*, xxxii (1989), pp. 627–41, F. S. L. Lyons, *John Dillon* (London, 1968), pp. 82–110; A. Warren, 'Gladstone, land and social reconstruction in Ireland, 1881–87', *Parliamentary History*, ii (1983); S. Warwick-Haller, *William O'Brien and the Irish Land War* (Dublin, 1990) pp. 81–158.

was done in the Common Grazings Acts of 1891 and 1908, was neither a successful nor a sufficient approach. Progress was made, however, and by the 1920s the assumption of the role of landlord by the State was a crucial innovation. The technical support given by the Board (later the Department) of Agriculture for Scotland has been a major contribution to life in crofting communities. Nevertheless, the environmental amenability of crofting has declined, as sheep-farming has increasingly come to dominate the crofting economy over the succeeding period.[12] The fundamental problem here has been the crofters' profound and complex attitude to land. One commentator has noted that psychological attachment and agricultural value were in inverse proportion.[13] The land had symbolic importance: it afforded the opportunity to pursue other economic activities, and it accorded status; but it was not so important, and it was not desired so much, for the purpose of carrying out specific agricultural tasks. The 1911 and 1919 Acts did not disturb this mentality; they merely provided ever-improving facilities for its extension.

It was the intention of both the CDB and the BoAS to create holdings which were sufficiently large to provide a meaningful income for the landholder. The crofting economy had always been based on holdings small enough to allow the necessary additional income to be earned from other sources; this allowed retention of population, in areas where agriculture alone could not provide sufficient income for a livelihood, but it exposed the crofting community to economic downturn when opportunities for wage-earning were not so plentiful or fruitful – as had happened in the 1840s and again in the 1880s. The forty years of government intervention which followed the crisis of the 1880s was an attempt to ensure that the crofting community was no longer so vulnerable. The political environment in which policy was implemented, however, militated against this. In periods and areas of high demand for land, the policy of creating larger holdings could only be carried out at the expense of satisfying no more than a small proportion of the applicants for land. Thus the potential for trouble in the crofting counties would always remain.

A survey of the size of holdings across the crofting counties was conducted by the BoAS in 1935.[14] The aggregate results are presented in the following tables, which show the percentages of smaller and larger holdings:

[12] J. Ritchie, 'Some effects of sheep rearing on the natural condition of Scotland', *SJA*, ii (1919); K. W. Braid, 'Bracken as a colonist', *SJA*, xvii (1934); Mather, 'Alleged deterioration of hill grazings'; C. S. Orwin and E. H. Whetham, *The History of British Agriculture, 1846–1914* (Cambridge, 1964), pp. 295–6.

[13] Mather, 'Government agencies', p. 39.

[14] SRO, Development Department, Highland Development Files, DD15/54/1/1–13.

Table 8: *Smaller and Larger Holdings in the Crofting Counties, 1935 (%ages)*

Acreages	1-5	5-15	15-30	30-50	50-75	75-100	100-150	150-300	300+	Others
Caithness	16.8	34.5	17.6	9.1	7.4	3.9	3.1	3.5	1.5	2.5
Sutherland	50.6	33.7	7.9	2.2	0.8	0.6	0.7	0.9	0.4	2.1
Ross	44.7	37.4	5.6	3.6	2.1	1.3	1.5	1.6	1.0	1.2
Inverness	29.4	37.7	16.0	8.5	2.3	1.5	1.4	1.5	0.3	1.7
Argyll	30.0	21.0	15.9	10.1	6.2	4.0	4.0	3.6	0.7	4.5
REGION	33.7	33.7	13.4	7.3	3.5	1.9	1.7	1.8	0.6	2.4

Table 9: *Smaller and Larger Holdings in the Western Isles, 1935 (%ages)*

Acreages	1-5	5-15	15-30	30-50	50-75	75-100	100-150	150-300	300+	Others
Skye	44.8	43.7	9.0	1.2	0.5	0.7	0.8	—	0.1	0.5
Lewis	48.7	49.8	1.1	0.1	0.1	—	—	0.1	0.1	0.1
Harris	54.2	38.0	6.1	0.8	0.2	0.2	—	—	—	0.6
North Uist	4.7	53.6	26.9	7.4	2.3	2.8	—	0.6	0.4	1.3
South Uist	5.4	32.0	34.2	24.3	1.0	1.6	1.4	—	0.1	—
Barra	20.3	39.8	24.4	14.3	—	—	—	—	—	1.1
REGION	37.8	44.9	10.5	4.6	0.5	0.6	0.4	0.1	0.1	0.3

The first table covers the whole region (except for Orkney and Shetland) on a county by county basis. The second isolates the Western Isles, which have been called the 'heartland' of the crofting community. The first table demonstrates the continuing preponderance of very small holdings after a generation of land settlement. Caithness, with a substantial proportion of larger holdings, was the least congested of the crofting counties. Inverness-shire and Ross-shire were extremely large and diverse counties; more can be learned about them when the island figures are considered. The large proportion of holdings under five acres can be seen most clearly in Sutherland, where there had been a considerable amount of land settlement activity and considerable trouble from land raids. Most of the figures for the islands accentuate the impression that these were areas of continuing congestion. Only in the Uists does land settlement seem to have been relatively successful; there the level of demand and the available land matched up more closely than in most other areas. Land settlement was pursued to its maximum extent in the Hebrides. This in itself was no guarantee of success, as the figures for the island of Lewis clearly demonstrate. The result of land settlement in that island can only be described as a perpetuation of congestion, and continued economic hardship when the opportunities for ancillary employment contracted.

The 1930s, of course, displayed these economic characteristics to the full, and the Highlands suffered along with the rest of the country. The achievement of tenurial security had not produced any pay-off in terms of economic security. Once again a campaign for special action for the Highlands was evident. The Highland Development League was led by the articulate Glenelg minister, Thomas Murchison, and the thoughtful Ballachulish doctor, Lachlan Grant. They drew their inspiration, however, as much from the contemporary example of the New Deal in the USA, and in particular the Tennessee Valley authority, as from the historic example of the Highland Land League.[15]

A sub-committee of the Scottish Economic Committee conducted an investigation into the state of the Highland economy and published its report in 1938. Its recommendations were directed towards the objective of making conditions in the Highlands 'approximate so far as possible to conditions obtainable elsewhere'.[16] This was to be achieved through improvements in the transport system, the application of scientific discovery to improve agriculture and the development of appropriate industry in the area. To aid progress towards these ends, the appointment of a Development Commissioner was proposed; he would be responsible to the Secretary for Scotland, and would co-ordinate development work.

The publication of this report stimulated consideration of the Highland problem to a greater degree than at any time since the mid-1880s. It is interesting to note that, throughout the course of this debate, there was no reference by either government officials or pressure groups to the positive benefits conferred by the policy of land settlement. Indeed, in the period immediately prior to the outbreak of the Second World War, we can detect the origins of the post-war policy of seeking an alternative to classic crofting based on smallholdings and bi-employment. There was also a growing realisation that the legacy of the 1886 Act – in terms of security of tenure – was one of rigidity, and that its inflexibility was in fact an obstacle to the changing structure of landholding.

Following the report's publication, the Scottish Office costed its recommendations. A programme of expenditure worth £113,780, which paid particular attention to the proposals for infrastructure developments and agricultural improvements, was presented to the Treasury; but the Chancellor of the Exchequer, Sir John Simon, faced with clamour for increased defence expenditure, could only agree to £50,000.[17] John Colville, the Secretary for Scotland, was furious at this

[15] Video Interview, F. J. MacDonald and T. M. Murchison, Glasgow University Audio Visual Services.

[16] Scottish Economic Committee, *The Highlands and Islands of Scotland: A Review of the Economic Conditions with Recommendations for Improvement* (London, 1938), p. 28; Hunter, *Claim of Crofting*, p. 42; R. Saville, 'The industrial background to the post-war Scottish economy', in R. Saville (ed.), *The Economic Development of Modern Scotland* (Edinburgh, 1985), pp. 13–16.

[17] SRO, DD15/15.

response. He had received many representations complaining that while the government was failing to act substantially in the Highlands, money was being spent on aid to foreign countries – a point he passed on angrily to Simon.[18] The Scottish Office was well aware of the complaints that the government was using the excuse of consideration of the Hilleary Report to delay action, but also knew that it could not afford to ignore the report.[19] However, in September 1939 the outbreak of war put an end to any formal consideration of the report. Any attempt to implement it was postponed indefinitely, though the Scottish Office was wary of making a public announcement to that effect.[20]

Despite the fact that nothing came of the 1938 report, two related points emerge from the way in which it was considered. First, the justification for remedial action in the Highlands was not purely the contemporary economic problems. The late 1930s saw economic hardship in many areas of Scotland, and the Special Areas legislation was designed to facilitate aid to stricken industrial areas. The government was concerned to clarify the position of the Highlands in relation to this legislation. A different set of circumstances operated in the crofting counties, and there was still widespread agreement that the Highlands merited special consideration.[21] While the problems in the industrial areas were seen to be due to 'severe and sudden depression', the Highland problem was said to be 'as old as the physical considerations which give rise to it'. The question was not what was the most efficacious way to apply aid, or how to design government action to put an industrial community back on its feet, but 'how to enable a scattered and huddled population to live tolerably under natural conditions probably more difficult than those existing in any other part of Great Britain'.[22] There is a slight change of emphasis here, from earlier definitions of the Highland problem in historic terms, to a new, physical, definition of it. There was a recognition that action taken under the older conception had created as many problems as it had solved.

This leads to the second point to emerge from government thinking in the late 1930s and 1940s. The experience of economic problems in the 1930s had convinced government officials that the classic crofting system was too vulnerable to be allowed to continue. This was made explicit in the course of a 1946 government investigation into the condition of the island of Lewis. The notion of a 'surplus population',

18 Ibid., J. Colville to J. Simon, 20 Jul. 1939; for representations to the Scottish Office on the subject of the Hilleary Committee, see DD15/14.

19 DD15/2, Notes of a meeting of officials at the Scottish Office, 7 Dec. 1938; DD15/11, Resolution of Crofters Unions, 2 Feb. 1939; DD15/15, Representations from local authorities.

20 DD15/2, Memo on draft letter to Lord Elgin from the Secretary of State for Scotland, 25 Nov. 1939.

21 This awareness extended to the SLPF, see DD15/12, SLPF to Secretary of State for Scotland, 27 Jul. 1939; GD325/1/415, SLPF Memo, Aug. 1937

22 SRO, DD15/12, Undated memo concerning the Highland Development Commissioner.

that is those who faced hardship when supplementary sources of income dried up, was resurrected. In considering the possibilities of developing or improving conditions, the government realised that among the obstacles it faced was:

> the fact that the existing layout of holdings is governed by a legal code which has security of tenure as one of its main guiding principles and which therefore militates against any aggregation or redistribution of the land into large sized holdings ... and [that] of the conservatism of the crofter and of the fact that he does not have an undivided interest in agriculture.

In short, it was concluded: 'The existing distribution of land in Lewis is unalterable by anything short of a legal revolution. This ties us to a system of small part time crofts.'[23] When Thomas Taylor proposed this legal revolution in 1953, however, the government shied away from it. Essentially, the question posed by the duke of Argyll in 1884 had still not been grasped: was the crofter a small farmer first and part-time worker second, or *vice versa*?

A broader investigation into the policy of land settlement in 1944 confirms this point. Although fringe social benefits, such as improvement in housing, had been achieved, there was a wider and deeper failure of policy:

> In our view, land settlement, as hitherto encouraged, has failed to establish within the Highlands an agricultural economy which either procures the maximum utilisation of land or provides an encouragement to the young generation to follow an agricultural career.[24]

As has been demonstrated here, the committee's conclusion that the policy had been piecemeal and driven by demand, rather than by objective prospects for success, was surely valid.

Thus the period from the 1880s to the 1920s is important not so much for the changes which took place, but for the general continuity which it exhibits. It has, however, bequeathed a questionable legacy to succeeding generations of Highlanders. The system created by the interplay of politics and ideology with respect to the Highland land issue may seem nowadays to have had an internal consistency, but its main characteristic has actually, and most notably, been its near-absolute incapacity for change.

[23] DD15/21, Note on agricultural position in Lewis and Harris.

[24] *PP*, 1944–5, V: *Land Settlement in Scotland: Report by the Scottish Land Settlement Committee*, pp. 44–6.

Bibliography

Manuscript Sources

A. Government Records

Edinburgh, Scottish Record Office
Allotments and Small Holdings Files, AF66
Board of Agriculture for Scotland Miscellaneous Files, AF43
Congested Districts Board Files, AF42
Crofting Files, AF67
Development Department, Highland Development Files, DD15
Emigration Files, AF51
Estate Management Files, AF83
King's and Lord Treasurer's Remembrancer Department, Scottish Office Files, E824
Lord Advocates' Papers, AD59
Roads and Bridges Files, DD4
Scottish Home and Health Department Miscellaneous Files, HH1
Scottish Office Correspondence, HH28

London, Public Record Office
Cabinet Committees, General Series, CAB27
Cabinet Memoranda, CAB24
Cabinet Minutes, CAB23
Photographic Copies of Cabinet Letters, CAB37
Photographic Copies of Cabinet Letters in the Royal Archives, CAB41

B. Estate Papers

Edinburgh, Scottish Record Office
Balfour of Whittingehame Muniments, GD433
Campbell of Jura Papers, GD64
Cromartie Muniments, GD305
Ivory Papers, GD1/36
Lothian Muniments, GD40
Mackintosh Muniments, GD176
Scottish Landowners' Federation Papers, GD325

Edinburgh, National Library of Scotland
R. B. Haldane Papers, MS 5908
Murray of Elibank Papers, MS8801
Rosebery Papers, MS 10017, 10019, 10063, 10145

Edinburgh, Edinburgh University Library
Scottish Liberal Association Papers

Cambridge, Churchill College
Thurso Collection

Inverness, Highland Regional Archive
Inverness-shire Commissioners of Supply Papers, R/13
Kilmuir Estate Papers, AG INV 10
Skeabost Estate Papers, AG, INV 11
Miscellaneous Papers, AG INV 14

London, British Library
A. J. Balfour Papers, MS Add. 49800–1, 49859–60, 49871
H. Campbell-Bannerman Papers, MS Add. 41227, 41230, 41243B, 52512
W. E. Gladstone Papers, MS Add. 44197, 44199, 44335, 44476, 44494, 44497, 44546–8, 44646–7
Marquess of Ripon Papers, MS Add. 43640

Oxford, Bodleian Library
Harcourt Deposit

Stafford, Staffordshire County Record Office
Sutherland Estate Papers, D593

Private Collections
Achnacarry Castle Papers
Ardtornish House Papers
Cluny Castle Papers
Dunvegan Castle Papers
Hatfield House Papers
Hunter of Hunterston Papers, Hunterston Castle
Inveraray Castle Papers
Lord MacDonald Papers, Clan Donald Centre, Armadale, Skye
Sinclair of Ulbster Papers, Thurso Estate Office
Skene, Edwards and Garson Papers, Edinburgh

PRINTED PRIMARY SOURCES

A. PUBLIC REPORTS

Board of Agriculture for Scotland Annual Reports, 1913–1925
Congested Districts Board Annual Reports, 1897–1912
Crofters' Commission Annual Reports, 1886–1912
Scottish Land Court Reports, 1913–1925

B. PARLIAMENTARY PAPERS

1884, XXXIII–XXXVI: *Report of the Commissioners of Inquiry into the Condition of the Crofters and Cottars in the Highlands and Islands of Scotland.*

1888, LXXX: *Report on the Condition of the Cottar Population of the Lews.*

1888, LXXX: *Report by the Crofters Commission in Regard to Applications for Enlargements of Holdings for the period from 25 June 1886 to 10 December 1888.*

1889, CCLXXIV; 1890, CCCLIV; 1891, CLII: *Evidence and Report of the Select Committee on Colonisation.*

1890, XXVII; 1890–1, XLIV: *Reports of the Committee appointed to inquire into certain Matters affecting the interests of the population of the Western Highlands and Islands of Scotland.*

1895, XXXVIII–XXXIX: *Royal Commission (Highlands and Islands, 1892), Report and Evidence, 1895.*

1896, XXXV: *Royal Commission on Land in Wales and Monmouthshire.*

1902, LXXXIII: *Report to the Secretary for Scotland by the Crofters Commission on the Social Condition of the People of the Lews as compared with twenty years ago.*

1906, CIV: *Reports to the Local Government Board on the Burden of Existing Rates and the General Financial Position of the Outer Hebrides.*

1906, LV: *Report of the Departmental Committee appointed by the Board of Agriculture and Fisheries to inquire and report on the subject of Small Holdings in Great Britain.*

1908, LXXXVIII: *Correspondence with reference to the seizure and occupation of the Island of Vatersay, 1908.*

1908, LXXXVIII: *Report of a Special Committee of the County Council of Inverness upon Applications for Allotments in North Uist and Barra made in September 1897.*

1910, XXI: *Report of the Departmental Committee appointed by the Secretary for Scotland to inquire and report upon the work of the Congested Districts (Scotland) Commissioners for the Improvement of Livestock and Agriculture.*

1916, XII: *Report of the Departmental Committee on Land Settlement for Soldiers and Sailors.*

1922, IX: *Second Interim Report of the Committee on National Expenditure.*

1928, XI: *Report of the Committee on Land Settlement in Scotland.*

1944–5, V: *Land Settlement in Scotland: Report by the Scottish Land Settlement Committee.*

HANSARD, *Parliamentary Debates, House of Commons.*

C. OTHER MATERIAL

Court of Session Cases

The Salisbury–Balfour Correspondence, 1869–1902, ed. R. Harcourt-Williams (Hertfordshire Rec. Soc., 1988).

D. NEWSPAPERS

Ayr Advertiser
Ayrshire Post
Celtic Magazine
Forward!
Glasgow Herald
Highland News
Inverness Courier
Northern Chronicle
Oban Times
Scottish Highlander
The Scotsman
Scots Law Times
The Times
West Highland Free Press

E. CONTEMPORARY COMMENTARIES

BATHURST, C., 'The land settlement of ex-servicemen', *Nineteenth Century and After*, lxxviii (1915).
BERNHARD, H., 'Land settlement in Switzerland', *SJA*, ii (1919).
BLAIR, A. M., 'Land and language', *Guth na Bliadhna*, xiii (1916).
BRAID, K. W., 'Bracken as a colonist', *SJA*, xvii (1934).
CAMERON OF LOCHIEL, DONALD, 'Speech to the 13th annual dinner of the Gaelic Society of Inverness', *TGSI*, xi (1884–5).
CAMERON, J., *The Old and the New Hebrides from the Days of the Great Clearances to the Pentland Act of 1912* (Kirkcaldy, 1912).
CAMPBELL, G. D., DUKE OF ARGYLL, 'A corrected picture of the Highlands', *Nineteenth Century*, xvi (1884).
CAMPBELL, H. F., *Highland Reconstruction* (Glasgow, 1920).
MACKENZIE, A., *A History of the Highland Clearances* (Inverness, 1883).
——, 'Report of the Royal Commission: an analysis', *Celtic Magazine*, Jun. 1884.
——, 'Landlord resolutions at Inverness', *Celtic Magazine*, Mar. 1885.
MACKENZIE, W. C., 'The Highland crofters and their needs', *Progressive Review*, cxlvi (1889).
MACLEOD, R., 'The Crofters' Commission', *Blackwoods Magazine*, 1889.
MALCOLM, G., 'The Small Landholders (Scotland) Bill', *Factors Magazine*,

vii (1906–7).

MAXTON, J. P., 'The problems of land tenure in the Highlands of Scotland', *Proceedings of the First International Conference of Agricultural Economists* (London, 1929).

MUNRO-FERGUSON, R. C., 'The Scottish Small Landholders Bill', *National Review*, l (1907).

NAPIER, F., LORD NAPIER, 'The Highland crofters: a vindication of the report of the Royal Commission', *Nineteenth Century*, xvii (1885).

PENNEY, S. M., 'The Highlands and Islands under commissioners', *Juridical Review*, xiii (1901).

RAE, J., 'The crofter problem', *Contemporary Review*, xlvii (1885).

RITCHIE, J., 'Some effects of sheep rearing on the natural condition of Scotland', *SJA*, ii (1919).

SCOTTISH ECONOMIC COMMITTEE, *The Highlands and Islands of Scotland: A Review of the Economic Conditions with Recommendations for Improvement* (London, 1938).

SCOTTISH LAND ENQUIRY COMMITTEE, *Scottish Land, Rural and Urban* (London, 1914).

SKENE, W. F., *Celtic Scotland: A History of Ancient Alban*, vol. III: *Land and People* (Edinburgh, 1880).

SPIER, J., 'The Small Landholders Bill', *Factors Magazine*, vii (1906–7).

STEWART, C., *The Highland Experiment in Land Nationalisation* (London, 1904).

[——], 'Agricultural reconstruction in France', *SJA*, ii (1919).

[——], 'The Congested Districts Board', *Scottish Law Review*, xxii (1906).

[——], 'The Congested Districts Board: its constitution and aims', *Juridical Review*, xiii (1901).

[——], 'Land settlement for soldiers and sailors', *SJA*, i (1918).

[——], 'Land settlement in Scotland', *SJA*, xv (1932).

[——], 'Land settlement in Skye – Migration schemes', *SJA*, vii (1924).

[——], 'Smallholdings in France: acquisition by military pensioners and victims of the war', *SJA* , i (1918).

[——], 'Small Holdings in Scotland', *International Labour Office, Geneva, Studies and Reports*, series K, no. 3 (Nov. 1920).

[——], 'Soldier settlement in Italy', *SJA*, iii (1920).

SECONDARY SOURCES

BERNSTEIN, G. L., *Liberalism and Liberal Politics in Edwardian England* (Boston, 1986).

BLACK, R. D. C., 'Economic policy in Ireland and India in the time of J. S. Mill', *Economic History Review*, xxi (1968).

BLEWETT, N., *The Peers, The Parties and the People: The General Elections of 1910* (London, 1970).

BOURNE, J. M., Review of D. Cannadine, *The Decline and Fall of the British*

Aristocracy, in *Twentieth-Century British History*, ii (1991).

BROOKES, D. (ed.), *The Destruction of Lord Rosebery* (London, 1986).

BROWN, J., 'Scottish and English land legislation, 1905–1911', *SHR*, xlvii (1968).

BUCKLEY, K., 'The records of the Irish Land Commission as a source of historical evidence', *Irish Historical Studies*, viii (1952–3).

CAIRD, J. B., 'The isle of Harris', *SGM*, lxvii (1951).

—— and MOISLEY, H. A., 'Leadership and innovation in the crofting communities of the Outer Hebrides', *Sociological Review*, ix (1961).

CAMERON, E. A., 'Public Policy in the Scottish Highlands: Governments, Politics and the Land Issue, 1886 to the 1920s' (Glasgow University Ph.D. thesis, 1992).

——, 'Politics, ideology and the Highland land issue, 1886 to the 1920s', *SHR*, lxxii (1993).

——, 'The political influence of Highland landowners: a reassessment', *NS*, xiv (1994).

CANNADINE, D., *The Decline and Fall of the British Aristocracy* (London, 1990).

CARTER, I., *Farmlife in North-east Scotland, 1840–1914* (Edinburgh, 1979).

——, 'Unions and myths: farm servants' unions in Aberdeenshire, 1870–1900', in T. M. Devine (ed.), *Farm Servants and Labour in Lowland Scotland, 1770–1914* (Edinburgh, 1984).

COOKE, A. B. and VINCENT, J., *The Governing Passion: Cabinet Government and Party Politics in Britain, 1885–86* (Brighton, 1974).

COULL, J. R., 'The island of Tiree', *SGM*, lxxviii (1962).

CRAIG, D., *On the Crofters' Trail* (London, 1990).

CRAIG, F. W. S., *British Parliamentary Election Results, 1885–1918* (London, 1974).

CREWE-MILNES, R., MARQUESS OF CREWE, *Lord Rosebery* (London, 1931).

CROWLEY, D. W., 'The Crofters' Party, 1885–1892', *SHR*, xxxv (1956).

CURTIS, L. P., *Coercion and Conciliation in Ireland, 1880–1892* (Princeton, 1963).

DARLING, F. F. (ed.), *West Highland Survey* (Oxford, 1955).

DAY, J. P., *Public Administration in the Highlands and Islands of Scotland* (London, 1918).

DENMAN, R. D., *Bibliography of Rural Land Economy and Landownership: 1900 to 1957* (Cambridge, 1958).

DEVINE, T. M., 'Temporary migration and the Scottish Highlands in the nineteenth century', *Economic History Review*, 2nd ser., xxxii (1979).

——, 'Highland migration to Lowland Scotland, 1760–1860', *SHR*, lxii (1983).

——, *The Great Highland Famine* (Edinburgh, 1988).

—— and CAMPBELL, R. H., 'The rural experience', in W. H. Fraser and R. J. Morris (eds.), *People and Society in Scotland*, vol. II: *1830–1914* (Edinburgh, 1990).

DEWEY, C., 'Celtic agrarian legislation and the Celtic revival: historicist implications of Gladstone's Irish and Scottish Land Acts, 1870–1886', *Past and Present*, lxiv (1974).

DUGDALE, B. E. C., *Arthur James Balfour* (London, 1936).

EMY, H. V., *Liberals, Radicalism and Social Politics, 1892–1914* (Cambridge, 1973).

ENSOR, R. C. K., *England, 1870–1914* (Oxford, 1939).

FOSTER, R. F., *Modern Ireland, 1600–1972* (London, 1989 edn).

GAILEY, A., *Ireland and the Death of Kindness: The Experience of Constructive Unionism* (Cork, 1987).

GARDINER, A. G., *The Life of Sir William Harcourt* (London, 1923).

GARVIN, J. L., *The Life of Joseph Chamberlain* (London, 1933).

GASKELL, P., *Morvern Transformed* (Cambridge, 1973).

GILBERT, B. B., 'David Lloyd George, land, the budget and social reform', *American Historical Review*, lxxxi (1976).

——, 'David Lloyd George: the reform of British landholding and the budget of 1914', *Historical Journal*, xxi (1978).

GILLANDERS, F., 'The economic life of Gaelic Scotland today', in D. C. Thomson and I. Grimble (eds.), *The Future of the Highlands* (London, 1968).

GOODLAD, G. D., 'The Liberal Party and Gladstone's Land Purchase Bill of 1886', *Historical Journal*, xxxii (1989).

GRAY, M., *The Highland Economy, 1750–1850* (London, 1953).

——, 'Crofting and fishing in the north-west Highlands, 1890–1914', *NS*, i (1972).

GRIGOR, I. F., *Mightier than a Lord* (Stornoway, 1979).

——, 'Crofters and the Land Question, 1870–1920' (Glasgow University Ph.D. thesis, 1989).

HANHAM, H. J., 'The creation of the Scottish Office, 1881–1887', *Juridical Review*, 1965.

——, 'The problem of Highland discontent, 1880–1885', *Transactions of the Royal Historical Society*, 5th ser., xix (1969).

——, *Scottish Nationalism* (London, 1969).

HARRIS, J. F. and HAZLEHURST, C., 'Campbell-Bannerman as Prime Minister', *History*, lv (1970).

HENDERSON, D. M., *The Highland Soldier: A Social Study of the Highland Regiments, 1820–1920* (Edinburgh, 1989).

HOBSON, P. M., 'The parish of Barra', *SGM*, lxv (1949).

HUGGETT, F. E., *The Land Question and European Society* (London, 1975).

HUNTER, J., 'Sheep and deer: Highland sheep farming, 1850–1900', *NS*, i (1973).

——, 'The politics of Highland land reform, 1873–1895', *SHR*, liii (1974).

——, 'The Gaelic connection: the Highlands, Ireland and nationalism, 1873–1922', *SHR*, liv (1975).

——, *The Making of the Crofting Community* (Edinburgh, 1976).
——, *The Claim of Crofting: The Scottish Highlands and Islands, 1930–1990* (Edinburgh, 1991).
HUTCHISON, I. G. C., *A Political History of Scotland, 1832–1924* (Edinburgh, 1986).
JAMES, R. R., *Rosebery* (London, 1963).
JONES, D. T. *et al.*, *Rural Scotland During the War* (London, 1926).
KAYE, K. J., 'The use of the countryside by the urban state: Scotland's north-west seaboard and islands', *SGM*, cvi (1990).
KEATING, M. and BLIEMAN, D. , *Labour and Scottish Nationalism* (London, 1979).
LENEMAN, L., *Fit For Heroes? Land Settlement in Scotland after World War One* (Aberdeen, 1989).
——, 'Borgie: a debatable gift to the nation', *NS*, ix (1989).
LEVIN, A., 'Peter Arkad'evich Stolypin: a political appraisal', *Journal of Modern History*, xxxvii (1965).
LINDLEY, F., *Lord Lovat: A Biography* (London, undated).
LOGAN, C. A., 'Attitudes to the Land on Lewis, 1886–1914' (St Andrews University M.A. dissertation, 1993).
LUBENOW, W. C., *Parliamentary Politics and the Home Rule Crisis: The British House of Commons in 1886* (Oxford, 1988).
LYONS, F. S. L., *John Dillon* (London, 1968).
MACARTHUR, E. M., *Iona: The Living Memory of a Crofting Community, 1750–1914* (Edinburgh, 1990).
MACCUISH, D. J., 'The origin and development of crofting law', *TGSI*, xliii (1960–3).
——, 'The case for converting crofting tenure to ownership', *TGSI*, xlvi (1969–70).
——, 'Ninety years of crofting legislation and administration', *TGSI*, l (1976–8).
MACDONALD, A., 'The Geddes Committee and the formulation of public expenditure policy, 1921–22', *Historical Journal*, xxxii (1989).
MACDONALD, D., *Lewis: A History of the Island* (Edinburgh, 1978).
MACDONALD, S., 'Crofter colonisation in Canada, 1886–1892: the Scottish political background', *NS*, vii (1986–7).
MACINNES, A. I., 'The Crofters' Holdings Act: a hundred year sentence', *Radical Scotland*, xxv (Feb./Mar. 1987).
——, 'Scottish Gaeldom: the first phase of Clearance', in T. M. Devine and R. Mitchison (eds.), *People and Society in Scotland*, vol. I: *1760–1830* (Edinburgh, 1988).
MACKENZIE, W. C., *The Highlands and Islands of Scotland: A Historical Survey* (Edinburgh, 1937).
MACLEAN, M. and CARRELL, C. (eds.), *As An Fhearran: From the Land* (Edinburgh, Glasgow and Stornoway, 1986).
MACPHAIL, I. M. M., 'The Napier Commission', *TGSI*, xlviii (1972–4).

——, 'The Skye military expedition of 1884–85', *TGSI*, xlviii (1972–4).
——, 'The prelude to the Crofters' War, 1870–1880', *TGSI*, xlix (1974–6).
——, 'The Highland elections of 1884–86', *TGSI*, l (1976–8).
——, 'Gunboats to the Hebrides', *TGSI*, liii (1982–4).
——, *The Crofters' War* (Stornoway, 1989).

MACSWEEN, M. D., 'Settlement in Trotternish, Isle of Skye, 1700–1958' (Glasgow University B. Litt. thesis, 1959).

MASON, J. W., 'The duke of Argyll and the land question in late nineteenth-century Britain', *Victorian Studies*, xxi (1978).

MATHER, A. S., *State Aided Land Settlement in Scotland* (O'Dell Memorial Monograph no. 6, Department of Geography, Aberdeen University, 1978).
——, 'The alleged deterioration of hill grazings in the Scottish Highlands', *Biological Conservation*, xiv (1978).
——, 'The Congested Districts Board for Scotland,' in W. Ritchie, J. C. Stone and A. S. Mather (eds.), *Essays for Professor R. E. H. Mellor* (Aberdeen, 1986).
——, 'Government agencies and land development in the Scottish Highlands: a centenary survey', *NS*, viii (1988).
—— and ARDERN, S. J., *A Bibliography of Rural Land Use in the Scottish Highlands* (O'Dell Memorial Monograph no. 9, Department of Geography, Aberdeen University, 1983).

MEEK, D. E., 'The land question answered from the Bible', *SGM*, ciii (1987).

MICKS, W. L., *An Account of the Constitution, Administration and Dissolution of the Congested Districts Board for Ireland, 1891–1923* (Dublin, 1925).

MOISLEY, H. A., 'The Highlands and Islands: a crofting region?', *Transactions of the Institute of British Geographers*, xxxi (1962).

MORGAN, K. O., *Consensus and Disunity: The Lloyd George Coalition Government, 1918–1922* (Oxford, 1979).
—— (ed.), *The Age of Lloyd George* (London, 1971).

MURRAY, A. C., *Master and Brother: Murrays of Elibank* (London, 1945).

NICOLSON, N., *Lord of the Isles: Lord Leverhulme in the Hebrides* (London, 1960).

NORTON, W., 'Malcolm MacNeill and the emigrationist alternative to Highland land reform, 1886–1893', *SHR*, lxx (1991).

O'DAY, A., *Parnell and the First Home Rule Episode* (Dublin, 1986).

OFFER, A., *Property and Politics, 1870–1914* (Cambridge, 1981).

ORR, W., *Deer Forests, Landlords and Crofters* (Edinburgh, 1982).

ORWIN, C. S. and WHETHAM, E. H., *A History of British Agriculture, 1846–1914* (Cambridge, 1964).

PELLING, H., *The Social Geography of British Elections, 1885–1910* (London, 1965).

PERREN, R., 'The North American beef and cattle trade with Great

Britain, 1870–1914', *Economic History Review*, xxiv (1971).

PUGH, M., *The Making of Modern British Politics, 1867–1939* (Oxford, 1982).

RICHARDS, E., *A History of the Highland Clearances: Agrarian Transformation and the Evictions, 1746–1886* (London, 1982).

—— and CLOUGH, M., *Cromartie: Highland Life, 1650–1914* (Aberdeen, 1989).

RIDLEY, J., 'The Unionist Opposition and the House of Lords, 1906–1910', *Parliamentary History*, xi (1992).

ROWLAND, P., *The Last Liberal Governments: The Promised Land, 1905–1910* (London, 1968).

SAVILLE, R., 'The industrial background to the post-war Scottish economy', in R. Saville (ed.), *The Economic Development of Modern Scotland* (Edinburgh, 1985).

SCOTT, J., *The Law of Smallholdings in Scotland* (Edinburgh, 1933).

SHANNON, R., *The Crisis of Imperialism, 1865–1915* (London, 1984 edn).

SINCLAIR, M. A., LADY PENTLAND, *The Rt. Hon. John Sinclair, Lord Pentland: A Memoir* (London, 1928).

SKRUBBELTRANG, F., *Agricultural Development and Rural Reform in Denmark* (Rome, 1953).

STANSKY, P., *Ambitions and Strategies: The Struggle for the Leadership of the Liberal Party in the 1890s* (Oxford, 1964).

STORRIE, M. C., 'Two early resettlement schemes in Barra', *Scottish Studies*, vi (1962).

THOMPSON, W. P. L., *The Little General and the Rousay Crofters: Crisis on an Orkney Crofting Estate* (Edinburgh, 1982).

TURNOCK, D., *Patterns of Highland Development* (London, 1970).

WALKER, G., *Thomas Johnston* (Manchester, 1988).

WARREN, A., 'Gladstone, land and social reconstruction in Ireland, 1881–1887', *Parliamentary History*, ii (1983).

WARWICK-HALLER, S., *William O'Brien and the Irish Land War* (Dublin, 1990).

WESTON, C. C., 'The Liberal leadership and the House of Lords veto, 1907–1910', *Historical Journal*, xi (1968).

WILSON, J., *C-B: A Life of Sir Henry Campbell-Bannerman* (London, 1973).

WILSON, B., Column in *West Highland Free Press*, 26 Mar. 1993.

WITHERS, C. W. J., *Gaelic Scotland: The Transformation of a Language* (London, 1988).

Index